THE DEAFENING SILENCE

Hans Hansen

MINERVA PRESS
LONDON
ATLANTA   MONTREUX   SYDNEY

THE DEAFENING SILENCE
Copyright © Hans Hansen 1998

All Rights Reserved

No part of this book may be reproduced in any form
by photocopying or by any electronic or mechanical means,
including information storage or retrieval systems,
without permission in writing from both the copyright
owner and the publisher of this book.

ISBN 0 75410 189 4

First Published 1998 by
MINERVA PRESS
195 Knightsbridge
London SW7 1RE

Printed in Great Britain for Minerva Press

THE DEAFENING SILENCE

Prey not on the gigantic swindle, but rather observe, think and become the truth.

> Anonymous

We look forward to the time when the power of love will replace the love of power, then will our world know the blessing of peace.

> William Ewart Gladstone

Preface

In this book I am attempting to illustrate the way I have experienced and perceived the world and the universe that we live in. Most of the experience and observation is in Africa, but interspersed with influences from outside. It is not that I particularly want to tell a story about myself and my life. It could for that matter have been a story about someone else, someone who has gone through similar turbulent times of which there are unfortunately many in our imperfect world of conflict. I have waited nearly twenty years before arranging the story into a book, mainly to allow for calmer times and so as not to aggravate open wounds and sensitive subjects.

Today I see interesting changes taking place in the world. There are new politics, new holistic thinking and New Age religion, which is of course not new at all, but the foundation of what over time has became formalised and fossilised thinking. The spirit is reawakening for the Aquarian Age. We are at a crossroad and new ideas seem to be easily accepted. The rationalists have no answers to long-term human problems because of their self-created limitations. Analysing the past, including its mistakes and the role of institutions past and present, is a sign of maturity. Humanity today stands at the gate of a different reality, an awakening to new values. Will we go through the gate to embrace our own 'Higher Self', or will we stay in fear of terror created by the ones who want to dominate society, be they terrorists or the institution that protects us from terrorists? Neither has a desire to see further human evolution. In Africa the churches and dictators have fulfilled that role to perfection, and I hope that era has passed. In the first world the fear is of a more subtle nature, but nevertheless fear should not be the force that controls humans. Society's stability should be encouraged because it is to everyone's advantage. Many doctors create many patients. Protection agencies see criminals everywhere and that force can eventually dominate society.

On the spiritual quest I take reincarnation as a matter of fact because at a certain level of consciousness that is how it appears to me and there is plenty of historical and written material pointing in the same direction.

Obviously my suggested political conspiracies or secret agendas are speculative. But the indications are there for all to see. I do not claim that all accusations and postulations are the final truth. However, the fact remains that two commercial airliners were shot down in 1978 and world leaders refused to condemn such actions. Only *deafening silence* was heard. Why?

Since we fell from the sky in a ball of fire, shot down by men, brothers of mankind, a strong desire has grown, a desire to tell others of the real tapestry of the world and of the path to freedom, real freedom. Spiritual freedom is like a surfer riding the wave, but riding the wave of light and accelerating into the mystery of the universe where colour takes form, form that words cannot name, but still somehow understood with feelings of humility and the uttering of the phrase 'O God your universe is beautiful!'

In our world of strife and conflict great men and women of wisdom do exist, hidden amongst humanity. Sitting around the fire at night, traversing the quiet path, they speak the voice of silence, and yet power is in their midst. They see the light at night. They are the Living Love.

All places and happenings described are true, written from memory, and any deviation from fact is not intentional. I offer my apologies to any one who may be offended.

H.H.

Denmark and Departure

Someone else's decisions can and often will change the course of your whole life, especially if the decision makers are your parents. They are not politicians; therefore they are not subject to democratic principles and do not have to justify their actions except to themselves. Do not misunderstand me. I am not even considering blaming them for their decision back in 1955, but it certainly led to what became a very eventful life with adventures and situations that one sometimes prefers to read about in the newspaper or watch on television. On the other hand, had they made no such decision to immigrate I would not have known 'the way of Africa', caught over five hundred million fish, grown coffee and cotton, among other things, and become involved in matters of a more mystical nature that have become important to me. I do believe, though, that by leaving your home country you lose the feelings of continuity, permanency and the security that old established systems offer. I suppose it is one of those paradoxes that life presents – you cannot have this and that at the same time.

My parents decided to pack up farming in Denmark and emigrate to Kenya, Africa, which was a British colony at the time. The year was 1955. For a change I thought my parents had come up with an excellent idea. I saw adventure. I had not read any of Karen Blixen's books yet, but for whatever reason I was already preoccupied with Africa. I had a good collection of newspaper cuttings, and the subject was often discussed at school. Livingstone's and

Stanley's adventures were realities. Cannibals with missionaries in big pots were also realities. We had obviously read about the savage Mau-Mau uprising and activities, but my father trusted the British and believed that they would be able to sort things out. He saw the British as his generation's 'world civiliser' – I suppose a leftover confidence from the Second World War.

I had just learnt in school that Admiral Nelson had burnt the entire Danish fleet in Copenhagen harbour one night to prevent Denmark from supporting Napoleon. We children believed that if that act of aggression and destruction by a one-eyed British admiral had not taken place, Denmark could have been a major colonial power. Now we only had a God-forsaken frozen Greenland with a few Eskimos, who apparently behaved like children, and who, beside fishing, had sex with all visitors to keep warm! No thanks, who would want to go there? Warm climate colonies such as the British held – that would be the answer.

If we had held a family vote on emigration in 1955, I would naïvely have supported my parents in the desire for adventure, but I did not have the responsibility for five children or the planning of such a venture. In a way I longed for a change from the trivial life on a dairy farm, filling bottles of milk from here to eternity, an occupation in which we children were actively involved. Between the ages of five and eleven my brothers and I participated in filling milk bottles every day with only the odd day off. The milk was cooled and tapped in litre and half-litre bottles, then placed in boxes of eight, twelve or twenty bottles per box before delivery to customers by the milkman on horse cart. My counting and tables to twelve were therefore perfect before I commenced school. We children also participated in other farm work and garden maintenance. Child slave labour maybe, but not the way I saw it then.

GALLERY ANN

requests the pleasure of your company

AT

AN EXHIBITION

THE

LITTLE PICTURE SHOW

1998

Friday 27th November from 3pm
Saturday 28th November from 11.30 am
Plot 205 Independence Avenue
Phone: 359416

The participation in the adult world gave us a sense of value. It gave us confidence and we knew that we were important members of society. Occasionally we complained, and once even went on strike. My father would then listen and discuss our complaints and grievances until they were rectified, just as one would do with paid adult workers.

One of the reasons for leaving the farm in Denmark was that the farm, 'Hestholm', was up for sale. My father had leased the farm in 1937 from A.P. Moller, founder of Mearsk Shipping. As it was only three miles from the German border in the south-west of Denmark, Moller had bought the land after the 1914–1918 war to keep it in Danish hands.

I suppose it had some historical value. The homestead was beautiful, thatched and fairly large according to Danish standards, set in a large garden full of trees and flowers. The buildings dated back to 1595, with half-metre thick walls, and were built on a mound in marshland. Some of the grazing land surrounding the farmhouse was below sea-level. A canal system in the lands collected the rain-water and led it to a central pump station. The water then pumped into a river with dykes from where it could run freely out to the ocean.

It was jokingly said that the lease agreement required my parents to produce at least five children, to increase the Danish population in the border region. I suppose this was a good excuse if you need one!

We 'Hestholm children' grew up with old-fashioned values. Loved by all – parents, workmen, animals, teachers – that was the way I perceived it. Perverts and child-molesters did not exist. We were told, though, never to accept lifts from strangers. We had no complexes and only few fears, and life was full of wonderful things, tulips in spring and other flowers during the rest of the year. As a four-year-old I pointed out an emerging tulip to my grandmother who was visiting, and asked her why the tulips had red faces when they came out of the dark ground. The dear old lady laughed so much that she tripped, fell, and broke her arm. Thunderstorms were hell for me as a young boy. I saw the sky turning inside out, and lightning sent shivers of fear through my body while I awaited the total collapse of the heavens. I do not know why. None of my siblings had that phobia. We usually said prayers at night for the Angels to protect us. My early belief was trust in adults, governments and some mysterious hidden God in the sky. He had written a book called the Bible and then left for heaven where he had some form of telescope through which he kept track of all people and wrote their deeds in a big book.

Out-of-body consciousness was something I experienced fairly often between the ages of three and seven. A large pulsating shadow with white undulating lines would appear on the ceiling. Then suddenly the observation point would shift. The 'observing me' would be in the pulsating shadow and I would see my body lying on the bed. My heartbeat would be audible, sounding hollow, and the surroundings appeared rather transparent with a bluish glow. After such an occurrence I would get up and find my way downstairs to my parents' room, attempting to explain what had happened. They tried to talk sense to a little boy who could not verbalise what had happened because his vocabulary did not cater for that type of experience. My parents must have been rather concerned because they arranged for me to attend speech therapy, conducted by a cousin of mine who was studying to become a teacher. It was not very successful because he only wanted to talk about 'common' things like horses, cows, pigs, and so on. I knew all those animals very well and had even seen them in strange positions, on top of one another, copulating. All I wanted was to talk about dreams, God and other things for which I needed explanations. After a few months he gave up, or maybe we gave up. I then commenced regular school.

My father did not allow us to repeat the silly anti-German jokes we had picked up from school. He said that although he had been interned by the Nazis during part of the war, this did not give us the right to condemn all Germans or make fun of them. Fortunately Denmark was not badly bombed during the war years, as the government at the time capitulated immediately. Later an organised resistance movement was set up to sabotage the Nazi activities. The Nazis were dedicated to building bunkers and canon positions along the west coast of Denmark during the war, expecting a British invasion from that side due to an excellent misinformation campaign by the British Secret Service. Our home was bombed once by a fire-bomb dropped by an English plane which had been on a mission over Germany and possibly hit by a German anti-aircraft gun. The pilot, desperate to get back to base, offloaded his heavy bombs somewhere in the dark. During a windy October night who can blame him? I wonder if he ever got back home, or if the North Sea became his final earthly destination? Anyway, the bomb did not explode. The sloped thatched roof allowed the bomb to land softly, no one was harmed, and the bomb was defused.

I can sympathise with a pilot in a damaged aircraft, something I had to experience many years later. In Africa my wife and I were shot down by a Sam-7 missile in a commercial jet liner. This is a story we will come back to.

I know that my father wrote a letter to us, his children, stating his reasons for participating in the resistance movement. As he said later, the winner writes the history books and some truths can become very distorted or never told. How true that is. Born in the constellation of Virgo, on an early September morning in 1942, I was only three years old when the war ended and do not remember very much of it, but many stories are as clear as if I had witnessed them. For example, the day the Germans stole our salted hams from the cellar, and the day it rained with silver foil strips, I suppose some anti-radar stuff, and the day my father was arrested by the Germans, are small glimpses on an otherwise blank screen. Shortly after the war my memory became more vivid though, and I remember even small events such as going to the nearby main road on an autumn afternoon to wave to the passing king and queen. Not having seen a car with lights on before I took it for a dragon. To escape I promptly dived into the nearby muddy river from where our observant maid plucked me out, my new sailor suit in ruins. I realised then that my reference guide might not be valid. Things are not always what they appear to be.

Like most children, I craved adventure and recall as a four-year-old climbing on to a wooden cart with steel-rimmed wheels. The horses and cart were ready to go to town and the driver had gone into the house to collect instructions and money. I saw my chance, released the reins, and told the horses to take me to Ridder Rap immediately. Ridder Rap is the Danish Sir Lancelot. My knowledge of him came from a Sunday newspaper cartoon series, read to me by a housemaid or some other adult. I awoke some time later to the doctor's announcement that although I had a wheel mark across my body, no bones were broken. The driver pursued the horses and managed to capture and control them in a field some distance away from the starting point. Apparently they had been rather bewildered by their young driver's actions and disappearance.

One thing I would like to reverse is the amputation of our cat's tail, of which I was the four-year-old instigator.

During a lunch I had overheard farmhands talking about the work they were presently conducting, namely amputating lambs' tails. I understood that the reason was to facilitate pregnancy when adult. I wished for nothing more than that our old impatient cat would produce some small cuddly kittens, and was now of the opinion that the cat's tail was in the way. With limited reasoning abilities I decided we had to relieve the cat of its problem. My brother Ulrich, three years old, held the cat while I performed the horrendous act. Fortunately my parents arrived shortly afterwards, but unfortunately not in time to save the cat. I was obviously bombarded with a lot of questions, but can't really remember what happened after that. There seems to be a black hole. I never saw the cat again.

At an even earlier age, two and a half years old, I managed to get hold of a croquet club and smashed all the windows within reach. Some twenty windows fell victim. Seeing my father approaching I screamed for help. 'I cannot control the croquet club, it is jumping for the window. You can see I am trying to stop it, but it will not listen.' My father took me by the hand and I started crying. The following day the repairers were called to install new glass.

Was the window-smashing act some sort of possession I suffered from? I don't know.

Later in life I saw people possessed. I have done a lot of private research on the subject and have not come to a satisfactory conclusion. More about that later.

Most of the cultivated land was worked by horses. We had sixteen big Belgian and Russian horses and two Oldenburger horses. They ploughed the land. They took us to church with bells on their feet. They took us to the beach, and they delivered milk to customers. Basically they did what tractors and a delivery van and a private car would do nowadays. We even had a sledge for the horses which was used in bad winters with heavy snowfalls.

We did have one tractor, an old petrol/paraffin Fordson, but prior to that we had a Lanz Buldock tractor. Before starting a Lanz Buldock tractor you have to heat the cylinder-head glow point with a blowtorch. One day, noticing that the new workman could not start the Fordson, my younger brother and I decided to give him a helping hand during lunch hour. We got hold of a pot, put some petrol in it, and held it below the carburettor. I struck a match and flames emerged from everywhere. Fortunately the workman came back from lunch just at the right moment and prevented catastrophe. Nearby he found a wet sack and managed to get the flames under control. We tried to explain that we had only wanted to help by heating the tractor so it would be easier for him to start it. We walked away from an obviously failed mission.

Normally the farm fields would be weeded by hand, but some new herbicide came on the market. I seem to recall it was mainly a grass killer, called sodium chlorate. Having a scientific inclination, my brothers and I mixed sodium chlorate with potato flour to manufacture smoke bombs. By restricting the burning process we could make small explosions. Where we got the recipe from I simply don't know. Only Heaven knows why our homestead was not left in ashes before we reached the age of intelligent reasoning.

Another act of well-intentioned destructiveness brought swift retribution. Ulrich and I were playing near an old-fashioned thrashing machine, now replaced by self-propelled combine harvesters. I had at some time noticed a man at the railway station, prowling around with a long hammer and hitting the rail-wagon wheels. I had been told that he was checking the wheels for cracks. Now, looking at the big cast-iron gear on the baler connected to the thrashing machine, I told my brother I would check the big wheels for cracks. One knock with the hammer and the gear wheel shattered. Believing that it was faulty I also 'checked' the other one with the same result. I was also shattered and felt guilty. Later that afternoon a picture of Moses came into my mind, Moses being punished by God for hitting a rock to get water in the desert. In our case, when my father found out he used a stick on our rear ends. This was the one and only time he ever used a stick on us, and water came into my trousers.

My initial knowledge of the Bible characters and stories had come mainly from my older siblings and first school year. My first public school teacher was an active Christian of the Danish Lutheran church, and he also preached in the local church, which we attended sometimes, on Sundays.

I had heard from young friends that if you go down a deep hole into the earth, God's starry sky can be seen during the day. Yes, we did have a very old deep well on the farm and one day I arranged for the necessary descent. Fortunately, again the Angels conspired to keep us alive for a bit longer and we were interrupted by a mature person before disaster happened. I knew nothing about mining then, therefore I did not know that poisonous gas can accumulate in deep holes, wells or mine shafts. You learn along the way, don't you?

Imagine if today's TV had been my tutor! A black hole would have been extracted from deep space by sound waves, superconductors and laser beams bending the horizons for a spectacular holographic sunset and gravity insulators propelling new continental drifts to get rid of the Russians. Cobalt bombs would have been in schoolboys' back pockets to control teachers and sapphire-tipped knives for genetic engineering on difficult headmasters.

Did the Angels indeed hear our evening prayers or was it a waiting game to see how far human kids would go before destroying themselves and their surroundings?

The old farmhouse was also the abode of ghosts. Over the years various apparitions were exorcised and stuffed back into the ground where they apparently came from. A pole or stake was then erected to prevent the apparition from raising its ugly head again. We had three of those poles, two in the barns and one in the lands. I do not recall anyone ever suggesting that we remove those poles.

The Devil was a strange creature, to my young mind. Why would an all-loving, powerful God want a Devil? Why not eliminate him forthwith, if you have all the power? The Devil with horns and a fork must after all be quite powerful, I reasoned.

I lost a finger at the age of four. Fascinated by and examining the knife on the old grain binder, while my older brother Chris and sister Karin fought for the seat on the machine, I suddenly felt something warm running down my leg. A small push by my brother or sister on the test handle had turned the mechanism of the machine. The knife had moved and taken my ring finger off, and blood was running down my leg. My father took me to hospital on a bicycle, and I felt like a war victim for weeks. The middle finger on the same hand was lost, four years later.

Our maid, a young girl, was hanging out washing. In a teasing play I pinched one end of the wash-line, running away as fast as I could, failing to register that the other end of the line was still tied fast to its pole. Exhausting the loose play of line caused me to somersault and simply pulled my finger off. This time the ambulance took me to hospital. The doctor asked if I had being playing with an axe. I said 'No', and told him that I had being playing with the maid. He must have been confused at that, and asked if I was a strong boy, giving me injections, on either side of the finger stump. After a while he asked if it was numb, and commenced cutting the protruding bone away, while explaining that there was not enough skin to cover the top of the finger. I survived!

In 1951 the cattle had foot-and-mouth disease, and we were quarantined. Our normal school attendance was interrupted, causing no dismay. Books were delivered to the farm entrance from where we picked them up. We had no other interaction with the rest of the world for a few months.

From time to time we had wonderful parties with beautifully dressed people in the decorated party hall with live music until the early hours of the morning. Harvest parties were for everyone: workmen, business people, neighbours and others all participated in an apparently classless Danish society. We children loved those gatherings and to see adults play like children was a second dimension of heaven.

There was also the real threat of nuclear war. For some youngsters it was a devastating reality. We often debated how long the world would last. We knew about the overkill philosophy which meant that there would be very few survivors, if any, if nuclear war broke out. Many predicted that 1970 would not be seen by most people. Atom bombs were exploded in the atmosphere on a regular basis by Russia and the West. The effect of radiation was not fully understood and therefore played down by the scientific fraternity.

In the summer of 1955, after the decision to emigrate to Kenya, my parents rented a house on a nearby farm. Most of the furniture and household goods were sold at auction, including antiques. My father undertook some temporary work, ploughing heather land for the soil conservation authority. Ulrich and I went with him, staying in a tent. That summer we killed five snakes, not in Africa but on the mainland of Denmark.

Immigration permits were granted in August, after many letters addressed to various authorities. My father was to work for one Colonel Bingley as farm manager from first of November. A 'His Master's Voice' gramophone was acquired and English lessons became the family's evening activity for the next few months. In October the family split up. This was not an easy event for a very close-knit family. The stomach played tricks on one, and tears would burst out for no specific reason. Our known world and security system had fallen apart. Only now did I realise that we in fact had lost our home. An uncharted, unknown world had begun. My mother and younger sister Anna moved north to stay with an aunt. My older sister Karin stayed with friends near her school. Chris commenced work for a farmer friend. Ulrich and I moved in with the owners of the house the family had rented for a short period.

Then came the day for us, Ulrich and me, to say goodbye to our father, not knowing if we would ever see him again. I silently began to doubt the whole philosophy of adventure. The price was too high. But I had no power to turn anything back now, and that would only have been even more devastating. So an acceptance of providence, a capitulation, became the way forward. My father cried when he left on the train for Copenhagen airport. We stood speechless on the platform, and it began to rain. Our newly-gained foster parents, the Mollers, took us by the hands and led us 'home'.

A state of suspended animation set in, but fortunately it did not last long. Our foster parents were natural psychologists and absolutely fantastic, giving love and understanding freely. We pursued our schooling and drove tractors in the afternoons, ploughing the Mollers' large fields. We loved the work. I drove a red Nuffield, my brother a grey Ferguson, hooting when we passed each other in the field. The gulls followed us up and down the turned-over furrow, picking up exposed worms. The black crows also came for a worm now and again, in between whatever else these black birds do. Mrs Moller would bring us coffee and sandwiches in the field, and we would rest and talk and then carry on till after dark. Here in Moller's lands, I had an experience I never will forget. Approaching a marl pit with a five-metre steep cliff, I lifted the plough with the tractor's hydraulic lift, as we normally did when preparing to turn. A sudden surge of unhindered power pushed the tractor forward to the point where the front wheels went over the cliff, spinning in the air. In a split second I felt some strange entity turning the tractor for me and catastrophe was avoided.

We stayed with the Mollers until just before Christmas 1955. The family, except my father of course, congregated at The Travellers Inn in Rebil, which was owned by another of my many aunts. Rebil is in the north of Denmark, the place where Danish Americans come to celebrate their Independence Day, the fourth of July. While there we received the sad news that the Mollers had been involved in a car crash and were badly injured. New arrangements had to be made. Ulrich and I joined up with Karin at Mejerholm. We stayed there for about six weeks and now had seven kilometres to school instead of two. In a winter of minus ten degrees the steel of the bicycle gets so cold that the skin of the palm sticks to it. But if one is faced with no alternative, to avoid upsetting already stressed people one manages. I do not recall missing a single day of schooling. In mid-February we moved back to our recuperated Mollers.

It had by now been decided that my mother, sister Anna, Ulrich and I should leave Denmark for Kenya by air in the last week of April. It was also decided that Karin and I should be confirmed in church before departure. Karin and my older brother Chris were to depart by boat from Italy via the Suez canal to Mombassa in July or August.

I had to have special dispensation from the bishop to be confirmed, because I was under fourteen years old. Normally in Denmark the age requirement for confirmation is fourteen. The permission was granted by the bishop, and I started the confirmation preparation. That consisted of two hours, twice a week, of talk and discussions with the local priest in his home on subjects such as ethics, religion and spiritual understanding, social science and community responsibility.

That winter Ulrich and I were exposed to a pervert, while on our way to a nearby forest for a walk. He was a national border guard on his afternoon patrol. He looked around, I suppose to ascertain that no one else was to be seen, and asked if we knew anything about sex. I said, 'No' and he promptly began relating the most hideous stories. He was a possible contributor to the Danish porn of the sixties! Obviously it was not a world shaker for a thirteen-year-old boy, but not the experience one would wish for a young mind. He obviously did not talk about love, holding hands, the single stolen kiss, the natural shyness of teenagers or any other feelings that can make humans so wonderful and special and apparently so different to animals. However, my confirmation preparations took care of those important subjects. As a matter of fact, I looked forward to those hours of altered consciousness, of intensified and stimulating thoughts. It was not religion and its preaching systems that I was interested in, but the mystical aspects, the questions. 'Who am I? What is the holy spirit? What is the soul? Did "I" exist before I was born?' I did not get any answers then, but did find out that one cannot get answers to anything without first putting the question, even if the question is only put to oneself.

Then came the day for which I had prepared. The ceremony took place in Tonder church, the biggest church in the area, with a history that goes back to the early Christian church in Denmark. The ornate decoration stems from its Catholic origin. On that day it was also full of flowers. Seventy youngsters, including Karin and I, were to be confirmed by a long-standing priest friend of my parents. He was a man who had ventured into China in his youth, who had that mysterious aura, which he could not hide even if he wanted to. I saw him as a holy man. After the normal service we had to go up to the altar in groups of ten, kneel down and wait for the priest to lay his hand on our heads. I heard him saying, 'We hereby confirm your baptism and in accordance with Holy Scriptures you will accept and pursue a spiritual life which brings eternal life in the name of Jesus Christ.' When it came to my turn and he put his hand on my head, I felt a sudden sensation in my lower back, like an electric charge. The sensation intensified as it crawled up my back and burst out of my head. My eyes went out of focus. And then the process began again. I did not know what to do so I surrendered, let go. That took me into a temporary spin of unknown feelings and momentarily I saw the whole universe as a gigantic crystal of brilliant colours, all vibrating in tune with an overwhelming, clear sound. I saw a full rainbow in the crystal and was awe-struck. Time disappeared, and I had no thought. After a while my eyes began to regain focus and I noticed that my group had left. I had tears in my eyes and wanted to wipe them away without anyone noticing. I stood up and looked around. Everyone behaved as though nothing had changed, so I quickly walked back to my seat, wiped my eyes and pretended nothing had happened. I spied on the other youngsters to see if I could detect any difference in their behaviour. There was nothing to see, but maybe they were keeping it to themselves as I did. That was how I resolved the dilemma for a long time. The church organ began to play and everyone looked down into their hymn-books and sang. The priest then gave a long talk, directed at my family. He expressed his sorrow that it was necessary for some people to leave their mother country to find fulfilment or for whatever reason drove them. Then he went on to suggest that society was too rigid, requiring its citizens to fit into the new great socialistic order, ignoring individual needs and creative thinking. 'Are we all meant just to be components in a machine-like state, living for the sake of the state, where we have experts to fix those of us who feel that life does have some hidden meaning? I am fully aware that today's schooling system and information media can brainwash anyone to be almost anything but himself. And maybe many of us are walking around under that hypnotic influence. Is it that overwhelming, one-sided influence that some want to escape from? I do not know, but I do know that the family leaving us will be an asset to whomever they come in contact with and will therefore be good ambassadors for our country.'

One more hymn had to be sung, and then we could escape. On the way out of church I felt that every one was looking at us and kept my eyes lowered. A good school friend came and reminded me not to forget to send him stamps from Mozambique and Bechuanaland. That broke some of the ice and I did manage to say goodbye to most of my friends.

We walked the two kilometres to Mejerholm, where the Rabecks produced a delicious lunch. During lunch a letter from my father was presented to me. I read:

Nakuru 15/3/56

This letter is only for you, Hanslver.
My own dear and good boy.

I understand that your confirmation is a week after the coming Sunday. This letter is only for you and Ulrich will have to wait for the next letter.

Dear Hanslver, it is extremely difficult for me to write to my two children on their confirmation and not be able to participate. I hope and pray that you will have a ceremony that will always stand out as being the day you felt close to God. Remember sweet boy, when you kneel at the altar, you are confronting God. Pray to Him that He will give you understanding of what is actually happening and that He will guide your steps in the future. I will be with you in thought, and let us also pray that we all will be reunited shortly. Let us hope that happiness will be restored in our lives and that the last year of sorrow will disappear from our minds, so that we again can be truly thankful for our existence. In my last letter I sent a photograph of myself. Please put that in front of you at the table when you have your confirmation lunch and feel that I am there speaking to you. You have been good to your parents in your childhood, and that I want to say thank you for, and now, as you enter manhood, be good and follow honesty and integrity, and never compromise with injustice. There will undoubtedly be times when temptation will be strong. Under such circumstances place a picture of your mother in the chamber of your heart and you will see the disappearance of temptations.

When we meet again soon let us be good friends who can talk about anything and everything. I am sure I have experienced many things that could be of value for you.

I will now wish happiness and all the best for the future.
With love from your father

By now I was tired. To top it all I had developed a banging headache, and all I wanted was to hide, so I went to bed. After a short while I fell asleep and numerous dreams entered my sleep consciousness. One dream was about a coffin that was to be buried, in a churchyard, but no one knew the name of the dead person in the coffin or even if there was a body in it. No one was prepared to check or find out so eventually they just buried whomever might have been in the coffin. They mumbled a few words to complete the formalities and everyone went back to work.

I understood the dream to be an illustration of triviality – a situation of fossilised tradition in which no one was prepared to investigate the meaning of life or death.

The next dream was about two young pilots who were having an aerobatic air show. I discussed with them how best I could photograph their display, and portray the feeling of speed and mastery over the machines. After numerous attempts I got fed up with the photographing, because it did not convey the flying feeling I was after. I explained to the two pilots that what they were doing I could do without a machine, and gave a flying demonstration feeling free and thrilled.

Years later someone told me that life can be compared to riding a bicycle. You have to keep on pedalling because the alternative is no momentum and then you will simply fall off. I have often wondered if my dream at the age of thirteen years was trying to tell me the same thing.

A few days following the confirmation my mother, brother Ulrich, sister Anna and I boarded the train in Tonder, bound for Copenhagen. The plane would leave Copenhagen for Kenya the next day at about lunch-time. Arriving in Copenhagen at the railway station we saw Chris. He had got time off from work and had found his own way there to say goodbye. He wanted us to see the Tivoli Gardens before leaving Denmark, so we had a quick tour of the fun-fair while Mother was waiting for the bus to the airport. One hour later we said goodbye to Chris and disappeared behind the departure door.

It was my first flight in a commercial aeroplane, although I had flown in a barn-storming plane some years earlier. We were allocated front seats. The plane was not full so we had two seats each. We waved goodbye to our homeland, not knowing when we would see it again. After short stops in Zurich and Athens, we had dinner and settled for the night. During the night I had another amazing dream. I dreamt that we were flying to Africa, but I was flying by myself, as in earlier dreams, without a machine. I felt like a dolphin in water. Just looking in a certain direction determined it. A huge archway opened in front of me which I had to go through. Coming closer I saw it was guarded by two men with fox heads holding clubs in their hands. They waved and said, 'This is the door of no return. Whoever passes here will never return to be the same again.' I responded that I was on the way to my father in Kenya, and they got out of the way and I passed through.

When I awoke at early sunrise everything was red, including the ground below us, as we were flying over red sandy desert. After a while breakfast was served. Then there was a brief stop in Khartoum. On our last leg from Khartoum to Nairobi the pilot invited us one by one into the cockpit to show us how the plane functioned. He even allowed me to hold the half-circle steering wheel. I turned a little and the plane gradually changed direction then went back again. I went back to my seat to buckle-up for the descent to Nairobi airport.

Kenya–Bingley

Our SAS DC-7c landed at Nairobi Airport in Kenya, one day in the last week of April, 1956. The morning was still fresh. When the door of the plane was opened a smell of newly cut grass mixed with the smell of drying paint welcomed us. Only a few people were standing on the lawn. And one of them was my father waving to us. What jubilation! He had not disappeared or got eaten or burned to parchment by the sun. He looked like himself, just as when he had said goodbye six months earlier. We rushed up and hugged him in turn, smiling with tears of joy in our eyes. Official papers were quickly stamped and finalised, our suitcases were collected and loaded on to the open Land-Rover, and we all boarded and drove off. We drove through Nairobi and stopped for breakfast in the Kikuyu reserve on the western outskirts of Nairobi. The smells of exotic fruits, shiny black faces under red fezzes, mist covering mountain tops, fields full of pyrethrum daisy flowers, tarred roads – what a place, not 'dark Africa' at all! After breakfast and a further twenty miles, passing dozens of black women with huge bundles of firewood on their backs, we came to the escarpment where the road wound into a huge valley twenty or more kilometres wide. What a view, a view that surpasses Naples. You do not die when you see it, but you do feel as though you have joined the eagles in flight, and the Angels are whispering their secrets into your ear… the secrets of the earth forces that have torn Africa apart from the Red Sea to Central Africa and extruded huge mountain ranges in the equator region, releasing new potential for humans to develop physically, mentally and spiritually, thereby contributing to the universal intelligence. The place is called the Great Rift Valley. I was already transformed. I wanted to shout to the whole world about this new land, but my parents, brother and sister were in the Land-Rover, and as social etiquette dictates, I kept my mouth shut. The flat-topped acacia trees in the bottom of the valley could only just be perceived as trees and the distant mountains, blurred in blue mist, looked like newly-made molehills on a rim-frosted lawn. I knew and felt that I had now seen the ultimate in natural beauty and could therefore happily join the ones who had seen Naples. Below the escarpment we made a brief stop at a little church reputedly built by Italian prisoners of war during and after the Second World War. The church was built in memory of the people who had died during the construction of the escarpment road leading into the Rift Valley. Over the altar I noticed a black Jesus on a cross. It seemed wrong, but why not? Jesus could have been black. I wondered whether it was easier for the missionaries to convert black people to Christianity if Jesus was portrayed as a black man.

Driving along in the valley, we passed the extinct volcano of Longonot, still looking like a volcano that had blown its top only a few years ago. Some modern prophets do believe that it will shortly blow its top again, coinciding with other geophysical activity. Herds of zebra could be seen in the dry grass from the road and the odd giraffe stuck its head above the acacia trees. The town of Naivasha, consisting of a railway station, a few shops, an hotel and a few houses, is situated almost on the shoreline of Lake Naivasha with huge mountains on the opposite side of the lake, scenery comparable with Israel's Lake Galilee and the Golan mountain. I am sure that had it been known to the biblical Abraham and his followers in earlier days, they would have preferred it to Israel's dry hills – what a different world that would have created. No wonder that great men of England wanted to colonise such a wonderful land! Gilgil was the next little town. It had a fairly large British garrison, protecting the Empire and maybe still fighting the Mau-Mau. At Embaruk we turned right, went through a viaduct under the railway and on to a dirt road. Driving through the viaduct reminded me of my dream in the aeroplane the previous night. I even turned my head, looking for the fox men, but they foxed me and failed to turn up. I had a feeling of déjà-vu. I did not know the word 'déjà-vu' in those days, but it was a feeling that I had seen the setting before. Another eight kilometres up in the mountains on a very slippery, red-soil, graded road, and we entered Colonel Bingley's Shangri-La. It was a small plateau only a few square kilometres in size, surrounded by hills covered in forest, with waterfalls and small streams. Four farms occupied the valley, and a police station, consisting of one white British policeman with his fifteen or so African askaries. To the west, about thirty kilometres away, we could see the rim of the Meningai crater, one of the world's largest craters, appearing just over the horizon. Meningai is an extinct volcano in the Rift Valley with the town of Nakuru built on its southern side. To the east and north beyond the visible forest was an even higher plateau extending all the way to the Aberdare mountain range.

Shortly after arriving at Mr and Mrs Bingley's homestead, after we were introduced and the Land-Rover offloaded, we were invited in for tea. It was a formal tea with cucumber sandwiches. Ulrich, Anna and I had been allocated rooms in the main house and my parents had a guest-house behind the main house. Both houses were made of poles and sun-dried bricks, whitewashed with the timber work painted black, with cedar-wood slate roofs.

Some of the rooms had ceilings and others not. Toilets were outside in small huts, consisting mainly of a deep hole in the ground covered with a wooden bench. One of the latrines had a huge double-horned rhino trophy behind the seat – we called it 'Mr Bingley's horny loo'. The other loo was referred to as 'Mrs Bingley's loo'. The kitchen was a two-roomed wooden shack situated about thirty metres away from the main house, right on the edge of the tropical forest. Here meals were produced on primitive wood-fired stoves in old black pots, but always served as if from a five-star hotel kitchen. Lunches and teas were served in shining silver. During tea we were instructed by Mr Bingley in the 'Do and Don'ts'. Do not ever go for walks on your own. Be totally quiet in the house after dark. Come to the inner room if unusual noise is heard or if the three dogs, Monday, Tuesday and Wednesday, are disturbed. Do not talk to the servants and workers except when relaying orders from him or my father. Do not eat or drink anything the Africans offer you. Do not kill snakes. Try not to get bitten by mosquitoes, to avoid malaria. Be careful not to get wet feet because jiggers can be dangerous. Jiggers are small worms that develop and grow in the toes. Do not touch the water in the dam because bilharzia can kill. It is a little creature that enters the human body via a snail, lives in the bloodstream and, when mature, departs via the urine. Disgusting how these creatures lie there, waiting to bore into a human body in order to multiply. We answered with military nods and 'Yes Sir', and at the time expected to comply with the instructions. During tea a peacock came to show off on the veranda, spreading his tail and shaking it in the late afternoon sunlight. Ulrich, Anna and I promptly followed the majestic bird out of the house to where the gardener was feeding the peahens and the peacock. The garden was outstanding, with bougainvillaea creeping up into tall trees and cascading out with red and lilac flowers, oleanders at the edge of the forest, and arum lilies growing along a little stream in the far end of the garden. We asked the gardener for permission to feed the birds, a way of getting into conversation I suppose. The next minute two saddled horses passed, apparently for Mr and Mrs Bingley's evening ride. The groom spoke some English and asked us to come and see the foal in the nearby stables, as soon as Bwana Bingley had left, which we did, disobeying earlier instruction. While there, the cook Mwangi came along. He also spoke a bit of English. I felt very relieved that one could actually communicate with these strange black people. Between them they taught us five Swahili words on the very first day in Kenya. Sometime during the evening one of us mentioned that we had learned five Swahili words. Colonel Bingley asked, with harshness in his voice, from where we had learned those words. All three of us felt like Adam and Eve transgressing some fundamental law! My parents had not approved of Bingley's earlier instructions and the restrictions placed upon us, but at the same time did not want to create waves. They explained that the Bingleys would leave for England soon, which was the reason we were there in the first place. My father was to manage the farm while the Bingleys were in England. I already looked forward to their departure.

The evening meals were prepared late in the afternoon by Mwangi in the kitchen, then placed on a table with pots etc. in the lounge, ready for warming in the huge fireplace later in the evening. The reason for that double work was a curfew which was still in force. All domestic and other workers had to be in their houses by six o'clock in the evening until six in the morning due to the Mau-Mau uprising which had started in 1952.

Mr Bingley showed us where the button for detonating light flares was situated, in case of a Mau-Mau attack. The flares themselves were placed just under the roof pitch. The nearby police station would then see the flares and come to our assistance, in time, we hoped, before we had all lost our heads. The Mau-Maus' main weapons were pangas, big knives, and they literally hacked their victims to death. Attacks would normally take place between six and eight o'clock in the evening, giving the attackers sufficient time to disappear before morning. No one knew who was a Mau-Mau except that they were likely to be Kikuyus. Bingley's domestic servants were all Kikuyus. Even the farm foreman was a Kikuyu. He had only one arm and was known as Mokono Moja.

One year earlier Bingley's son, daughter-in-law and two children had been killed by Mau-Mau on their farm near the Aberdare mountains, about forty kilometres east of Dundori, where we were now staying. The story was a classic one, in which a domestic servant's mother had died and the servant had asked for leave to arrange the funeral. A replacement servant from a neighbouring farm was then hired on a temporary basis. Then one evening hot soup was served, not on plates as normal, but in the faces of the white adults who were expecting nothing of the sort. At the same instant a gang of five or six men entered the house swinging their sharpened pangas, full of dope and other unspeakable substances, killing everyone that was around the dinner table, including the dog. The orgy did not stop with the killing and a slaughter followed, to be discovered by police and neighbours the following day. Bingley had seen the hacked remains of his son and family, after being notified by the police. As a retired colonel and hardened fighter from Burma, he did not show emotion, but said, 'Life must carry on as normal. We have learnt a lesson and have to carry on protecting the British empire.' I think by hiring mainly Kikuyu workers after his son's death, Bingley was trying to prove to and convince himself that he could forgive and forget. Or was it more calculated? If a Kikuyu accepted work on a white-owned farm had he in fact rejected the first Mau-Mau oath and what they stood for?

On that first evening in Kenya, before dinner, Bingley had mixed his usual drink, whisky in milk. It looked obnoxious, curdled milk with alcohol. He made a point of teaching me how to mix it, so for the next couple of weeks that became one of my duties. After dinner we went to bed very aware of all the new sounds, particularly one dominating, rolling, low-pitched sound. Bingley told us that it was the call of bushbabies. I visualised pink European babies stranded in treetops, screaming their heads off, waiting for a stork, whereas in fact they are adorable little animals with big eyes.

The farm was a mixed-farming operation, with most of the income generated from a dairy herd. Other activities included rearing pigs and growing barley for pig fodder, and some maize was grown, mainly for labour rations. The African workers mainly ate cooked maize meal, their staple diet. It is called *'ugali'* in Swahili, and is not liked by most Europeans because of its glue-like consistency. Sun hemp was grown on fallow lands for soil improvement. Pyrethrum, a daisy-looking flower, was cultivated for pesticide, its effectiveness not surpassed to this day.

The next morning at breakfast Bingley recommended that we took anti-malaria pills. He did not take malaria pills himself because he had lived in the country for many years. I could not see the relationship between the number of years you had lived in a place and contracting malaria, but anyway there were no pharmacies except in Nakuru some forty kilometres away. We never took pills for malaria.

Ulrich and I followed my father around the farm and got to meet most of the thirty or so African workers within the first week. We also learned more Swahili words. Anna and my mother looked after the house and kitchen or they escaped into the garden, depending on Bingley's whereabouts. Mrs Bingley had a daughter on a neighbouring farm and spent a lot of time there. Mr Bingley left the farm frequently in his Chevrolet pick-up, preparing their holiday I supposed.

A week or so after our arrival Bingley suggested that if Ulrich and I wanted to get up early in the mornings and go for a ride, he would see that the horses were ready for us. We should just tell him before four o'clock in the afternoon the day before if we wanted to ride. It seemed that he had relaxed somewhat on the matter of us exploring the surroundings and talking to the Africans. Maybe he realised that he could not protect or control us after he had departed for England anyway. Our answer was an unanimous 'Yes please, every day.' The following afternoon he shouted out through the back door, where various workmen and servants were conferring and awaiting instructions, 'Horseman, the horses must be saddled up by seven o'clock in the morning. The young Bwanas are going for a ride. Take them up to Bwana Dunlop's farm then over to the police station and back.' 'Yes Bwana', a black smiling face replied.

For the next few weeks the horses, the groom, Ulrich and I saw the farms and surrounding countryside from many different angles, including from ground level. We rode everywhere. One day we stopped at a hut situated under some acacia trees. One of the tractor drivers came out of the dilapidated termite-eaten hut and asked if we would like to join him for a cup of tea. The horses were tied to a flat-topped acacia tree and we entered the hut. The smoke and other unidentifiable smells nearly knocked me out. We sat down on some tree stumps while our host prepared tea. I silently prayed that Bingley would not turn up unexpectedly. He did not. Our new-found friend and host apologised for not having cups and with no embarrassment served the tea in an eight-inch-long mayonnaise glass, an old pea tin, and a test-tube glass. The tea was rather disgusting, like sweet washing-up water. But our upbringing forced us to drink it and to say 'Thank you'. During tea the driver showed us a black and white photograph of his thirteen-year-old son who lived with his mother near Lake Victoria. He was very proud of his son who, to me, looked like every other thirteen-year-old black boy I had seen so far. He also informed us that he was a Catholic and had a big certificate to prove it. He was given the certificate and a blanket when he dropped his previous membership of the African Inland mission. I later found out that he lived separately from other workers because he belonged to the Luo tribe. They are known in slang as 'engosi mulefu', which means 'long skin'. All tribes in Kenya are circumcised except the Luos. Circumcision in Africa is a cruel ritual during which the foreskin of the penis is cut off without anaesthetic. It is normally performed at the onset of the teenage years, but the way it is done varies from tribe to tribe. Some tribes, including Kikuyus, also circumcise the girls. I hope such barbaric behaviour has been outlawed by now. No people who want to be known as civilised humans can condone the burning or cutting of female sex organs, for whatever reason or excuses their male-oriented society can dream up.

It disturbed me that initially I could not see personality differences amongst Africans the way I could with whites. All Africans I had seen so far had the same type of eyes and I could not evaluate their moods easily. Even worse, they all looked so identical. I concluded that facial expression would only become distinguishable when one got to know the individuals or race well. With humans that fortunately happens fairly quickly. Look into a pigsty and you will see that all pigs seem to be identical. Get to know the pigs and they will develop appearance differences. If you get to know the pigs very well you will probably discover that they have mood swings and that some of them might even hate you because of your devouring look.

During our rides we developed friendships with the dairy foreman's children, an eleven-year-old boy called Lasso, and a girl, Getchemma, of about twelve. The dairy foreman was a well-educated, brown African who belonged to the Kipsigis tribe, who have Arabic features. His handwriting was beautiful and his written records meticulous. His name was Ade-Me-Sou. After horse rides we would meet Getchemma and Lasso somewhere in the forest and talk for hours, and in that way we became fairly fluent in Swahili in record time. I also found out that belief systems, upbringing and historical background make people very different. These two black youngsters believed that many animals were controlled by some dead person's spirit. Birds, snakes and monkeys were favoured by spirits but sometimes other animals as well. The possessed animals would exhibit behavioural traces of some dead village person and one would know who was in the animal although it was not often discussed. Lasso could get terribly defensive about the African spiritual belief system and say, 'Just be careful that the monster does not come out of the snake and eat you. Your God was a spirit and then became a man. You have a devil that was a snake, so!' I could see his point. Perhaps he knew more about the Bible than I did? They also saw smaller free spirits, appearing as small, round, blue lights hovering over the little farm dam during early evening and night. Getchemma seemed to have no objection that she, being a girl, would shortly be sold to some unknown man and would be expected to produce numerous babies. Failing that she would be returned to her parents to live in shame for ever, amen. That slavery system was taken for granted and accepted as being her lot in life. I often wondered what the missionaries were doing. Why had they not taught the Africans the principle of Love? Real love between a man and his wife, the way my parents loved each other.

In the evenings Colonel Bingley told us fascinating stories of early days in Kenya, usually ending the talk by saying, 'You must remember I have been in Kenya for forty-two years, and I know.'

He told us about Lord Delamere, who had come to Kenya before the turn of the century via Somalia on camels, battled with warlords and gangs, crossed the desert country and arrived at Eldama Ravine, lush evergreen forest and grassland on the opposite side of the Rift Valley. We were regaled with stories about even earlier explorers such as Joseph Thomson, W. Mackinnon and H.H. Johnston who came to East Africa in the 1880s and were the founders of the British East Africa Company, which was later sold to the British government in 1895 for £250,000. I am still amazed at the speed with which the railway, telegraph and roads were planned, completed or installed in the early years of Kenya. Names such as Lord Scott, Sir Girouard, Sir Grigg, Lord Delamere's brother-in-law Cole and others were mentioned, including Cecil John Rhodes and his determination to develop central Africa. I cannot recall their specific activities but I revered these great men who had toiled to make Kenya and other parts of Africa habitable for white people, stopped tribal warfare, introduced schooling and medicine and thereby opened the door for civilisation in Africa. I believe that Africa should be thankful for being introduced to new ways of existence by those early civilising pioneers, even with their possible shortcomings. Why would Lord Delamere, and others, rich men, risk their lives and battle to establish farms in the middle of Africa? Most of them came from the upper echelons of society in England. Why would they come, by free will, to countries that initially and for the foreseeable future could give them nothing but hardship, disappointments, unknown diseases and possibly death in wars with the indigenous tribes? Bingley said that Lord Delamere always consulted and debated sheep and cattle breeding as well as other matters with his Masai neighbours. He said that most of the early white settlers were liked and respected and seen as protectors by the African population. I believe many early settlers were transported by the sacred beauty of Africa, the open spaces, the simplicity and the local acceptance of the natural order, and that many felt a calling, a type of missionary work, a symbiotic relationship, which would help uplift the black people in time. Maybe this is a more realistic ideal than trying to convert the indigenous to believe in a trinity God, a God divided in three parts, where the human part has to be killed, and the bloody murder weapon adored, in order for you to be free from suffering and bondage! This is a belief that most thinking people have a problem with. Bingley did not say what had gone wrong to stimulate the Mau-Mau uprising, but obviously had his own thoughts on the subject.

One evening Karen Blixen, the author of *Out of Africa* was discussed. She was Danish and was then living in Denmark, but had lived in Kenya for a number of years. Mr Bingley did not like her at all. He said that she was immoral and a nuisance to the British people in Nairobi at the time, and that her boyfriends were also of dubious character. My father looked up to the ceiling and sighed with obvious disapproval. Perhaps he was just supporting a fellow Dane, I thought. Later, out in the lands, he informed me that the Bingleys were not married, that they lived together and therefore had no right to talk about immorality. Years later I was exposed to the saying 'Are you married or do you live in Kenya?' The renowned 'Happy Valley' was less than an inch away from Bingley's farm on the map.

One day Ulrich and I walked well beyond the police station, over Mr Dunlop's farm southwards to uninhabited hills that overlooked the Rift Valley and Lake Elementaita, a distance of approximately ten kilometres. Unfortunately we were seen by a police patrol, picked up and escorted back to the farm where Bingley was informed. That event hastened the inevitable return to school. My parents were of the opinion that missing one term of schooling in a new country would do no harm, but the situation had now changed due to our walk. It was decided that Ulrich and Anna should commence boarding school in Nakuru as soon as possible. My situation was different. I had completed standard seven and a high school, or some other training ground had to be found. But where? After some deliberation and sleepless nights it was decided that I should help on the farm for a year. I was quite happy with that decision.

School uniforms were acquired in a Nakuru shop and Ulrich and Anna were driven off to school one Sunday afternoon looking rather miserable. We did not speak English well, although by now we understood everything.

Then, out of the blue, Bingley informed us that he was no longer going on holiday. The British Empire needed his service, and he was on standby awaiting further instruction. An unlikeable chap in Egypt had apparently come into power and Colonel Bingley, at sixty-five years old, would have to go and protect British interests in the Suez Canal region! I visualised old Colonel Bingley on a camel riding over the desert dunes, swinging a long sword and reinstating King Faruk to his rightful place. That did not happen. Instead British troops were withdrawn from Egypt. Fortunately holiday plans changed again and Bingley *did* leave for England by boat via the Cape of Good Hope.

During his absence things went well. We ploughed, sowed and harvested wheat and barley crops. Being on the equator and with two rainy seasons the climate could be compared to a natural greenhouse. Pyrethrum was hand-picked by African women, dried in wood-fired flues and then once a week delivered to Nakuru, coinciding with visits to the school and shopping for the farm and house. I helped maintain machines, fencing and the water supply. I weighed pigs to check their weekly gain, drove the Land-Rover around on the farm, checked the milk-records book, castrated piglets and gave cows penicillin for mastitis. Thunderstorms would often bring work to a close by three in the afternoon. We would then wade in red muddy soil, like red paint, up to the farmhouse, have a wash and sit on the veranda watching the thunderclouds disappear eastwards and the sun reappear low in the west, distributing its rays to reflective water drops before finally setting in a sea of colours. Some of Bingley's machines were very antiquated. The combine harvester was an old ox-drawn machine that should have been in a museum long ago. Whenever we mentioned that any of his machines were old and needed fixing, Bingley would say they had lasted for forty-two years, and why should they break now? His logic was different to what we were used to in Denmark.

One morning we found that four steers had died during the night. A veterinarian was consulted and the cause of death was found to be anthrax, a highly contagious disease spread by spores which affect the brain and nervous system of the victim. It can also be transmitted to humans. During the afternoon six labourers dug an almighty big hole into which the four dead animals were dumped and covered with at least one and a half metres of soil. That same night, around ten o'clock, the three dogs started an unusual performance. My father and I got out of bed, dressed and drove down to the farm buildings with the dogs in the back of the vehicle. When we stopped the dogs took off towards the burial ground of the four animals. We followed and discovered that three Kikuyu workers, who had helped to bury the animals, were in the process of digging them up again and had already taken some of the carcasses for consumption, possibly even eaten some cooked on a nearby fire! We immediately drove to the nearby police station to report the incident, in case they should sicken or die. The white policeman, not amused at being woken in the middle of the night, recorded the incident and asked if we wanted to lay charges against the workers. My father said no, but asked what to do should they get sick. The policeman replied that had we given them the meat we could be charged for manslaughter in the event of death. The next day all came to work as if the night episode had not taken place. Like a page of nightmare in a book torn out and forgotten. They did not get sick and even after long explanations of the dangers refused to be taken to hospital. They survived and I realised then that the African immune system is made for Africa.

A few days later I took pipe fittings to the same meat eaters who were now digging a trench in the forest for a new water pipeline. Kariuki, the heavier of the three, a strong middle-aged balding man wearing sandals made of motorcar tyres, got out of the trench. 'You remember when we used to cut to pieces Mototo ya Musungu, children of the whites, with pangas,' he said loudly to one of the other workers, but obviously intending me to hear. 'That is how it is done.' He made a quick movement with his hand holding the panga. Then he called me to come closer. I hesitated. 'Come closer,' he hissed. I approached him smiling. He made the same movement as before, but in slow motion said, 'You hit Mototo ya Musungu like this. The flat side of the panga must come in contact with the body first, then you turn the panga sharp side towards the flesh and pull back. It will make a much bigger cut than if you just hack at the enemy.' After he had completed his demonstration I detected some anticlimax and said, 'Kariuki, Mau-Mau is over, it is finished.' 'And all for what?' he replied bitterly. Members of his family had been killed and he wanted to know who would compensate him. I did not understand what he meant and asked if I could borrow his panga to cut a small branch to put the pipe fittings on. It was a contrived diversion, as the killing conversation was uncomfortable. He became a good friend of mine. In the following years we went hunting, explored and debated many things together.

I never told my parents about Kariuki and his panga demonstration. They had enough on their minds. Karin and Chris would arrive soon. My father's position with Bingley was to terminate at the end of the year so another position would have to be found.

One Sunday before the Bingleys returned, my parents had gone to see Ulrich and Anna in Nakuru and were to be away all day. The British Queen Mother had come to Kenya and was to award achievement prizes to some children at Nakuru primary school. Ulrich had been nominated and was to shake the Queen Mother's hand, a good reason for my parents to attend such a function. After they left for Nakuru I went riding, then had lunch prepared by Muzee Mwangi. It was a beautiful lunch as usual, for he knew no other way. After lunch I rested on the lawn in the shade and fell asleep. In my sleep I saw – a dream I suppose – an enormous space station consisting of two huge pipes joined in the middle with a cross piece forming a large 'H'. After a short while more of the same type of craft appeared. Then out of the big 'H' came smaller single cylinder-shaped craft. With their appearance the entire sky began to vibrate. I noticed that the vibration emanated from loudspeaker-like devices mounted on the spacecraft. Then the sky changed colour and I heard voices saying, 'The time will come when enough is enough with man's non-consideration of his reason for existence. Live, observe and appreciate, but be aware that the day the sky vibrates, as now will be the time of evacuation. Other signs will be the sun darkening, the moon turning red during the night and stones falling into the sea.' One of the smaller crafts landed in the garden and a human-looking creature came out. He came towards me. The dream faded and I do not recall any more. I awoke around four o'clock in the afternoon with a headache. I began to wonder if dreams had meaning or messages, direct or in symbolic form. I did describe the dream to Getchemma and Lasso and asked what they dreamt about. Getchemma was quick and told us that her last dream was about Mr Bingley. He had arrived in the camp of Mokono Moja, a small group of huts, but Mokono Moja had turned into a snake and Bingley had drawn his pistol ready to shoot. But after a while he had realised that he would in fact shoot his foreman. I thought, 'You and your bloody snake! Every time you tell me something there is a bloody snake involved!'

My brother Chris and sister Karin boarded their ship in Genoa, Italy, on 16th July, 1956, and passed through the Suez Canal only a few days before the canal was nationalised by General Nasser, the new communist-oriented president of Egypt who had helped to oust King Faruk in a 1952 military uprising. General Nasser became president of Egypt in 1956 and demanded payment for ships going through the canal. The shareholders of the canal, England and France, had refused to hand over the canal revenue to Nasser. He then nationalised the canal without compensation and declared martial law in the canal zone. That led to a short war. England and France wanted to take the canal back using Israel, Egypt's enemy number one, as the aggressor. England and France then intervened between the warring parties to keep the canal in neutral hands, but, as history illustrates, had forgotten to ask big brother USA! President Eisenhower of the USA got annoyed and told Prime Minister Eden of England to stop hostile action against Egypt immediately. Eden resigned and the new decolonisation era began with the wind of change under England's next Prime Minister Macmillan. Rightly, if England could not count on her ally when in need, who could she count on? However, Macmillan and Eisenhower developed a close relationship, choices were few, and world history changed in a few weeks. And all that happened while Colonel Bingley was on holiday.

Had Chris and Karin left a few days later their ship would probably have joined so many other ships on the bottom of the Suez Canal. However they disembarked in Kenya's main port of Mombassa early in August and took the train to Nairobi where my father fetched them. Chris and Karin stayed with us on Bingley's farm for only a few weeks. Karin found a job at a kennel a few kilometres from the farm. Chris was to work for the new owner of the farm where Bingley's son and family had been killed by Mau-Mau – a Dane by the name of Pedersen. My father had corresponded with Pedersen before we left Denmark. In fact he had been instrumental in our coming to Kenya in the first place. The second Sunday after Chris's arrival we took him to the Pedersen farm. On the way, driving east through forest and on to a large plateau, I could see a single mountain in front of the Aberdare mountains some thirty or so kilometres southwards and thought, If we have to move from Bingley that is where I want to stay. I even made a deal with the Angels. I would do all the things that they would want me to do, if they saw to it that at some stage I would live near those forest covered mountains. I had a passion for mountains. They extend your horizon, Mau-Mau or no Mau-Mau.

Bingley returned from his holiday at the beginning of September, just before my fourteenth birthday. I decided that being fourteen I had now joined the ranks of adults and vowed to behave accordingly. Bingley displayed pleasure at being home. He was grateful for finding the farm in good order and that we had fixed the dilapidated manager's cottage and moved out of the main house. He informed us that he was considering semi-retirement and suggested that we discuss a new long-term management contract. He seemed happy and talked about his holiday, world events and the future. One morning, while I was feeding calves, he put his hand on my shoulder and told me that he was so happy to be home, and that he would like to teach me African farming. He added, 'You want to stay in Africa don't you?' His voice was almost intimidating. I answered him with an affirmative, but pleasant times ended abruptly. While the Bingleys had been away my mother had overseen the nursing of the sick and had also inaugurated a women's sewing club. She was a trained dress designer from Denmark. As weeks passed Bingley became irritated by the Africans relying on us for work instruction and their social welfare. I think he felt superfluous and in the way, and definitely not ready for retirement. He had also heard that my parents and I had attended Mukono Moja's father's church service on a Sunday afternoon, where a talk was given about a white man named John Boyes who had become Honorary Chief of the Kikuyus many years ago because he had given credit and dignity to his black friends. Something they apparently craved for. Why not? They did not have much else to look forward to in their primitive lifestyle. Bingley became more hot-tempered by the day and would for no reason, and quite uncalled for, say things like, 'You can't trust a bloody nigger, can you? These people will lie whenever they have a chance.' He would slip into his own frustration over the behaviour of the British queen fraternising with new African leaders. 'I have lost all respect for my Queen and the British empire, and people will go down the drain if we start placating and patronising this new communist, the way the Queen does!' he thundered.

One Friday, having organised the work force for the day, to pick pyrethrum, my father asked permission to use the Land-Rover to fetch Ulrich and Anna who had a long weekend off from school. Bingley's reaction was violent and shocking. Red-faced, he shouted that the farm was not a 'kindergarten', that the children should stay at school and that the Land-Rover was not to be used for personal reasons. Well, we left him, heads bowed and went home for breakfast. My mother, furious when she heard the news, said, 'How *dare* he!' She quietly disappeared into the bedroom from where we could hear her crying. Father waited a few minutes before following her. I left the house through the back door and went up the mountain into the forest under the vines that link the trees in a vast web. The continuous cooing of African doves sounded louder than ever before. The black and white colobus monkey from high up silently surveyed the intruder. I walked in amongst the trees and vines and found a place where I could lean against one. With hands covering my face I cried. I sobbed and cried more and asked God, 'Why? Why?' My mind then produced a picture of the horror of Bingley's son and family cut to pieces, blood-splattered curtains, body parts stuffed into the fireplace and other limbs scattered here and there, and the dog's head on the table between smashed plates. I saw Bingley standing in the doorway. He looked like a dead man who had been dragged back from a war where everyone had been killed. It suddenly occurred to me that the man could be insane, scarred beyond repair, dead inside. He could not afford to feel! I felt sorry for him and began to cry again. I cried and all the trees cried with me and the wind passed through my hair and said, 'I am sorry.' I stood up. My mind was made up. I would walk the eight kilometres to the main road, get a lift to Nakuru and bring Ulrich and Anna back. On the way out of the forest I saw my father in the pyrethrum field with Bingley – I joined them. Bingley looked stressed. Minutes later my mother walked across the field and came right up to Bingley. Three feet from his face she called him a bloody insensitive bastard, a cold dead fish with no feeling! 'No wonder the world hates you, you made it that way for yourself. Do not make us suffer because you have suffered. Your forty-two years in Kenya are worth nothing if all you have learnt is to become insensitive and hateful. We will be leaving shortly you can count on that!' Bingley looked bewildered and full of rage, no one had never spoken to him like that before, but he said nothing for a while. Seeing my mother, normally kind and well-behaved, standing there in the daisy field was more that he could handle. I think he had sense enough to understand that she was speaking the truth. He probably even admired her for it. When he did speak he apologised for causing distress. It was agreed that the Land-Rover was to be our vehicle for private use until we departed. He wished us well and hoped to be of help in the future! One problem was resolved, but now my father had to find another job urgently. Friends were consulted and informed by post and asked to help to look out for a farm manager's position. No newspaper with job offers existed in Kenya in those days. Word of mouth was the only way to find a new position. After a week or two we were informed that Italian millionaires had recently bought a big estate on the foothills of the Aberdare and were looking for a manager. The following weekend a Hussar friend, with whom my Father had been in the Danish cavalry before the Second World War, arrived on foot. His Morris Minor had slid off the muddy road five kilometres from the farm. He was to go with my father to witness and evaluate the Italian job offer. In Kenya a verbal agreement was binding if you could prove what was agreed.

Therefore a witness was essential, especially when dealing with Italians who speak so expressively with their arms. Rope was put into the Land-Rover and the three of us set off in a real tropical afternoon downpour to rescue the stranded vehicle. We found the car on the road where he had left it in a ditch. My father turned the Land-Rover around, reversing close up to the front of the Morris Minor. The Hussar joined the two vehicles with long rope and climbed into the driver's seat, waiting expectantly to be towed. My father moved forward with the Land-Rover and unknowingly severed the Morris Minor's bumper from the rest of the car. After fifty meters he looked back and saw that he was dragging the bumper only. I had been pushing the Morris Minor at the same time. The scene was just too comical for Father. He climbed out of the Land-Rover, laughing so much that he lost his dentures in the mud. Seeing what had happened the Hussar remarked, 'Very well you have lost your dentures, but look at my car. If it ever had any dentures you have pulled them out!' That led to a new outburst of laughter in competition with the ongoing thunder. The result was that both middle-aged men fell in the mud and literally had a red mud bath in the warm tropical rainstorm. After a few minutes they had controlled themselves sufficiently to continue with the breakdown service. I laughed with them to my heart's delight. It was a fantastic healing event. Both men had gone through extreme hardship mentally and emotionally. My father's friend had recently divorced and had other personal dilemmas in his life. Years later his farm was expropriated, like many other Kenyan farms, for African resettlement. He left for Greenland to work on an American army base. He died of cold one evening in the snow. I am sure that he remembered his mud bath with my father in his last minutes before the cold of Greenland sent him to sleep for ever.

The following day they drove to the foothills of the Aberdare to see the Italians. After a few hours of driving around on the ten-thousand-acre estate, over an unexpected plate of spaghetti, a contract of employment was agreed upon, commencing in two weeks' time, the 1st November, 1956. The farm truck would collect our personal possessions and it was arranged that Antonio, another farm manager, would collect my parents on the same day. Bingley was notified and accepted our early departure. Everything went according to plan and the loading of the three-ton flat-nosed Albion truck did not take long. We did not have many possessions, a few beds, a table, chairs and kitchen stuff. The driver, named Cairo, had come via Navasha-Gilgil and up the road from Embaruk and we were to go the other way over the hill to Kipipiri. I knew that the address was PO Box 8 Kinankop and that it was somewhere near the mountain where I had asked my Angel to accommodate me. I sat next to the driver in the truck, and Antonio and my parents followed. On the outskirts of Bingley's farm the African labourers had turned up to say goodbye. They all stood there waving in work clothes, and shirts full of holes, some with two hats on, one to cover the hole in the other, and the traditional sandals made of motor-car tyres. Women were in long dresses and head scarves. Kariuki shouted, 'Will see you shortly.' Ade-Me-Sou with his wife, Getchemma, and Lasso were there. They wanted to come along, but my father had persuaded them to stay because Bingley needed them. It was a rather sad moment saying goodbye to people one had grown with even if only for a short period. Our passing through the well-wishers coincided with Bingley's return from Nakuru. Alarmed, he stopped and asked what the problem was. In unison and harmony, the Africans sang 'Hakuna Matata', meaning 'No problem'. And on that beautiful note we left for the next adventure.

Nine years later my parents revisited Bingley's valley. Bingley had left. The farm and neighbouring farms had been subdivided for African resettlement and Mukono Moja had one of the small new shambas. They had tea together and a talked about the old days. Mukono Moja was now the head of their little church.

Kipipiri Estate: Working for Italians

Driving on gravel roads at a speed of thirty kilometres per hour uphill and a bit faster downhill in the three-ton Albion truck allowed Cairo and me to have a long conversation during our sixty or so kilometre journey. Cairo was a Kikuyu, about thirty years old, newly married and a very good driver. I kept pumping him for information about where the farm was. 'Is it near the Aberdare mountain?' I asked. He looked at me with amazement and said, 'You will see when we get there, Bwana.' I wanted to know if it was the place I had made a deal with the Angels to take me to, but I could not tell him that! Three hours later we headed straight towards 'my' mountain. Driving across the Ol Kalou open-grassland plateau towards Kipipiri I could see that there was a pass between the Aberdare and 'my' mountain and asked Cairo if he had been there and what its name was. The mountain and valley were covered in very dense forest with some huge trees protruding well above other trees. Cairo followed my eye direction and ran a commentary on whatever could have interest as we were driving. The valley between the Aberdares and Kipipiri was called Neptune Valley by the white man, because it rained every day. He did not know if it rained so much because of the name or if the name had come from the rain. He said it was a place full of the spirits of the departed, not necessarily friendly, and would not recommend a casual walk there. I asked him if God lived between the spirits? His frustration was obvious and he promptly informed me of my ignorance and explained that God lived on top of Mount Kenya and was called Nyaga, the highest God that controlled the land and the heavens. The high priest could confer with Nyaga, but everyone else had to rely on the local priest, medicine man or witch-doctor for guidance and help if troublesome spirits bothered them. We drove on a winding narrow road through a very deep ravine carved out by thousands of years of heavy rainfall on the mountains and surrounding plateau. I had seen mounds and big heaps of straw-like substances on the road, and finally saw the reason, a herd of elephants! They plodded along in front of us till we reached the bottom of the gorge where they disappeared into the thicket. Coming out of the ravine we turned left on to the farm road, a Podo-treed avenue. We drove right up on the slopes of 'my' mountain, passing numerous very tall Australian eucalyptus trees, to the very place I had asked the Angels for some months earlier. Two kilometres more and we reached the farmhouse on a rise with a fantastic view to the west and north. High mountains with forest were behind the house, to the east and south. To the immediate north of the house was a sheer drop into a ravine. The house was surrounded by acres of gardens with Kikuyu lawn and cut hedges. There were defunct fountains and pools, fruit trees and pavilions surrounded by roses all in various stages of mismanagement and dilapidation. It used to belong to Lord Delamere, serving as his summer retreat and sawmill, nearly three thousand metres above sea level, Antonio later informed me. Cairo was very proud that I liked the place, and I am sure he felt like the owner. My parents and Antonio had overtaken us and arrived long before Cairo and me. They were standing admiring the views in front of the magnificent carved-oak door with an iron-mounted coat of arms, almost covered by an overgrown bougainvillaea lending a Mediterranean feel. The front door led into an open courtyard surrounded by a veranda with doors leading to each room. I counted twelve doors. The courtyard also had a fountain without water. The bygone charm and grandeur had been swept away by lack of occupancy and maintenance. Because of the Mau-Mau uprising it had stood empty since 1953 with one short exception. The Aberdares had been recognised as some of the worst infected Mau-Mau areas because of the close proximity to the forest and the traditional Kikuyu land. We were now guinea pigs to see if any killers were left in the forest! The Italian owners and Antonio lived fifteen kilometres away and had their house on more open ground. We offloaded the truck and moved our stuff into the courtyard. I made some coffee on an open fire. Everyone needed a short break. Cairo drank his coffee and left. He had his new wife to look after and it was already late afternoon. We had no electricity and no paraffin, only a few candles. I walked around to the kitchen side of the house. The kitchen, pantry, firewood room and change room all had their entrances from the outside, the back that faced the forest and mountains. A little bundle of firewood caught my attention. I collected some and took it into the room we had selected to sleep in as it had a fireplace. The evenings get very cold at high altitude even near the Equator. Returning to collect more wood, I found a large cobra had positioned itself on the firewood. I jumped back and noticed that the entire white-washed wall behind the snake was full of writings in charcoal. I read from the top:

> Seek thee first the Kingdom of God and the rest shall be given to you. We have found our Kingdom and the rest we want now. I am the spirit of Ngugi that makes the white man's cattle sink to their knees. My

panga is sharp and one hack – cows lie down like grasshoppers with no legs. New Queen of England give us our land back! Our Saviour will lead us to our glorious future that will be like our past history, before we had the dirt of the white man with us, and we ruled all of this land. Our God on Mount Kenya with Jomo Kenyatta, The Messiah, will fill our stomach and we shall be great as in the past. We are the children of Israel.

I took a deep breath and decided to leave the snake alone and tell my parents not to go into the firewood room because I had seen a snake there. That night, sleeping on a mattress on the floor, a lot of thoughts swirled through my head. How could these people change the meaning of the Bible so radically? Why had I never heard that the Mau-Mau thought they were fighting a religious war? Or was it the Kikuyo leaders who used religion as a political instrument? Who taught these Africans Christian religion in the first place? The missionaries. Were they aware of how their teaching was interpreted by the author of the wall writings? I decided to find out slowly in my own way. My mind also wandered back to my childhood in Denmark, to the history or fantasy stories we were told, and recalled the times that I had wanted and tried to imitate various characters from those stories. Could it be that the Africans here had learnt the Bible stories and now wanted to enact them for their own show? The next morning I asked my father if the Germans had held some different belief to us during the Second World War. He was not aware of that. As far as he was concerned they were Christians like us. My mind was in turmoil. Did the Bible teach us to kill or did it teach us to love? It could not do both at the same time. Did the missionaries teach warfare or did they teach compassion? Maybe the missionaries were divided, some following and teaching the spiritual messages of love and 'be not overcome by evil but overcome evil with good'. Perhaps others and their supporters like the wall-writer saw the British as the new Romans and therefore felt they had the right to revolt, take horrible oaths, defend the primitive and ultimately kill. We have seen that type of theology with the example of the Mau-Mau, and its descent into total barbarism and satanic behaviour in order to reach its objectives – is that really what Jesus taught his followers? As I understood it, that philosophy belonged to Darwin. Namely, killers keep on killing until compassion is weeded out and the best killers will survive and inherit the earth. Is that not exactly what humans will come to if we lose sight of our highest spiritual ideals? I have seen enough in the world to know that barbarism, hatefulness and evil sustain nothing. Total disintegration is the inevitable outcome and if you take revenge, be sure to dig two graves, one for your enemy and one for yourself! The spiritual signpost is clear. Either we join Darwin's gigantic killing machine or we rediscover the spiritual path and destiny.

At eleven o'clock the next morning Guidici and Manusardi came to our new home. We had moved furniture in and taken cognition of our immediate surroundings and were ready for discussions with the owners. Guidici was just under thirty years old, good looking, and he spoke English well. His family was in the steel mill industry in Turin in northern Italy. He was related to Manusardi, second cousin once removed or something like that. Manusardi was tall with a dark complexion and near forty. His family was involved in the clothing industry, also in northern Italy. They handed over a Land-Rover for our use and we went for a grand tour in the immense gardens. One garden led into the next, peach garden, rose garden, plum, apple and vegetable gardens, tennis courts and fowl run. While walking around and talking about developing the estate Guidici and Manusardi started a rather lengthy argument with typical Italian hand and arm support. It transpired that the argument was about the date of their next elephant hunt near Kilimanjaro. That was an important priority in their lifestyle and they needed the truck for the elephant hunt in December. It was concluded that we should drive around the estate and familiarise ourselves for the next month and then decide on development plans. We could also get the gardens under control with the seven workmen allocated for that purpose and possibly repair the poor water supply from the mountain. I would be paid to help and later next year I should commence working in the estate workshop where Caterpillars, combine harvesters and other machinery were serviced and repaired. Antonio was in charge of that section at the time. We walked to the water reservoir in the forest higher up on the mountain slope. The mist hung just over the treetops and everything was dripping wet with lichen draped over branches of trees. A troop of black and white colobus monkeys quietly watched our approach. The tall trees protruding from the forest canopy were cedar, too large to have been taken out for the sawmill in earlier years. The canal system that fed the water reservoir extracted the water from a stream some thousand meters higher up. Where the mountain side was too steep for the canal to be dug, the canal ran in a timber trough anchored to the mountain side. The timber trough was rotten and other parts of the canal had been damaged by elephants so very little water came into the reservoir. From the reservoir a ten-inch pipe took the water downhill to propel turbines for electricity and to turn the machines in the sawmill, but all that had fallen into disrepair. I liked the forest and ventured the suggestion that if I had four forty-gallon drums of road tar and two hundred empty grain bags and two Africans to help I would fix the water supply. The two Italians became exited and enthusiastically promised delivery of requirements the following day – and so I began working on Kipipiri.

The following day with the help of one of the gardeners I cleaned out the firewood room, killed the nearly two-metre-long cobra snake and washed the wall. Thereafter, I cleaned the kitchen, which was black from smoke – some vagrants had slept on the floor on cardboard and the remains of an open fire were still visible. In the afternoon my father and I took a walk to the lower part of the gardens and found a beautiful three-bedroomed cottage covered in vines and bougainvillaea. We also discovered numerous horse stables and other outbuildings all made from cedar timber, which is resistant to termites. Any other timber building would have disappeared in a few years, eaten away by millions of termites. I also had a peep into the water turbine electricity generator house, but seeing wires and parts all over the floor quickly closed the door again. What a shame, the disintegration of what was once a magnificent, functioning estate.

As promised, empty grain bags and drums of tar were delivered and two African workers allocated to work with me. The job turned out to be easier than I had visualised. Heating of the tar was a lengthy process on the first day, but to keep elephants away from our work area we had to keep a fire going for the duration of the work anyway and that also kept the tar hot. We had no problems dipping the bags in hot tar, carrying them on poles and laying them in the wooden troughs. The only mishap we had was that one drum of tar slipped out of control and careered down the mountain slope between the trees, landing in the stream fifty metres below. We had to cut the drum open to salvage the tar in smaller containers. The elephants eventually got used to us and our constant fire. Those Gentle Giants would watch us for a while with their small ones kept in the background, and after they had evaluated the situation they did what they wanted to do in the first place, which was swim in the fifty-by-fifty-metre reservoir. I have a special affinity with elephants, and it was aroused then. We would sit quietly, observe and study those remarkable giants and I was filled with awe. It was as though the forest had turned into a huge hall where the elephants were the main speakers and everyone else sat around in trees and on the ground waiting with great expectation for the next move or wise word. Finally, when the elephants had completed their almost holy task, every one would wait absolutely quietly to see them disappear into a tropical forest tunnel of monkey rope, vines, trees and bushes. One day while sitting there I heard whistling. It came closer and closer and the next minute I heard *'Jambo Bwana.'* It was Kariuki! He had absconded, left Bingley and wanted to work with us. Later I discussed the issue with my father and it was agreed that he could start work with immediate effect. In less than three weeks our canal repair work was completed, water was flowing and I was given a lot of praise from everyone concerned.

In mid-December a report was handed to Guidici on my father's plan for the development of the estate. Pyrethrum, sheep, pigs and cattle should be the main activity with some grain production, depending on the next year's crop yields. The previous wheat crop had been a write-off because of persistent rain during growing and harvesting time. Kipipiri had an annual average rainfall of one thousand five hundred millimetres with low evaporation due to high altitude. The temperature would not exceed twenty-four degrees and very seldom would go below freezing. The soil on the plateau was a yellowish clay and could only be ploughed with Caterpillars and even they sometimes got bogged down in mud. The slopes closer to the forest were of well-drained dark loam and suited for pyrethrum. I was to work in the main workshop from the beginning of January, and my superior would be an Indian Singh mechanic, complete with turban.

The whole family was together for Christmas and picnic tours were taken to different parts of the estate. A grand canyon was the western boundary with unspoiled African nature and wildlife. The river at the bottom was full of fish. Dense bush and forest covered the slopes where baboons and other monkeys had a fantastic time watching humans. Part of the valley floor was grass plain, hosting kudo and other buck. Evidence of wild boars, leopards and hyenas was frequently seen, but the animals themselves were nocturnal and tried to evade the human predator. Elephants would come there on occasions but they seemed to have become forest dwellers. Even rhinos were spotted in the valley, according to Antonio. We called the place by the obvious name of 'The Big Valley'. A tourist attraction had it been known! Kenya's nature is outstandingly beautiful with colossal contrasts, especially for those, like us, accustomed to a flat Denmark.

During the Christmas period Antonio and a friend were supposedly shot at in the ravine approach to the estate two kilometres from our house. The Mau-Mau had obtained guns, home-made or stolen. Antonio's Land-Rover was full of bullet holes and the windscreen was shattered, but no harm had been done to the occupants. The incident was immediately reported to the police and during the investigation it transpired that Antonio and his friend had shot at the Land-Rover themselves to create a situation where we would become afraid and move. He felt that his position was threatened. But, as happens everywhere else in Africa, someone had peeped from a nearby bush and reported to the police what he had seen. The whole episode was quickly forgotten and Antonio paid to have the company Land-Rover repaired. Our relationship grew and improved over the next months and later I shared my lunch meals with him.

Cairo, the truck driver, lived in Kipipiri village, which was about one kilometre downhill from our house and consisted of about twenty small three-roomed stone houses and another twenty huts. There was a Duka (shop), selling matches, maize meal, paraffin, sweets and other basic consumer items, mainly for the African market. Every morning Cairo would drive most of the workers fifteen kilometres through two gullies and forest to Aberdare estate where Antonio, Guidici and Manusardi would take teams of workers to different places, then in the late afternoon bring them back. When I commenced in the workshop I joined the morning commuters and after a few journeys Cairo asked me if I would like to drive the truck, which I did. I became a stand-in driver. At the workshop we did normal oil changes and other maintenance work but also changed pistons, crankshafts and bearings on Caterpillars, Land-Rovers and other engines. On a few occasions I would go with the third Italian partner, an older man, a veterinarian by profession and speaking Italian only, to Nakuru for spare parts. If it happened that the Nakuru dealer did not have the required parts we would then proceed on to Nairobi and later back to the farm. It was a round trip of nearly four hundred kilometres in one day, some of it on dirt roads, just for a wheel bearing! In the workshop we welded seed drills, ploughs and harrows. The electric welder was powered by a tractor as no electricity grid existed in Kenya at that time except in towns. Pipes and radiators were mended with acetylene welding or soldered. Rewiring of Land-Rovers and tractors was done when the electrical system ended up in smoke due to rats eating the insulation of wires and cables. Singh was a good teacher and a good mechanic. Morris was the African mechanic who did most of the blacksmith work. During coffee and lunch breaks we would discuss, among other things, the state of emergency due to the Mau-Mau terrorist activities, religious and spiritual matters. Singh and his brother, who was also employed as a workshop helper, were rather neutral on the political side, preferring to make jokes and saying that they had no complaints about the local African farm girls as long as the Kikuyu did not spoil them in circumcision rituals. They sometimes referred to Indian writings which I understood to be very, very old and which contained mystical information, some of it similar to Jesus's teaching they said. Morris, on the other hand, was of the opinion that we were witnessing the fulfilment of the Bible. He maintained that we were living the last chapter of the Bible, namely Revelations, and at every available moment introduced the subject. He would bring his Bible along and point out events that he saw happening and those that would happen in the future. The Apostles' Letters and John's Revelation were his guide. When on a few occasions I suggested that maybe we should not take the Bible too literally, he would look at me in total disbelief and sulk for a while. His religious indoctrination was complete. His interpretation was that state and other authorities would eventually collapse, children would turn against their parents, everyone would have to go back to their individual home countries, traditional morality would be abandoned, music would become evil, men would sleep with men and they would get hollow eyes. He read me Revelation 6:12–13:

> And I beheld when he had opened the sixth seal, and, lo, there was a great earthquake; and the sun became black as sackcloth of hair, and the moon became blood; and the stars of heaven fell unto earth, even as a fig tree casteth her untimely figs, when she is shaken of a mighty wind. And the heaven departed as

a scroll when it is rolled together; and every mountain and island were moved out of their places.

That sent cold shivers down my spine and torpedoed me back to my dream on Bingley's lawn about heaven shaking and changing colours. This Bible scripture was telling a similar story. What was going on? I had to think about that, so to change the subject I said, 'How come reading and believing in the Bible hasn't stopped the Kikuyu from being cannibals?' Without hesitation he answered, 'Don't use the word Kikuyu for Mau-Mau and troublemakers. Yes, I believe that some Kikuyus have taken war oaths by eating human brains and other disgusting things. These few people have become obsessed with hatred, focusing on issues that their leaders have made up, and to become unscrupulous killers they destroy anything decent in themselves by eating humans and other equally horrible things. They also use the Bible to see what the destroyers must do to hasten the speedy return of the Messiah. They are made to believe that they are fulfilling prophecy by being malicious and destroying everything that the white man owns, because, as they say, the downtrodden and poor shall inherit the earth and that is what they are after.' Morris, in his long talks, explained many of my questions, but I was still mystified as to how you could get that type of movement to grow between otherwise friendly people. Is the human really nothing more than what his leaders and teachers tell him he is? And what happens if leaders and teachers are limited themselves, have ulterior motives or are outright evil? I thought about the last world war and what the Germans had done, gassing and burning people. I was frightened of my own questions. I had to know who ran the human earthly show and why?

My father's development plan was accepted by Guidici and Manusardi shortly after Christmas and implementation commenced immediately. He had taken over half the labour force and some machinery and was planting hundreds of acres of pyrethrum. Our relationship with Antonio improved and one day in April he suggested that I should have my daily lunch with him instead of bringing my sandwich box. I should pay him, but only a few shillings a day. Antonio was a bachelor, living in a stone house with polished cement floors, very sparsely furnished, with no curtains. He prepared meals himself which consisted of macaroni, spaghetti and more macaroni. When I came into his house for the first lunch, I looked at the table and saw only one plate on the table with one spoon and one fork. Embarrassed, I asked if I had misunderstood the 'eating together' bit and the thought entered my mind that maybe he was having me on, that this was some practical joke. He then said 'Please, please me only one plate, me eat, you look, then you eat me look.' It worked until more plates were obtained, but eventually I tired of pasta with garlic, salt and butter sauce, as delicious as it is, and a new arrangement was made.

From July I toiled in the workshop during the mornings then walked the five kilometres home through the forest for lunch. In the afternoons I worked on repairing the water turbine and the single-phase, direct-current electric generator, with Kariuki's help. I also assisted my father measuring and designing cattle-dip tanks, pig houses, sheep runs and layout of pyrethrum fields. Like the previous year it rained and rained for months. Neptune had truly moved in. The sky was constantly grey, mist and low clouds covered the mountains and lichen, algae and moss grew profusely, making the forest even more mysterious. Rivers overflowed, fields became waterlogged and farm roads were washed away. Singh resigned when he realised that the wheat crop was rotting in the lands due to another year of persistent rain. He could foresee the inevitable change of farming method and that would be without a large workshop. He was also aware that cattle and sheep would be introduced in due course to roam the fields presently under wheat. An Italian mechanic took over Singh's position. He was from Somalia and was a character for whom one could truly feel sorry. He was middle-aged with loose teeth and lost them all in the course of a few months. When he heard African children or babies crying or screaming in the nearby worker's camp, he would stand in the doorway of the large workshop and shout towards heaven, using all the Italian swear words that only an Italian can dream up, one string of words followed by the next like the rosary of the Devil. I had it translated by a African ex-Somali worker. It transpired that he had left Somalia in a hurry due to fighting or politics and had left his African wife and children behind, never to see them again. He would burst out in tears and walk up and down the workshop floor like a lion in a small cage. His eyes projected his despair, unresolvable dilemma and his suffering. He would walk out and shout '*Porco Dio*,' come back into the workshop, make himself some tea and sit and stare into the teacup to see if he could find a solution. But he would only see the darkness of his own soul. After a while he would get involved in work and forget himself. The only thing the man wanted was to be allowed to look after his children and wife in a country that he had been taken to by his parents and loved. Now he was heartbroken, elderly with no teeth and no one really cared if he was dead or alive. If he shot himself no one would miss him. He did suggest to me that one day he would do that. What could I say? I could not offer advice. I could not console him. I had nothing to offer him. He stayed for five months and then disappeared. Kenya had no social service to pick you up from the gutter. The few taxpayers could not support a social service. A heap of bones in the forest could have been anyone's and in the humid climate of Kipipiri they would be covered by vegetation within a month if not eaten by a hyena.

Cows and Boran bulls were acquired from far and wide and herdsmen hired. Ade-Me-Sou had heard through the bush telegraph or the legendary African drums that we now had cattle and arrived with wife, Getchemma and Lasso, expecting to work. He was hired and became chief stockman. Getchemma, now looking older, was nearing the age of marriage when African parents turn their daughters into cash or other assets. During a school holiday my sister Anna was persuaded by Getchemma to ask me if I would meet her behind a certain ant-heap near some bushes on a Sunday afternoon to fulfil her sexual ambition before she was sold to a stranger. I declined the offer and remained a virgin for many years to come. Getchemma was sold for five cows, three goats, four blankets and a bicycle. With her pierced ears, holes big enough for a tennis ball to go through, she disappeared with her new husband never to be seen again. The cows had calves and enjoyed the humid climate that produced the lush pastures, green Kikuyu grass. What else does a cow want but to lie down, ruminate and sleep? No chance, as far as engineer Guidici was concerned. He asked if the cattle were sick as they were lying down at lunch-time and suggested instructing the herdsman to make them stand up and eat. My father had to embark on a lengthy explanation regarding the function of the multiple stomach during rumination. Because of language restrictions on both sides, a certain amount of graphic demonstration was required! Guidici departed looking like a schoolboy who refuses to admit that he knows nothing about the subject in question.

Guidici usually had two rifles strapped down in his Land-Rover when he travelled around the estate. During one of his usual morning meetings with my father, on this occasion discussing sheep purchases, my mother burst into the cedar-panelled office and breathlessly announced that while she was pruning roses in the quarter-acre rose garden, three rhinos had come through the cypress hedge like three locomotives freewheeling downhill. They passed her, with their poor eyesight had not seen her, and were now eating their portion of fresh vegetables from the vegetable garden. Guidici located me in the water-turbine room. I dropped my pliers and was given an .308 rifle. We leapt into his vehicle and returned to the house, but the rhinos had gone, leaving a five-metre path of destruction behind them. We followed them for four or five kilometres and at one stage we could hear them, but no eye contact was made. What we would have done with a .308 rifle if they had charged us is anyone's guess. It would have easily perforated an ear, but would certainly not have stopped a rhino unless a very accurate shot had penetrated the heart. I did indeed shoot a wild boar in the heart with a pistol once. The boar had sneaked into the chicken run under the wire and eaten all the chicken food. Exhausted, with a full stomach, he had fallen asleep until a loud bang from the pistol sent him running for ten metres. Then darkness came over his eyes and he died.

The day of the rhino, Guidici and my father asked me to take Manusardi's dog at the first opportune moment into the forest and shoot him. The dog was full of veld sores, non-healing sores, and no one really loved him or wanted him. Kariuki was to come with me so we could dig a hole and bury the dog. The dog was old and Kariuki held lightly on the leash. When I pulled the trigger the dog turned his head slightly. A little neat hole in the outer ear appeared and he took off at great speed. In that moment I saw the Gods of Heaven descending to earth. The God of remorse, the God of sorrow, the God of anger, and the God of frustration all had a go at my inner organs. I felt sick. I had to face the music and went up to the house, arriving minutes behind the dog. Manusardi, who was conferring with my father, said, 'Hi Guidici. The dog has been fighting with a wild boar, look at his ear. He is also too old. I better put him down.' No one said anything and in relief I looked at heaven and blessed the Angels for removing the weight of that deed from me. Wild boars had killed numerous African guard dogs in vegetable and potato fields.

The management of the estate changed and with most work allocated from Kipipiri village the commuting stopped. Workers would cut stone with chisels in a quarry formed from compressed volcanic ash for new buildings. They sawed timber and cut fence posts in the forest, and planted and reaped pyrethrum flowers. The pyrethrum produced well and dried flowers were taken to Nakuru on a regular basis. This was handled by Cairo, who would also buy farm requisites like pig fodder supplements and groceries and pay bills. Normally the Albion truck would be loaded in the afternoon for early morning departure. One morning the truck's covering tarpaulin was missing. Removed during the night by the one who blends with the night. The local witch-doctor was consulted to help locate the thief for a fee of one hundred shillings. After lengthy debates with askaris, neaparas (foremen) and other interested parties all possible candidates were assembled, ready for the witch-doctor's early morning interview. A pumpkin was produced from his kit bag and a face cut in to the yellow flesh. He placed it on a plank in front of the fourteen guilty-looking men, and a red handkerchief resembling a tongue was stuffed into the rather grotesque mouth. He then took a seven-inch nail, a hammer and *bang* the nail was hammered though the effigy's tongue. He yelled, 'Now spirit of our fathers and grandfathers speak! You, evil one, your tongue is nailed and you cannot speak, so let any one who can speak, speak, and he is not guilty. He whose tongue is bleeding stay silent that no one will see evil blood and the nail that is in his tongue. Let the spirit that is in you speak now.' He stood up, walked up and down in front of the men as though inspecting the guard, and sure enough number four from the left was dumb and deaf. He confessed stealing the tarpaulin and returned it. He was also to pay the one hundred shillings to the doctor. He later disappeared in disgrace. The ultimate sin is being caught.

Very little wheat was harvested due to the persistent rain in 1957. Antonio left for Italy to get married and on his return found new employment. Ade-Me-Sou's wife, for reasons best known to herself, committed suicide by hanging, it is believed that she was pregnant. We found her hanging in the forest with her knees touching the ground, looking like a scarecrow. She had used a piece of steel fencing wire which she had looped around her neck and tied to a branch of a small tree. She had jumped off a little stump on a mound. The wire had cut right into her flesh and it was left there. She was buried quietly with no traditional ceremony. Ade-Me-Sou stayed on for another six months and left, broken-hearted, for retirement in the tea-growing district of Kiricho, the Kipsigis home area in Kenya.

Eight hundred Marino sheep were bought from different places, some from Equator Farm, some from near Mount Kenya. Corridale rams were introduced some months later and what a performance! Unexposed to this aspect of animal farming, Guidici stood there with eyes on stalks, saying, 'Have you seen he is now on number five, now another,' and so on. He eventually kept the running commentary, on how various ram were doing, to himself, because the rams did not take much interest in his enthusiasm. He expressed amazement that lambs would be the result of such a performance – nature is remarkable! Two weeks later he asked when we could expect the first lambs!

The sheep were looked after by herdsmen during the day, Masai hired for that purpose. At night all the sheep were ushered into small, guarded, moveable pens to protect them from falling over cliffs, getting stuck in mud or being eaten by leopards or hyenas. Most of the grazing area was open flatland, but bordering on steep, deep gullies with dense forest or bush, a haven for big cats. We lost five sheep in as many weeks to leopards so I decided, with Guidici and my father's consent, to stay out at night near the sheep with Kariuki, who was now chief guardsman, and my .308 rifle for a week or until the leopard was shot or offenders eliminated. A little 'A' frame tin shack downwind from the pens was our night shelter. We had a fire going to boil water for tea and to keep warm. The rain would pour down monotonously, making a racket on the tin roof for hours. This would induce an hypnotic trance in us, and we would suddenly awaken, feeling the fixation of leopard eyes. Kariuki insisted that he saw an almost black leopard on various occasions. We would venture out into the pitch black every hour to walk around the sheep pens. The sheep looked rather daft and stupid in the torch-light, with no expression in their eyes and water dripping off their faces. No point asking them where the leopards are to be found, I decided. No leopards were shot in that first week, but later one managed to jump into the pen and killed another sheep. A few days after that a huge leopard was caught in a box trap and was, sadly, killed. It was almost black. On another night a hyena was tracked around the pens for hours. With a powerful torch we followed its reflective eyes and eventually shot the determined killer. The evening after Ade-Me-Sou's wife killed herself we went out to guard sheep as we had done for the past five days. It was becoming routine. But around eleven o'clock that night, as the rain was pouring down, I fell asleep, not to wake up before morning, and had a long visual dream about Africa. It was during the dawn of history, before man knew that he existed and was just another predator among many. I saw a group of people involved in a hunt on the open savannah. A herd of gazelle had been spotted and everyone concentrated on those thin-legged animals. It was late afternoon, the heavens beginning to display colour in a dust and smoke-filled cloudless sky. A gazelle was killed and a brawl about ownership of the dead animal began. Most of the men had starving children and wives waiting anxiously for food at their temporary resting place near a dried-out river. The brawl culminated in injury and death. The clan in disarray, a small group collected their few possessions from the camp and began a long and treacherous journey to another part of this great expanse of land. They settled in an area full of food and had generations of children, many of whom died at birth. But more were born. Snakes and baboons also ate some of the children. Lions, leopards and hyenas were always waiting to snatch a screaming unattended infant. If a mother was distracted for only a few seconds, the baby was no more. Later they learned to strap the babies to their backs. One day, after many rainy seasons, when the clan had grown to great numbers, the Chief was worried about food supply because another clan had moved in close to the hunting area. Elders consulted one another in secret and finally the oracle decided that the competitors must be killed. Early one night when the moon was lying on its back, low in the western sky, a surprise attack was launched. Hundreds upon hundreds of men, women and children died on both sides and animosity now existed for ever. The two clans had an uneasy cessation of hostilities while both sides determined to increase their numbers by having as many children as possible for forthcoming winning battles. Over the years they had many children. While mothers died and children died, the living produced more children so they could fulfil the wishes of their fathers and forefathers. The desire of forefathers and fathers became the tribe's motivating factor and they lived and died and performed the past generation's desires, trapped in the past with a handicap no one had the power to resolve.

I woke up cold and noticed that my rifle had been moved. I looked at Kariuki who said, 'So, Bwana had a long disturbed sleep. I could have killed you in your sleep, stolen your rifle, run away and hunted with your rifle until everyone had forgotten about you.' 'Kariuki,' I said 'will you shut up with your stupid nonsense. My Guardian Angel will strike you dead before you lay a hand on me you fool.' Motivated by the night's dream I added, 'My Guardian Angel and I live in the ideal projected future. Not like your lot trapped in your forefather's unfinished business.'

Kariuki nodded and said, 'I was just testing you, the same as when I did the panga demonstration at Bingley's, you remember? Africa is not a place for weaklings. Now that I have tested you I can reveal a little of myself where no one hears us. I have been to many places and seen many things. I have served with the Rhodesian and South African forces in Abyssinia during the last big war and had a good time with those white Africans as they called themselves. I have been to Burma with British and Kenyan soldiers. I have seen men killed and I know what makes a survivor. I do not read books, but I can read people. I have never really been a Mau-Mau and do not believe in their cause, but for my own safety I can't say that openly. I prefer to have my stomach intact and not taken out while I sleep by a gang that works for Jomo.' He then entered into a long talk about his life with the Rhodesian forces in Abyssinia and Somalia in 1942, where he saw how white men behaved under stress in war situations. Then returning to the Mau-Mau he said, 'All for what? We all know that the British government consists of mostly respectable people. They have introduced new ways of life that have helped us here in Kenya. We have jobs, we can buy things in shops, we can travel by train and on roads, we can have ownership of our lands and we have no local wars. They have made Kenya into a nation. Before that the whole place was divided between many different warring tribes. We have to be reasonable and accept that the British also had our welfare at heart right from the beginning when the first white people came here. Maybe a few individual settlers are unscrupulous and rough, but so what, they will die when they get old. The British Legislative Council in Nairobi will listen to us if we have grievances and with time we will have more influence. We will become included in government in Nairobi and in time we will have even more say. They are now talking about elections – what do we know about elections? It all takes time to make people understand new ways. Take Ghana or Uganda. They run themselves with British help, and the same will come here if our leaders do not make war for their own ulterior motives.' He continued, 'You see, the Mau-Mau is a war between ourselves. It is a pecking order situation, to see who has most power and can get everyone to succumb to their command. They will employ any means of terror to achieve that power. The first in the intimidation game will probably win, especially if the masses of people are whipped up to believe that the enemy is some foreign power. The British have wide shoulders. They can carry that burden for a while until the day they get tired and hand over to whoever appears to be the strongest. Do you understand?' With the night's dream still fresh in my mind, yes I did understand. 'Kariuki,' I said, 'it seems to me that religion and the spirit world play an enormous role in African thinking. Can you tell me what you know about that? Wait, I will make tea first.' I made some tea and handed Kariuki a cup with lots of sugar and milk, the way he liked it. We sat quietly watching the eastern morning sky over the mountains turn pink before sunrise. There was no mist covering the mountain for a change, but all low-lying areas and ravines were full of mist. The country side looked flat with an eerie white sheet obscuring all indentations. The spirits and other creatures of the African underworld had a golden opportunity for an ambush in the valley or a naked dance with whomever descended below the misty levels. Sounds of distress or a hyena's call would temporarily be ignored by the one who wants to survive. We had our tea and Kariuki explained. 'The African spirit world is real, do not underestimate its power. Most Europeans call it superstition and think that we are just too easily influenced by certain suggestions. In a way that is true, but if powerful occupying thoughts fill your head for no reason and you lose the normal self-control then the spirit world is responsible. They become so powerful that you start seeing images. You whites fill your heads with ideas and trivial things such as buying tomatoes, hanging out the washing, money for this or that and many other thoughts that crowd out any powerful, spontaneous thought emerging from the spirit world. This is a good thing if we talk about evil spirits, but a sad thing if the spirits of kindness and love are kept at bay. Religion, with all its strings attached, is another way to fill your head with thought, thereby preventing unwelcome visitors, but unfortunately it can also keep out true spiritual development. But it all depends on oneself, on what you want. If you have hatred in you, you see yourself as a slave and will be used by evil spirits who are attracted to the negative. If you have love in you, you focus on co-operation and harmony and no evil spirit can use you so therefore leaves you alone. The evil spirit is filled with hatred and wants to take revenge so will hover around persons who may be willing to perform revengeful acts. That is why evil Mau-Mau oath-taking works. The same forces work in other fields. If a farmer is envious and always believes that he is getting the bad end of the stick, he then blocks out the good spirit's influence. He concentrates on his shortage and therefore eats the first crop that matures, the biggest cob or the biggest calf, instead of using it for seed or to improve his herds, with the result that all his animals eventually look like starving dogs, and his crops are deprived of the best seed and come to look like plants grown in a desert. Right thinking is very, very important and can make us co-creaters with God, the power that sustains everything.' Kariuki's early morning talk in a mixture of English and Swahili made an unforgettable impression on my young mind.

Christmas 1957 saw the whole family together with the exception of Chris who was now employed by a Jewish farmer in Kitale, north-west Kenya close to the Uganda border. He became the explorer for the family of new frontiers with new opportunities in the highly fertile and remote part of Kenya. Ulrich battled along at Prince of Wales High School, professing that he enjoyed it, though he was reluctant to return at the end of the holidays. Anna was set to excel herself still further at Nakuru school. Karin had left the Kennels and joined us on Kipipiri as manager of the sheep section. Once I was asked to drive and chaperone Karin to a party at Ol Kalou where she met up with her boyfriend, Dennis, renamed by me 'The Menace'. I waited with much patience until midnight, having no interest or inclination to participate, and saw the laughing and dancing young people as misguided fools who had not discovered the beauty and mystery of the natural sounds of the African night. Ten years later, I danced all night! At twelve o'clock we drove home in silence. My career as chaperone was over. Just before Christmas Guidici, Manusardi and Monzini had moved into our house – the main house – and we moved into the beautifully renovated manager's cottage at the far of the garden. After restoring the entire power system, which included replacing old wiring chewed by rats, I triumphantly opened the turbine and switched on electric power for all to see. In the main house, at Guidici's request, along the inner courtyard veranda I hung sixteen converted paraffin lamps which gave the yard an atmosphere of an enclosed laager, a perfect setting for a wonderful Christmas party!

During the Christmas week, when most people in the rest of the world celebrated, our village shopkeeper, a devout Christian, became a self-styled Father Christmas, handing out stolen goods as free gifts to all and sundry. For two hours he distributed from the shop sweets, biscuits, condensed milk, sugar, soft drinks and bicycle tyres, all the while ranting about Biblical matters – 'You shall not want.' 'He divided the bread between his disciples.' 'Let the children come to me, let them not thirst' – and out went some bottles of orange juice. 'The birds do not gather so come and have what has been gathered' etc. Eventually with the help of Kariuki and Cairo we managed to calm him down. He continued babbling and ended by saying, 'Yes, crucify me, you have waited long enough.' Then he passed out. We returned him to his well-kept house and left him in the care of his wife. Kariuki discreetly whispered, 'Here you can see it, demons have moved in. The man is possessed.' The following day he poured petrol over his dog and set it alight. We realised that the man really was deranged and with some resistance managed to get him into the Land-Rover and drove him to the Naivasha police station. My father went into the station while I waited in the vehicle with the possessed. An officer approached me as I was sitting behind the steering wheel and requested my non-existent driving licence. I explained that I was only fifteen years old and not entitled to a license yet. We paid the fifty-shilling fine on the spot. The police took care of the shopkeeper and saw him admitted to a mission hospital for mental treatment.

The Masai Christmas party culminated in bloodshed. When Masai fight, even cats, dogs and birds leave the scene. They can sense trouble in the making as they can detect earthquakes in advance. One of the brawlers had his skull cracked with a rungo (knobkerrie). We took him to hospital in the Land-Rover, his head resting on my lap. Each time he inhaled the top of the skull expanded. In horror I visualised fumes and things that go bump in the night coming out. After five days in hospital he discharged himself and walked the forty kilometres home to take up his herding responsibilities. Humans do have an enormous ability to heal themselves if they are ignorant of the immensity of their disease.

January and February are the months with least rain and referred to as the dry season, but in the Kinankop and Kipipiri region that only meant that it did not necessarily rain every day. On one clear Sunday afternoon Kariuki and I went walking. I had taken my .308 rifle and two bullets with me and would shoot a buck for meat if the right opportunity arose. In the forest amongst heavy undergrowth we discovered five elephant skeletons. They had been bombed and killed by British jet fighter planes pursuing Mau-Mau. Elephants, generally speaking, do not look like Mau-Mau, but I suppose from the air, looking down at cloud-covered mountains, anything that was dark and moved in the forest below would be a target. Poor elephants had to pay the ultimate price of humans' inability to sort out their squabbles in a civilised manner around a table. As far as I am concerned human warmongers should be chained together until they learn to co-operate. We walked past the stone quarry and into a gully. Between the bushes on a small grass patch I saw a buck with horns. I decided to try to get close enough to make a clean kill, and not repeat the hole-in-dog-ear incident. Coming in very close I aimed and pulled the trigger. The buck fell. I had one more bullet only and when I noticed the buck move I used it for a head shot. At that very moment a newly born calf came out of the nearby bush, still with the curly hair on its back wet from mother's licking. It tottered up to its dead mother, then, confused, came over to me because I moved. That was me finished! I had reduced myself to nothing but a murderer of the calf's mother. I could not hold the tears back. I called Kariuki and said, 'Do something,' hoping that he could reverse the deed. I took my bloody rifle and stuck the muzzle into the soft ground next to the dead animal. If the dead buck had had a helmet, I would have put that on my rifle in final respect. My body was shaking with emotion and self-anger. I had a problem controlling myself. Why should I feel guilty and sorry, I asked myself, is it not only an animal? Yes, but it had a baby. How can others shoot animals without feeling remorse? The dialogue kept on hammering in my mind. Kariuki detected my distress from the corner of his eye and came closer. I told him to go away and leave me alone. 'Do what you have to do,' I managed to say, meaning kill the baby. 'Take the buck and go home, I will follow.' I sat there trying to justify my terrible act. Eventually the only thing my mind felt right with was to say a prayer aloud, so I did. 'Thank you buck, you have died. I have killed you so that I may eat you and live, thank you.' The echo of my statement sounded hollow, but it made a colossal impact and I felt that I could handle the murder. It made more sense than Jesus on the cross ever did to me. My hunting career was over and I now hold an aversion to the two words 'enjoy hunting'. They simply do not go together in my vocabulary, and I even feel sick sitting here writing about it. I do not condemn others for their hunting instinct as long as they ask themselves, 'What am I doing and why?' Maybe they will find out for themselves as I did. As a farmer later in life I did produce pigs and cattle for slaughter, but I never forgot my little prayer.

On the way home I passed a troop of baboons and I sat down to watch, envying them their apparently simplistic lifestyle, but noticing how big daddy wielded his power over other troop members. Crawling up and out of the dangerously steep gully I had to be careful not to step on loose material and slide back to injury or death. Near the top I had to lift myself up and out holding on to a small tree right on the edge. As I did, the tree and embankment gave in, but just at that very moment a black arm reached me from the top and a voice said, 'Guardian Angel at your service!' Kariuki had been concerned about leaving me behind and had waited at the point where I had emerged from the gully – what a fortunate coincidence! I had a friend for life.

Over the Easter period we saw three accidents on or near the estate. Manusardi turned over his Land-Rover. He walked away unharmed but the vehicle was almost a write off. A tractor and trailer belonging to a neighbour carrying fourteen football players freewheeled at high speed down a gully road. Half-way down the driver lost control and seven people died. The tractor and trailer was not worth recovering. I helped to load bodies into the Land-Rover without getting sick. Somehow my emotions stepped aside and practicalities and the job at hand became paramount. The third accident involved a friend, Peter, who lost control of his VW Beetle in the heavy rain. It slid down a muddy road until it eventually stopped on a bridge at the bottom of the valley, with a front and rear wheel hanging over the edge of the bridge, wheels spinning in the air. The spirit of the turbulent river twenty metres below had eyed the vehicle, for as the driver stepped out of his door the centre of balance moved in favour of the abyss. The car was immediately swept away by the river never to be seen again.

When Peter eventually arrived, soaked and dishevelled, for the expected traditional Danish smorgasbord à la Africa, we found that unfortunately my mother's seventeen-year-old African kitchen lad had eaten most of the canned seafood. He explained that when he had opened the cans he had tasted one small fish, liked it and thought that Memsahib would not notice and object if he took another one because there was plenty. And so he carried on till three quarters of our lunch had disappeared into his later apologetic mouth. He promised never to do it again and kept the promise as far as canned seafood was concerned. Our cat was extremely annoyed and did not see any humour in that episode. He went out and caught a rat.

During our late lunch, stories were told about what happens when one is ignorant of the local language and gestures. Our Danish friend was harvesting wheat and the African combine harvester driver requested grease, using hand gestures to illustrate a small container. However, our friend thought that the clever African driver had learned some Danish words. '*Grise*' in Danish is 'pig'. The next thing the driver said in Swahili, '*orna hapa*' means 'look here'. '*Orne*' in Danish denotes a boar. Our friend became totally confused and looked around not understanding why a whole piggery invisible to him was seen by the African in the wheat field. Eventually, when he understood what was requested, he instructed a farm-hand to take a nearby bicycle and go to the farm workshop to collect grease. An hour later the farm-hand was back with a twenty-litre grease container in one hand and the bicycle in the other, totally exhausted and marked as if he had been in a fight. It transpired that the obliging guy did not know how to ride a bicycle and pushing it had been a major battle, hence his numerous scratch marks. He had therefore decided to carry the bicycle in one hand and the heavy grease container in the other all the three kilometres back.

This type of story was often Sunday afternoon entertainment. It was not meant to be derogatory towards the African, but simply humorous. By the way the Africans did exactly the same, telling stories about the peculiar behaviour of the Musungus (Europeans) whose priorities were most odd in African eyes.

On the farming scene, the sheep produced nine hundred lambs to everybody's delight, and the cows had calves according to nature's law with humps on their back, a Boran characteristic. Porkers from a thirty-sow piggery were delivered to Uplands bacon factory on a regular basis and the pyrethrum did very well with a pyrethrum content of nearly three percent, which was excellent. We also produced two hundred tons of barley for the pigs and breweries.

Cairo managed to make his neighbour's daughter pregnant and was summoned by the local farm court of eight elders to pay compensation to the girl's parents because now she was second-hand and could no longer fetch full price. Eight goats, a raincoat and half a bag of sugar was paid.

Kariuki kept me informed of most squabbles, intrigues, cliques and hierarchy formations in our farm village. He also took me to observe a circumcision ceremony, when adolescents become adults and one in spirit, according to tribal belief. They call one another 'brother' and walk around in sackcloth with no fixed abode for a month, usually with a hand in front of their private parts to prevent the sackcloth rubbing against the injury which often becomes infected.

Manusardi left for Italy to get married. On his return we arranged a mock ambush at the entrance to the estate. Masai, in full regalia, served 'welcome home' sherry on a silver tray. That also ensured that the newlyweds arrived at the house at exactly six thirty when I had one hundred and twenty men and women with burning torches lining the two-hundred-metre avenue to the house. It was like a tunnel of light, a spectacular sight that created a festive feeling. Later drinks and meals were served to all involved.

A few months later, out of the blue Guidici announced with distress that no more money would come from Italy for development. A fairly large sum had been invested in sheep, cattle, wages and other development. The estate would break even this year and make a profit the following year in accordance with the original plan. But due to Guidici and Manusardi's distress signals a contingency plan was made. The labour force was called in for meetings and it was mutually agreed to cut the monthly wages bill temporarily, to protect and secure the estate's future. But when Guidici and Manusardi and another devious Italian newcomer known to us only as 'cousin' airily demanded the Albion truck for a month's hunting safari, my father lost his cool. Hands and feet said more than words and we were given two months notice to vacate Kipipiri, the place we had grown to love in two years, and where my friends were. It was all over! Chris wrote from Kitale that he had found a farm for lease in that area and so opened the next chapter of my African adventure.

Saying farewell was a handshake, eye contact, walking away, looking over the shoulder and waving to Kariuki, Cairo, the Masai and all the others. Many said that they hoped to join us in Kitale, an African way of being kind. Africans have an ability to say what you like to hear, especially when you are confused and filled with apprehension.

Harvesting Wheat

We crossed the Rift Valley, passing Nakuru, and went up the west bank of the Rift to Molo and Mau Summit which resembles Devon, south-west England, with its rolling open grass or wheat fields, and avenues of trees leading to well-built farmhouses and forests on nearby hills. My father's Hussar friend was employed as manager on Mau Summit farm while arranging to move on to his own farm. We slept there. The following day my parents drove the one hundred and ninety kilometres on dirt road to Kitale, passing the Equator. I stayed behind to help drive the combine, harvesting wheat. The old self-propelled machine should have been put on pension with Bingley's old machine before I was born. Two days in the workshop made the machine operational. The first day in the golden rippling wheat fields was wonderful, and I had a feeling of achievement as each swath ate into the standing wheat. Many bags were dumped in six different locations to be picked up by the transporter. Then the owner of the farm arrived and requested that the bags be dumped in one place. I objected, reasoning that the brakes on the old machine were not powerful enough to hold the machine with eight bags or more going downhill. The brakes were not designed for that type of load. As predicted, turning downhill with only six bags on the platform, the large machine became a law unto itself. It jumped out of gear, the brakes useless. Turning would tumble the machine and further downhill a ravine was waiting. The third alternative was a nearby eucalyptus tree. Here we come! The machine's front part was badly damaged, but repairable. The owner resigned with excuses and apologies, never to be seen by me again. It was one of those experiences where a quick decision without consultation saved lives and machine. But during the following night the machine ran out of control again. In a dream I saw a seed planted in a landscape called 'the cradle of evolution'. It grew and grew and produced diverse seeds. Each generation saw improvements in the 'new seeds', collected and absorbed by humans, and finally the harvest of humans was at hand. The machine was driverless and a law unto itself, threshing humans like wheat straw. Every one of the multitude of humans was gathered and threshed. In the bags were 'Hearts' and 'God's requirement', and the rest was dumped and burned. The dream was vivid. I looked into the bags and saw the hearts and the spirits. I saw the hordes of humans entering and what was left behind. It was a shocking dream, and it was frustrating not to have anyone to share it with. Who would want to discuss that type of dream anyway, I asked myself. Logically I reasoned that the previous day's incident was responsible for generating the dream. But I was still intrigued by the impression that every living thing produces something to be harvested and used by Life, that this occurs higher and higher on the ladder of spiritual evolution, up to the final human harvest. I asked myself many questions about possible Biblical influence and my thoughts wandered in different directions, finally concluding that a dream is a dream and no more, forget about it. At that very moment a new thought came forth – life, living things, converts physical matter into spiritual stuff, whatever that is. I had breakfast and left for Kitale on the next minibus.

Kitale, Mitoni Mitatu Farm: Farm Assistant

The road to Kitale was dusty and hazardous, with sharp corners and a loose surface. We drove at high speed through cultivated pine forest, natural forest and hills covered in grass. Passing the equator the air was very cold due to high altitude. Then there was a gradual descent to the plateau of Uasin Gishu. I remembered Bingley telling me that it used to be inhabited by Masai a long time prior to white occupation, but on the arrival of Europeans was found to be deserted. There are still traces of older settlements, such as stone bomas and cattle pits near permanent water. In about 1904 the plateau was offered to the Zionists but was rejected as unsuitable for their purposes by a commission under Major Gibbon. In 1906 the first South Africans settlers arrived in ox wagons, and ten thousand acres each were allotted to the Breda brothers. The following year a general settlement began, mainly with settlers from South Africa. Now in 1959 workable lands were occupied by many second-generation settler farmers. Another sixty kilometres and we arrived in Kitale, after having crossed Hoey's Bridge over the Nzoia river which separates South African Boer-dominated Uasin Gishu from the more English Trans-Nzoia district, where Mount Elgon's crater rim protrudes four thousand three hundred metres into the sky, dominating the western horizon and the Cherangani mountain range thirty kilometres to the north-east. Kitale town was well laid out, with a main street with shops and stores, hotels and a cinema. Other parts of the town housed engineering companies, soap manufacturers, a farmers' co-op, a seed company, fuel companies, a creamery, hospitals, a railway station, a labour officer, schools, agricultural research stations, courts, a police station, open markets, doctors, churches with graveyards and various clubs, bars and long bars where patrons could fortify the weakened spirit after a hard day's work with well-deserved extended drinks. Life was good to hundreds of farmers and business people who were kingpins in the prosperous Trans Nzoia region. Everything was in place for a whole and happy society. The Africans appeared content with their unsophisticated but emerging new lifestyle, and nearly all had small holdings or farms bordering Trans Nzoia. The only obvious surface discrimination was at the watering holes, the clubs. They were reserved for members only – no Jew, no Dog, no Dane, no African, and no Englishman either, unless he was signed in by a member or had become an accepted member in his own right. An internationally-accepted club rule.

My parents collected me from the minibus terminal, the local photographic shop, and we drove the few kilometres to the west of Kitale where they had leased a maize and cattle farm from an ex-Belgian Congo chap who had been jailed for fifteen years for murdering his cook in an angry brawl. The place was derelict, and the thatched, sun-dried brick buildings were busy creeping back into the ground from where they had been extracted. My mother cooked meals on an open fire, the roof was rotten and rain-water filled containers in the lounge and bedrooms. Some lands were partly cleared of bush but of the thousand arable acres only two hundred were presently under cultivation. But it was not a bad place to begin. Whatever one did was an improvement. Four weeks of demolishing, burning, cleaning and clearing changed the appearance of the farm, but there was still much to be done. Lands were ploughed and prepared initially by Ulrich and me. We worked day and night to be able to sow the maize, with the first rain expected at the end of March. Ulrich had left Prince of Wales to help my parents. Karin became a probationary nurse in Kitale hospital, to prepare for her nursing education and career in Denmark. Anna moved to Eldoret Girls' High School, also later to return to Denmark for university.

In March, 1959 at sixteen and a half years old, I was asked to caretake a farm for six weeks while the manager went on annual leave. During that time the general manager hired me on a permanent basis and the previous manager became a tea planter near Nairobi. The farm, Mitoni Mitatu, was twelve kilometres east of Kitale and owned by E.W.D. Elmer, a strange man who had been interned in Japan during the Second World War and had also lived and travelled in China. My status was 'assistant to the general manager' and I was in charge of the daily running of the farm. The general manager, Jacobsen, lived some six kilometres away and had another farm to attend to as well, where Chris was now manager. Jacobsen would give guidelines and long term objectives, and assist in the purchasing of requirements. My job was to delegate work to forty workers and see that it was done correctly, scrutinise and repair machinery, count and inspect cattle and keep the records. I lived alone in a two-roomed African hut, with a kitchen and bathroom in a nearby brick building. I had a cook who aspired to be a District Commissioner, an ambition he did not spare me from hearing about frequently. He also informed me equally frequently that he did not steal! Water was collected from a little stream in forty-gallon drums by ox wagon and heated in a donkey boiler, which is nothing more than a drum in a chimney with a fire underneath. My bath water was then poured into a zinc bath by hand. Drinking water was always boiled. There was no electric light and no telephone. Here I lived in solitude for two and a half years. I did have an old Peugeot 203 to run around the farm in, although I was still too young for a licence. I drove to Kitale for grocery shopping and haircuts in the late afternoons every fortnight, when the police would obligingly pretend not to see me. The farm office was in Mr Elmer's tin shack. He had gone on an around-the-world trip after his house had burned down some months prior to my arrival. He had erected the tin shack among the remaining ruins and ashes – 'The place of spooks', the Africans called it. Often during nights with a full moon I would hear a crash on the office tin roof, which was only a few metres away from my hut. Initially I suspected burglars, but what would they want my office papers for? One night, under a full moon, listening to crickets scraping their legs together and a distant dog barking, I waited on guard in the shadow of a cluster of banana palms, expecting to see intruders. Only fruit-bats and fireflies gave my position away, but not to the one I was waiting for. Suddenly, the crash. I ran towards the shack and saw there a duck in the process of regaining consciousness. It had obviously mistaken the shiny moonlit tin roof for a sheet of water, dived in and been stunned. After recovery it took off for the sounds of water (I hoped) in preference to moonshine on a tin roof. After a long day's work I would have my evening wash, eat and then sit outside alone, listening to the silence. I learned to isolate the sounds of the African night from the stillness and had pure immense silence, in which the hum of the Milky Way could penetrate the inner ear with songs of love, songs no one resists once they are experienced. The search for the source is never ending – it is the eternal striving for the music of the Spheres.

When you move on to a new farm the existing African labour force, in this case forty-five of them, expects that you will know their names, wives and children within a very short time, a week or two the most. Not to do so would indicate a lack of caring and interest. Therefore every morning a roll-call was conducted before work commenced. Obviously this also kept track of absentees. Some names stick at first hearing. Here it was Ngugi. He was the cattle foreman, a Kikuyu with three wives and numerous children. He had been placed by the authorities in employment away from traditional Kikuyu land because of earlier subversive activity. He was referred to by other workers as 'the tamer of snake' and also accused of witchcraft. On one occasion a black cockerel was crucified on the door of his hut, head down with nails through the feet and wing tips. He did not freak out at this, which made me wonder about the perpetrator. I suspected that he had done it himself to gain power over the other workers by not being petrified with fear. At times I wondered if in fact he was not the very one who had painted with charcoal on the wall of the firewood room at Kipipiri. Ngugi had a flowing handwriting and so had the wall writer, unusual among Africans in those days. Our labour camp on Mitoni Mitatu was raided by Kenya-based British security forces, the GSU, on more than one occasion. What they were looking for I do not know. I never asked Ngugi about his possible involvement with the Mau-Mau. He was conscientious and kept meticulous records of our six hundred head of cattle. Another name I took immediate note of was Kahawa, meaning 'coffee'. I hired him shortly after my arrival as *askari*, farm watchman. He was a member of the Bugishu, a cannibal tribe from Uganda. Not a nice-looking man, short and stocky with a Bismarck beard, and blacker that the darkest night, he would scare away any criminals just by his presence. He was born in a coffee plantation, hence the name. He was a good story-teller and actor but I never found out if his stories about African traditions and beliefs were concocted for my benefit alone or if they truly reflected African legend and myth. He told me that the early kings and people of Uganda thousands of years ago had come from a land near Egypt where they had descended from the stars. The people later copulated and had children with baboons and that is why the baboons today distinguish men from women and only raid camps or fields when they have seen all the men leaving. This also explained why no Bugishu male would thatch roofs. They did not want to be seen crawling! I told him that it is believed by many Europeans that all humans have evolved from monkeys. His comment to that was that the white race had only recently evolved because we still had straight hair like monkeys, as opposed to the curly hair of the African, which no primate has. All of this was said in good fun with plenty of laughter. I recall him saying that before the British came and stopped the internal tribal wars and protected them from invading Muslims from Sudan they had been ruled by the Mugabe. Mugabe means 'king'. Kahawa was a good watchman and served me well until I left Mitoni Mitatu.

Lands cleared of bush by a multitude of hands and white termite mounds flattened by a plough pulled by a span of sixteen oxen, the Arabica coffee plantation was extended with the magnificent Silver Oak (Gravilia) as shade trees. The maize area was increased to one thousand acres and Rhodes grass for seed and sunflower crops was established. One year we produced over one thousand tons of maize, more that ten million maize cobs all picked by hand. Army worms could be problematic, and spraying unfortunately became necessary. The worms would crawl everywhere, even up the coffee trees, and the sheer weight would break branches. Even the train from Eldoret would have difficulty climbing uphill due to worms on the rail line, causing the wheels of the locomotive to slip. The most effective method of spraying was to find some worms that looked sick. We squashed them in a bucket of water, then strained the water before spraying the liquid on to other worms who would get sick and die. These were the early days of biological control I suppose. The cattle herd was improved by introducing new bulls. They were delivered to the farm by a local transporter named Erik Christensen, a Danish man who had come out to Kenya in the early fifties. I learned later that he is related to Karen Blixen, author of *Out of Africa*, and as he openly admits, there has always been the thirst for excess in the family. He can only speak for himself, but he has become a legend in his own right among Africans and whites from Kitale to Bulawayo in Zimbabwe, formerly Rhodesia. His nickname is Bwana Stuma, meaning 'The Strong One'.

E.W.D. Elmer's return from his travels filled me with apprehension, because his dog had died from old age during his absence. When I met old white-haired Mr Elmer in his faded safari suit full of burn holes in the pockets from his pipe, I thought it better to tell him of this immediately. He stared at me while I waited for an outburst, then said, 'I hope you kept the skin?' An unexpected reaction! After I apologised he said, 'Well, he had to be buried in something, I suppose it was a practical solution.' I realised that his priorities were rather different to mine! A few days later he came to the cattle dip where I was engaged in counting and inspecting cattle. He pulled a little dried-up banana out of his pocket for me to eat. It was black, impossible to peel or eat, had probably been in his pocket for weeks, but it was a well-meant gesture. One evening, driving home from a visit to his sister's farm, he spotted a dead stork on the road. He asked me to stop the vehicle and assess if it was fresh or rotten. If fresh, we could take it with us and prepare it for tomorrow's lunch, he suggested. I declared it very rotten.

He was a true casualty from a concentration camp, always seeing starvation as a probability. Old tyres, bent nails, tin cans and all other scrap was hoarded by him in case of emergency, which he foresaw. He had been overexposed to human cruelty, and psychological counselling was not available for colonial settlers who had fought for British interests. Fortunately for me he bought and moved to another small farm, but sadly years later he was murdered by a gang who stole his watch. He was a kind-hearted man and had helped many people, black and white, out of tight financial situations. As for his life philosophy, I think he belonged to the average, and reasoned that physical life was too hard and cruel to allow for a higher order with a loving God at the helm.

At times, after a day's work and supper, I would be sitting alone outside my hut in pitch darkness contemplating the pain and suffering I had witnessed. I would, after a while, let myself drift into a state of capitulation to sadness and sorrow, and would just flow to see where these feelings would end, going with the young or old in despair to the end of the road into the 'eternal calmness'. I visualised Bingley, Ade-Me-Sou, the Italian mechanic and old Elmer. Maybe unbeknown to them conflict and tension enhance awareness expansion, especially if interspersed with times of joy and contentment. I would see life as a mixing of opposites, a joining of tensions, and that is the very process that generates awareness. I felt that out of tension the new is born. But I also realised that suffering is related to awareness level, and that great awareness equals great suffering. Grief for loss of a loved one can only be experienced if you have a loved one to lose. I concluded that the spiritual stuff that life produces, the 'Hearts and God's requirement' in the bag, has to be activated by human feelings of Love and thereby gain consciousness. One part of the mind observes other parts and all have to be loaded with the feeling of love to be able to be the storehouse of wisdom. Because only in love are 'they' sustainable. In conflict everything changes until sufficient awareness is created in harmonious order, and you have a non-physical being filled with love. The Higher Self? If not filled with love, it would be in conflict, therefore in a state of change and therefore in the process of developing consciousness. And in that light I saw Jesus on the cross. He had rejected conflict and had thereby transferred consciousness to the Higher Self, or transcended to his 'Father in Heaven'. His words 'What I can do you can do' and many of his other statements began to make sense. I felt that I had pulled the plug on traditional Christianity, because I saw no conflict between the God force and the Devil but recognised the Devil as no more than human psyche in conflict. If Jesus had taken up the battle with the authorities he would have reverted himself to conflict. He would then have been a devil in the eyes of the high priest and the Romans and his messages of love would not have been sustainable. A new spiritual sun had risen on my horizon where God was outside conflict, where human life had meaning and it was up to us humans to self-direct and develop our potential. The Devil had been degraded to a human problem and God had become spiritual and lost 'his' religious status in my sixteen-year-old mind.

Chris and I took our annual holiday in August. We caught the train to Kisumu, the original rail link to Uganda, completed in 1901. Our steam locomotive was named Sir H.H. Johnston, the 1899–1901 Governor of the Protectorate of Uganda. The railway line snaked through hilly forests and bush country dotted with farms here and there. Tunnels took us under hills and huge steel bridges spanned ravines, eventually reaching flat sugar fields before the Lake Victoria harbour town of Kisumu. Lake Victoria's water level was very high in 1959 due to excessive rain and the harbour area was sandbagged to prevent flooding. After our comfortable and luxurious train journey we boarded the SS Usoga, an elegantly aged steamer, to sail a five-day round trip on Lake Victoria. It had splendid cabins with shiny brass door handles, towel rails and water taps. Floors were polished and staff were at hand to wipe or clean any disturbance of the perfect order. Crew members dressed in white walked around to ensure the passenger's comfort. In front and below were merchandise and third-class passengers for Uganda and further afield. Three hours of sailing out of Kisumu no land could be seen in any direction. The sun was about to set, turning thunder clouds into images of castles with silver roofs that reflected sun rays of many colours to the darkening heaven. The horizon merged with the still water in a golden rippled glow to the gentle sound of steam power, and the Union Jack fluttered behind on a white pole. Sundowner time and drinks were served in heavy glasses on silver trays by smiling waiters. Our white ship was heading for Port Bell near Kampala in Uganda, finding her way in darkness with only distant lightning interrupting the warm black African night. Conversation of beauty and tranquillity was on everybody's lips. A girl in a white flowing dress, silhouetted against the flashing lightning in the dark sky, spread her arms like a bird, and a sudden surge of romantic feeling befell me. I was still very young and in silence I shared her happy moment. How exciting to wonder what life has in store for another day! Her dinner-jacketed escort arrived and we all followed into dinner. It was a marvellous five-course meal with flowers and candles on the tables. The white piano remembered Strauss waltzes, hands gently gliding over the keys. I was shy, straight from the solitude of the African bush, but loved it. Early morning saw us sailing into Port Bell, a mooring place with a little steam crane. There were no passport controls, and the British flag was flying. Boxes were offloaded and bags of coffee put on board. At midday, after a short walk, we boarded ship again and waved goodbye to elephant grass, African children and banana palms. Next port of call was to be Bukoba.

A new passenger joined us in Port Bell, a Government official going on long leave to England. He lived on one of the seven rounded hills with flattened tops that make up the city of Kampala, a landscape that is characteristic of most of Uganda, interspersed with undulating green valleys and glimpses of water here and there. It is a country with an eternal harvest time, with prolific plant growth everywhere. Kampala accommodated about three thousand whites. The total white population of Uganda was about ten thousand, mainly engaged in civil administration or missionary work and a few involved in large tea and sugar estates. Uganda did not have settlers farmers like Kenya. During afternoon discussions he predicted that Uganda would become independent within a few years and was also of the opinion that Tanganyika was heading the same way. Those countries had not been colonised, they were protectorates.

'If we, England, had not protected Uganda from northern tribes nearly a hundred years ago and introduced civilised standards, Uganda would not have had stable conditions in which to develop a relatively modern organised state. Remember, in Africa before the white man's arrival, power always shifted between warring clans or tribes. Sufficient historical evidence exists to confirm that.' Those words rang a bell in me and I remembered my dream about the African cultural demand to fulfil ancestral spirit desires and thereby not being able to let go of the past. Trapped in the past, I had expressed it to Kariuki. I said nothing but kept listening. He confirmed that cannibalism, despite active Christian missionary work, was still part of old traditional tribal ritual and witchcraft also in some areas. Another passenger commented that the missionary was often too involved in issuing progress reports to sponsors on how many souls had been saved, to the point where they had forgotten the real Christian message. Early Christian missions had quarrelled and their message had become 'Only through us can you be saved from evil forces that will consume you'. With that the African really saw Christianity as an extension to his existing tribal system. All the gory blood-letting stories from the Bible were likened to witch-doctors' fear tactics to intimidate people and gain control over them. 'Where is the Christian message of love and compassion?' he asked. No one answered and the subject changed. It was a subject that made people uneasy. I did not know enough about the matter to open my mouth, but remembered the wall writings on Kipipiri and also remembered from school days the crusaders who wanted, in the name of Christ, to liberate Jerusalem from the infidels, killing and maiming people. So activity in the name of Jesus Christ was not necessarily always good. Was it true that the missionaries had forgotten the spiritual messages of Christ about love and compassion? In a later conversation I learnt that a long time ago French Catholic missionaries were ordered to leave Uganda by the British because of their strong desire to dominate. They apparently moved to Rwanda to establish their order, where over the years they have possibly taught thousands of local Africans to live and let live in peace and harmony. Unfortunately 1995 proved otherwise.

Our captain said that Kenya's independence was still many years away because the Africans were of too diverse an origin and too different. Masai and Kikuyu would never get on, not to mention fifteen other tribes. Jomo Kenyatta was in jail for subversive activity and no other leader existed. He believed that Kenya would be a colony for at least another ten years and then an African government formed with white participation. Little did he know that a

Lancaster House conference in London followed by a general election in February, 1961 would lead to Jomo Kenyatta being Kenya's first African president three years later.

That evening we had dinner at the captain's table. A memorable dinner in good company. Later, standing on the deck looking into the dark night with stars on the heavenly orb, I felt totally at peace with no worry in the world, loved every minute and appreciated my fortunate position. I knew that I had worked very hard for years and deserved this holiday. I was in such a frame of mind that I just had to think about Beauty, Love and Compassion and that would stimulate some inner part of my mind to ecstasy. A vision of myself floating in the air over the water alongside the ship sent me into an even greater intoxication of delightful uplifting experiences, comparable to my confirmation experience, but now with no resistance or fear. My Guardian Angel and I were floating together in a paradise, an experience no one had ever told me existed, and it could be achieved and experienced without drugs or alcohol! I felt that the more clear the body is of toxic substances, and that included some foodstuff, the greater the exhilarating moments where Heaven and Earth become one.

We sailed past two small islands, palms trees waving in the warm wind, before anchoring at Bukoba harbour where a huge stack of bagged coffee beans awaited us. We were now in Tanganyika, an old German colony that England had inherited after the First World War. A short walk along the waterfront took us into the town centre. Like most East African towns in those days it was neat with tree-lined streets, newly painted houses, flowers and grass trimmed and cut. People, mainly Africans, were milling around attending to life's necessities. Women with children on their backs were coming and going – a chaos of unperceived order. Walking back towards the harbour on a clean sandy beach a hippo had taken up a game of 'catch me if you can' with a hawk. The bird would swoop down right over the hippo's head, and the hippo would open his huge mouth, trying to snap the bird out of the air. The performance was repeated many times while they were moving closer and closer to us. Chris and I backed away until we were blocked by reeds. Our only way to escape being trapped between the hippo and water – a situation you do not put yourself in if you want to see the sun tomorrow – was to run towards the hippo and pass him on the land side by a few metres. Although hippos are big and appear clumsy their land speed is too fast for my liking and their teeth too large and penetrating for our delicate, soft human bodies. Hippos do not eat humans but they seem to have developed a dislike towards man – who can blame them? Man's behaviour towards most animals in Africa is despicable. I had developed great respect for wild animals and knew their unpredictability, especially if one blocked their real or imagined escape route. Late afternoon we boarded the ship for Mwansa on the south-east side of the lake. During the night I dreamt of a large gold treasure hidden on the bottom of the lake, placed there grain by grain by flowing river sediment over millions of years, one day to be found and cast into golden crowns and worn by 'the Golden Helmeted Ones'. The purpose of the helmets was to protect the bearer from thought pollution, negative thought wave transfer from other humans. To have a nervous system that resonates with the Universal Energy Flow you must safeguard yourself from excessive exposure to conditioned negative human thoughts, so the dream advised.

I did not have a diving kit to investigate the bottom of the lake, so in the morning visualised myself walking around with a golden helmet. Fortunately because I was visualising it no one could see the helmet, so there were no embarrassing comments or questions to answer! Reflecting on the dream, it obviously meant that gold, being wisdom, is accumulated grain by grain in a 'crown' – Higher Self – and safeguards one from bombardment of non-fruitful human philosophies and belief systems.

Mwansa harbour, boasting Bismarck Rock, a huge balancing boulder bulging out of the water, fashioned by an uncountable number of water droplets over thousands of years, saw us stuck on a mudbank. Long ropes were taken to shore and hundreds of Africans pulled the ship in to the quay to offload passengers and receive fresh supplies from wealthy hard-working Asian traders. Then we were off to Musoma, situated to the west of Serengeti plains on the east side of Lake Victoria, and finally on the fifth day back to Kisumu where we boarded the train to return to Kitale.

Back on Mitoni Mitatu in solitude I felt as though I had been put in a coffin and had joined the dead who refused to communicate. Fortunately that feeling of solitary confinement and despair disappeared after a week or so and my own company became sufficient again. A few weeks later I began to feel weak and could not eat or drink. During a walk, and escaping from demands into the maize land, I noticed that my urine was very brown. I had not noticed before because my toilet was the traditional long drop contraption. My sympathetic cook took off on his bicycle to call my parents for help. Now delirious, I was taken to hospital, and for two weeks filled with vitamins and plenty of water. A severe attack of hepatitis was diagnosed but fortunately it was the type you recover from. The nurses at Kitale hospital were charming, young and very beautiful, but sadly I was too sick to appreciate fully their loving help, care and concern.

After my seventeenth birthday I took my driving licence examination for motorbikes and was immediately provided with a BSA motorcycle for farm use and evening visits to Erik Christensen in Kitale or to my family. I felt freer and was glad I did not have to play 'cat and mouse' with the police in my old Peugeot. Only one more year and a car licence could be applied for.

One day, on the thoroughfare road on the farm, I saw a white person carrying a bundle of water-pipes on his shoulder. Stopping, I realised that it was Peter, the friend who had lost his VW in the river near Kipipiri. He had also moved to Trans Nzoia and was now working on a dairy farm installing a new milking parlour. On the way home from Kitale he had became involved in a heated argument with his new employer and had demanded to be dropped for cooling-off purposes. His equally eccentric employer had said, 'Take your damned pipes and we will see you when we see you,' and left him to walk the ten kilometres home. I took Peter back to the farm where in the yard a distressed tractor driver announced that the tractor and trailer had disappeared in mud near a river and only the top of the tractor was visible. I joined Peter for an on-site inspection and sure enough the driver and helpers had managed with wheel spin and excavation attempts to get the tractor well and truly stuck. Peter asked for my span of sixteen oxen to help pull the tractor out, but that proved futile as the oxen could hardly move themselves in the muddy soft ground. Eventually Peter had to dismantle the tractor and carry it out by hand. Peter's life was patterned and extraordinary events followed one after another. Maybe we all followed some hidden pattern, like a theatre script? All very well, but who and what are we playing for? It could be very desirable to change the script if repetition of the same pattern became the norm, which I could see in some people.

My sister Anna came to stay with me in the hut for a week during one of her school holidays, before going to university in Denmark. She slept on two chairs pushed together. We had a great time driving around the farm on the motorbike and in the evening, giving the cook time off, made various concoctions in the kitchen to the cook's dismay. He went so far as to call our maize flour bread 'concrete blocks'. Not far off the truth, but he was also very jealous of his kitchen! During that time our donkey water boiler sprung a leak and an African contract builder was hired to demolish the boiler-brick chimney and rebuild it with a new two-hundred-litre water drum inside. The contractor was of the same tribe as my watchman, namely Bugishu. During the course of building I asked him if he had ever eaten human flesh since he was of the cannibal tribe. His reply was quite simple. 'I have no reason to deny what I have tried. It tasted like porcupine meat and came from a young girl who had drowned in a river. She was from some other village. A friend cooked it, and I only found out after seeing fingers in the pot.' What can you do to an honest man who is dressed in a white shirt and black trousers and who can read building plans and write? I was a bit shocked and wondered where his next meal would come from, but did not pursue the matter.

A year after my holiday on Lake Victoria, Ulrich and I ventured on a holiday into Uganda. Again we went by train, but this time to the River Nile, some thirty kilometres downstream from the massive Owen Falls dam wall which holds water back in Lake Victoria and from where electricity is generated and transmitted to Kampala and Nairobi. We boarded a river paddle-steamer in Namasagali where the Nile is at least two kilometres wide. Twelve hours of sailing, appreciating a grand red sunset, avoiding drifting papyrus islands and millions of lake flies polluting our otherwise wonderful deck dinner, took us to a landing place where a bus was waiting. It was very well organised in those days. We had to go overland to Lake Albert to circumvent rapids and Murchison Falls – a fifty-kilometre journey. At the harbour in Butiaba, Lake Albert's main harbour town, hundreds of elephant tusks stolen from elephants were lying in warehouses and in heaps outside. They had been shot by hunters who still believed that Africa was forever filled to the rim with animals to be shot for what was perceived as fun, not realising that when animals have been exterminated in fun, humans, goats and cattle move in and multiply faster that anything history has known before. From Butiaba we sailed with a launch to Murchison Falls and here a small part of Africa was still filled with animals. The river banks teamed with elephants, rhinos, hippos, buffaloes, giraffes, gazelles and enormous crocodiles who pretended to be sleeping. Their mouths were wide open, waiting for birds to clean their teeth or for the movement of cool air to dampen their forever hostile attitude to all and sundry.

After a short walk and we arrived at a place where the mighty Nile water is squashed in between two rock faces only a few metres wide, and plunges many metres down, eventually watering the fields of Egypt. If that gap in the rock formation had not been there to let the water flow through, where would the pyramids and the Egyptian be? I found it an interesting thought and realised again that everything is where it is because of something else. Which meant that everything is dependent on something else for its existence, that humans in Egypt or anywhere else have evolved out of a particular environment. Developing life-forms are governed by an inherited blueprint system that determines their development and progression. Why should the earth at large not have a similar blueprint or code pattern for its past and future development? I thought that logical since it produced dynamic life systems and patterns and the ultimate non-physical blueprint should be of value to the final outcome. I saw an inter-beneficial relationship between the river, animals, clouds and the Egyptians, where everything assisted everything to evolve greater abilities in order to see itself through man. So creating a higher consciousness, that is if not distorted by wrong conditioning, philosophy or belief that dictates we have reached the end of the physical and spiritual evolution, or distorted by some even more hideous suppressive systems. The thought came to my mind that we could be evolving Gods. Our Higher Self is forever waking up to new insights and thereby growing. Returning to our river launch we nearly walked straight into the jaws of a three-metre-long crocodile despite my lofty philosophical thoughts, which I found humorous. The crocodile probably saw that our guide had a rifle in hand and slithered away to watch tourists with all their photographic paraphernalia from below water level. I could sense the hungry ray emanating out of those robotic-like, oblong, yellow eyes. The crocodile and the hyena have no mercy or feeling for anyone, even for their own kind. They seem to be 'evil' personified but are still a part of the jigsaw puzzle. The young female hyena, with an extended 'penis' as long as her legs and her ghostlike laugh, is enough to send the Christian Devil with cloven hoof running for shelter.

Why the Christian Devil is associated with a snake is a mystery. Snakes can be tamed to some extent and can become fairly friendly, but when a snake opens his mouth and garbled words and music-like noises emerge, then I will admit that the animal world becomes a strange place. During the process of clearing bush land for cultivation on a farm we discovered an old graveyard. According to local African history it was a battlefield where hundreds of people had been killed and later buried in shallow graves. Bones and skulls were uncovered in great numbers but no one felt that we should abandon the site, until one day only a three-metre-high, crippled, burned out, old tree stump was left. I was called to the site because a snake, guarding the long dead and protecting their spirits, was protesting, so

I was told. I thought, Here we go again with African superstition, but I was quick to learn. Accompanied by warnings of dire consequences from distant bystanders, I walked up to the tree stump from where the racket emanated. As I pushed away dead bark a black snake with an open red mouth recited a long story that sounded like a group of Chinese gabbling, ending with a composition from a chicken run during egg-laying time. I was gobsmacked and had nothing to add or subtract from African superstition. I had never heard about talking snakes from reliable sources before. We left the tree stump as it was but after a month a wide snake spoor was seen leading away into a forest area some five hundred metres distant. For the local Africans a belief system had been reinforced and I wondered if the living kingdom indeed had some hidden connection that was not necessarily severed at death. That theory would be impossible to verify, but I felt that all life somehow has some common connection and ultimate purpose.

We boarded our launch heading downstream for Lake Albert and Albert Nile, stopping here and there to watch animals bathing, drinking or just having a relaxing siesta under the natural parasol of Africa, the flat-topped acacia tree. On the boat a small polished brass plaque said: *'Warning. East African Railway and Harbours are not responsible for any act of God that befalls you'*. Were they suggesting that being eaten by a crocodile or trampled by an elephant was an act of God? Replacing the word with 'The Devil' did not sound right either! Why not be more precise such as, 'Warning to Stupid Tourist! If you fall overboard or become fodder for any animal except at the hands of our own kitchen staff then it's your own bloody fault.' At Pakwach, a little town at the inlet to Albert Nile, we boarded PS Lugard II, a paddle-steamer that would take us to Nimule in the Sudan and back. We had four barges on tow with cargo including live goats. Our cabins were excellent and clean and about two metres above water-level. The gleaming brass porthole could unfortunately open. One evening before going for dinner, Ulrich opened the porthole for fresh air and heard strange noises outside so asked me to check. Sticking my head out through the porthole I looked into the face of a hippo who was waiting for what I received on my head – a bucket of potato peel and other muck from the kitchen above! I had to bathe again and change my white shirt. The next day a paddle had to be repaired after being bent on a hippo's back. Floating islands were also problematic because the paddles would become entangled in papyrus roots if not avoided. When breakdowns occurred our engineering team was efficient and quick to get the old lady going again. The engine-room with the three-stage steam-engine was kept clean and shiny. In Rhino Camp we saw what later was to be prevalent everywhere, abandonment and decay. Here a cotton factory and mills had fallen into shambles. The west Nile district is very fertile and the Nile rich in fish, including the colossal hundred kilogram Nile perch, but the people were rather backward and seemed to be in a static state of fatigue with no evidence of business activity. On entering the Sudan the Union Jack was hoisted to the sound of a bugle and saluted by local police. This impressive style suited the Arabic-looking natives. Ongoing passengers had to take road transport to Juba as the Nile is not navigable along that stretch because of rocks and rapids. We turned around and headed southwards.

In Pakwach we changed ship to the 860-ton SS *Robert Corydon* which would take us back to Butiaba via Mahagi Port, a small town in the then Congo (formerly Belgian Congo, now called Zaire). It was a sorry salute here. The Congo was in turmoil. A number of white refugees with babies in prams joined us in whatever they were wearing, leaving their houses, farms and personal possessions to escape hordes of hate-filled Africans bent on destruction and violence who wanted the white Belgians to take the tarred road with them as they left. Catastrophe had befallen a prosperous, fairly well-organised country in the name of freedom – a new free-for-all orgy. Political slogans and promises had filled the ignorant with expectations of totally unrealistic proportions that no one could ever fulfil, and true chaos followed – 'the way of Africa'. Socialists were jubilant that the new world order was marching. There was Patrice Lumumba mania for a short time and then *bang*! A self-styled saviour is dead, but a few setbacks here and there should be expected and allowed for. But in Africa the spirit of Darwin is strong and only few survive at the top. A handful of white settlers could have been a great asset to an independent Congo, but no, a precedent was set. Independence and the white man were out, the very ones who had the same aspirations for the nation as the local Africans. Who really cares if Congo goes down the drain? The politicians and the media would have little to talk and write about if we all lived in peace and harmony! It is also very convenient to have backward countries in which to try out new political experiments, assisted by 'experts' who go 'home' when the experiment fails! The missionaries had disrupted the African spirit and had forgotten in their soul-saving business and in upholding their own importance, to incorporate Christ's message of love and compassion. Now, with no compassion in a newly gained political hierarchy, individual humans became unimportant and crocodiles were very well fed by humans who adapted the law of Darwin to suit their own ends.

The refugees came with us to Namasagali. What happened to them after that I do not know. I suppose they went back to Belgium with dried tears and their African memories intact – they had nothing else.

Ulrich and I travelled to Eldoret by train and then walked. A lift took us ten kilometres out on the sixty-kilometre stretch to Kitale. From here we walked again, expecting to get a lift. No car turned up for hours, but a herd of three-horned giraffe left their flat dry grassland and took up position on the tarred road blocking our passage. It was lunch-time and very hot, especially for two white youngsters with suitcases and no hats or water, who would have to walk ten kilometres to a bush lodge before dark if no lift materialised. The giraffes kept looking at us with their huge eyes as if they had never seen humans before. A Morris Minor salon car had recently been kicked and severely damaged by these beautiful animals.

Three hours later a truck gave us a lift and we passed our territorial long-necked friends.

Back home on the farm I really felt appreciation for our recently ended holiday in Uganda, for the things we had seen and the thoughts that seeing produced. My thought pattern, my way of thinking, was changing. I saw whole thoughts or whole ideas, not just small fragments of bookkeeping-like thoughts. Thinking of maize, for example, would immediately trigger off a long process of related activity, planting, spraying, weeding, harvesting and selling, not in linear form but on a mental screen simultaneously. I found that way of mental seeing fascinating and played with more complex subjects when I had time to myself. Managing the farm, keeping books and checking records took most of my daylight hours. The crops were looking good. The huge fields of green maize, all the same height, swayed and bent to the warm gentle breeze, behaving as if they belonged to a common organism controlled by a collective spirit. Like a flock of migrating Quealea birds, or a school of fish.

My motorbike took me everywhere on the farm, inspecting fences, chasing baboons and monkeys out of maize fields, herding cattle and checking on workers. One morning, riding through our well-established Rhodes grass field at relatively low speed, I suddenly lost control of the bike. The front wheel jammed as if the brake had been applied, and the bike tumbled over. I flew over the handlebars, landing with my feet on the front wheel from where a fat yellowish puffadder snake stared at me, trapped between the mudguard and wheel. I had no means of ridding my bike of the monster, so walked home and instructed the mechanic and Ngugi the 'snake tamer' to collect the bike and dispose of the fat snake. Late that evening my legs and hands turned red and began to swell alarmingly. I had not felt any snake bite and could not see any marks, but around midnight decided it was advisable to dress and ride the six kilometres over to Chris. I did not like the idea of dying completely alone, which would happen if I had been bitten. The thought arose that here I was on my private mission to find out what life was all about and now it could end because a stupid snake had been too lazy to move. Was a snake in the way just a snake in the way, or was it part of the script? I had found out that dreams and nightmares contained some hidden messages. Why should happenings or 'wakemares' not also contain some messages? Chris sleepily drove me to hospital where I was given a bed, an injection and antihistamine cream. Two days later I had completely recovered but never found out the cause of the swellings. But it did indeed set off a whole chain reaction which led me to decide to go to college in Denmark.

The day I came home from hospital suspicious Cook knocked on my door and said that a stranger wanted to see me. Africans are very vigilant in recognising and detecting people who do not belong to the area and come from far afield. Opening the door there was Kariuki. *'Jambo'*, *'Habari'* and a whole beautiful song of ritualised greetings followed. It was good to see him again! He had resigned from Kipipiri and remarried. His first wife had died before I met him on Bingley's farm, killed in a Mau-Mau attack on reluctant recruits. Now he had come to Trans Nzoia to see if any of the Hansens had a job for him. I hired him on the understanding that I would resign from Mitoni Mitatu shortly but that I would arrange to take him to my father's farm, which Ulrich and I would be managing for five months while my parents travelled to Denmark on holiday. Come October, I would leave Kenya for college in Denmark. Kariuki's position on Mitoni Mitatu would be head guardsman. That meant checking on everything and everyone, to let me know if anything untoward was going on, such as growing dope plants on their small allocated vegetable plots, brewing and distilling high concentrate alcohol from which the drinker would usually go blind, stealing maize, slaughtering new-born calves or any other misdemeanours, including witchcraft or black magic. I was so pleased that he had come. It gave me a feeling of continuity and someone to talk to besides my cook-cum-District Commissioner-in-waiting.

With one of my early salaries of thirty pounds a month I had bought a transistor radio with short wave bands and had become a keen listener of the BBC world service, especially News Reel at five o'clock East African time. That gave me a link to the world, and international politics fascinated me. I began to see politicians in a different light to my conditioned upbringing and realised that many had their own interest at heart, instead of the interest of those they represented. The socialist leaders, despite their philosophy that all should be equal, were seemingly entitled to privileged positions and remuneration. Some are more equal than others! Communism and Hitler's fascism appeared, according to information that I could gather, to be out of the same mould, the desire for total control of society by a few unscrupulous men. In those systems I saw no counter-balance. I also realised that rule by uneducated mobs would probably end up with the same result after a natural pecking order had weeded out all non-Darwinians. Western democracy was definitely the best system of government invented so far.

Kariuki believed that Kenya should have more than one party representing it at forthcoming London conferences. This would be a way of having brakes and control over a possible dictator emerging. Why have UHURU if the new masters are no better that the departing ones he asked?

Politically Kenya was heading for *Uhuru*, although the date for independence had not been set yet. Jomo Kenyatta, after having been tried for Mau-Mau activity, was to be freed and would lead the Kenya African National Union into government. '*UHURU na MOJA*' was their slogan, which meant Freedom United. It literally means freedom and one. All ingredients were in place for what Kariuki had anticipated, leading to dictatorship. The Kenya African Democratic Union did not fare well because of their more realistic and milder slogans. They wanted to build more 'bakeries' instead of cutting up the existing cake. In pre-independence talks the British government had agreed to finance land purchase for redistribution to the landless. Some white farmers became despondent with what they perceived as expediency policy. Knowing that their beautiful, productive farms would be cut up into small shambas, with no consideration given to long-term commercial food production and land degradation, they sold their farms and left Kenya. Africans wanted land and farms, but as in other races, not all Africans are farmers. Some just wanted the trees on the land for charcoal, and after that the wind and the rain could take what they wanted. Many Kenyan farmers of British origin had come from India, where they had been through the mill before leaving their homes and farms when India obtained her independence in 1948. They therefore had no desire to be part of a painful prolonged transfer of power to the 'new scientific socialism' that Kenya's KANU party was opting for, encouraged by many countries unable to appreciate fully that by destroying the relatively small agriculturally productive sector the country would become poorer, thus inhibiting further investment and development. If the country had to be propped up by aid from rich countries that could only lead to the usual dependency syndrome. My family and many others accepted the changing circumstances with the attitude that there was a chance the new dispensation would work, at least for some time. Expectation amongst the African population was running high because of unrealistic promises made by some African politicians and trade unions believing that 'Uhuru' would propel them straight into first world conditions. To avoid a new uprising and repetition of the Congo scenario the British government had to manoeuvre fast, but at the same time it had to be sure that security and stability was maintained. At the Lancaster Conference in London the independence date was set for 12th December, 1963. In February, 1961 everyone voted by sticking their fingers into red paint and making a cross for one of the two parties. We carted farm workers to voting stations by tractor and trailer. The election took place in an orderly fashion which was a good indication for the future.

Late one afternoon, sitting with Kariuki on the river-embankment watching cattle coming to drink in Nzoia river, I told him some of my experiences and thoughts while travelling on the Nile and Lake Victoria the previous year. After a long silence he spoke. 'Bwana', he said, 'you have become an African.' Not the answer I had expected at all! I had no desire to become an African, thank you! Imagine being an African woman, a slave just above the cattle! Always carrying something and being pregnant. I looked at the red sun halfway below the horizon. It was time to go home – night comes quickly in the tropics. Kariuki had noticed my intention to depart and interrupted. 'We have talked before about Africans and their beliefs and spirit world, please do not for one minute believe that we Africans are all the same. In the white race I have seen plenty of variations in the way people behave and the way they think. You remember I told you that I do not read books. I read people, and now again I say you have become an African. Do not worry about the dark. I have a torch you can use when I have finished my story.' I knew that I was browned by the sun but not black yet. 'What I am saying is that the way you explained your Nile experience and dreams show that you think like an African Muganga, a medicine man. You talk as if the Nile has a spirit. You have even come so far that the river influences your thoughts, in other words you accept that the river has an influencing spirit. Lake Victoria also influenced you and gave you a message that has changed your thinking. We Africans who think and wonder about our natural world have come up with exactly the same feelings and awe for rivers, forests, lands and hills, for they all have their own spirit. But sure, Bwana, when the people hear the talk of the medicine man and the spirits of our world many perceive it all wrong.

'They only think in terms of their own physical needs and therefore the spirits become a reflection of their own minds. That is not all bad because the destructive person sees the river spirit as a punisher if he misuses or destroys the river and likewise with forests and so on. You can't make a person understand the spiritual world. They have to experience it before it becomes real. It would be like telling the birds to understand the air they fly in. Man cannot understand God, but we can experience God's spirit reflected in creation, the river, forest, mountains and sometimes man. Maybe eventually when our heart is right, God's spirit will join with our spirit directly and we will truly be children of God. Face it, we are also a reflection of God, so we are reflections observing and harvesting reflections and thereby gaining expanded awareness. That process becomes simpler if the physical world is divided into spirit entities, because then you can be in one place in your mind observing another and the mind develops internal communication. The masses of people often reflect the spirit of a powerful man. They return energy to that man or to the institution represented by actively focusing on him or it. That is man's unfortunate position, and we can only break out of that individually, by focusing and giving our energy to higher ideals. I will go further and relate the same principle to Christianity and other churches. Preachers I have listened to talk as if the spirit of God is a man. They have lowered God to man's level for us to understand spirit as a "Him". Our present wrong thinking has thrown us out of the "Garden of Eden", if you like it that way, and many have forgotten that we have the possibility to re-enter the Garden. Even more have forgotten that they have forgotten. Here is the torch. It is time to go.'

Yes, if that was what made an African or an African medicine man, then I had to admit to myself that I was heading the same way. With my European conditioning process, as short as it was, there were still many aspects to ponder on, but I felt like I was looking out through a frosted window and knowing that as soon as the frost melted the vision would be clear. I was looking forward to college in Denmark and sharing my African experiences and new thoughts.

My last harvest on Mitoni Mitatu was excellent, 'nature's spirits' had done their work well. I was paid a substantial bonus and left with a good reference.

Managing my parents' farm with Ulrich while they were in Denmark went smoothly. The farm now had substantial pig and dairy herds. Maize and sunflower were grown in the lands. Acres of sunflowers at flowering time are a delightful sight. The round yellow faces nodding to one another when caressed by a gentle breeze looked like a Walt Disney cartoon. We could almost hear them saying, 'We are honoured to share our name with the sun. Let us therefore shine and spread our colour to all who have learnt to appreciate beauty that illuminates the mind of the beholder.' The bees and the birds were delighted and appreciated the sunflower's nectar and seeds. Margarine and edible oils are the physical end-product of most sunflower seeds consumed by man, enabling him to generate the energy to plant more sunflowers to repeat the cycle of life.

Two Turkana African farm workers from the northern arid and barren Lake Rudolf area, members of a proud nomadic livestock-rearing tribe related to the Masai, the type with dried mud and feathers on their heads, were caught in the maize field helping themselves to sacks of maize cobs. They carry with them a long thin stick to scratch the scalp when small inhabitants become too much of an irritation. The two were taken to the police station and I had to appear in court as a witness to the theft. In court the judge explained to me that these men did not steal as such, but helped themselves to food that is in plentiful supply. Therefore he could not sentence them because of their ignorance of European law. I did mention to the judge that the two had at election time come home with red fingers and had therefore voted. He smiled and said, 'Case closed.' I did not particularly want anyone to be fined or jailed, but felt that the sower of seeds was entitled to some of his harvest if not all. Taking these men to the police had been a demonstration to all that 'self-helping' was not acceptable. On return to the farm that evening all the Turkanas danced by jumping up and down in their mud-red loin cloths and the event was forgotten. This dance is graceful and most peculiar, resembling the action of the Crested Crane. It is performed by stretching the neck, flapping the wings and leaping into the air.

As arranged Kariuki joined us and took up the position of chief askari and protection officer. Only one nasty incident took place before I left for Denmark. Our pet bush buck, who had been bottle-fed and had become a loved member of the family, who lived in the lounge jumping on furniture and generally behaving as a spoiled baby, was murdered and eaten by unknown prowlers. Only the skin and some bones were recovered from near the slaughter place in a clump of dense bush.

Twenty kilometres to the west across the border, Uganda's independence came about on 9th October, 1962, with no upheaval or unrest. Ulrich, my parents and I spoke to some Ugandans on their independence day after crossing the Suam River Bridge border post. They were of the opinion that England had administered their country well and now hoped that Uganda's leaders would do the same. Little did they know that the tyrant General Idi Amin was growing up in the army and would turn Uganda into a bizarre mess, a massive killing ground, expelling tens of thousands of Asian businessmen, and that he would demonstrate to the world what evil, power-hungry megalomaniacs were capable of if not restricted. It was said at the time that the maniac kept human body parts in his fridge. Years later he did admit to cannibalism.

Towards the end of October I left for Denmark on a BOAC Britannia aircraft. We were supposed to have flown via Benghazi in Libya, but circumstances dictated a different route.

Pyramids in Egypt

Pyramid means pyra = fire, mid = centre = energy centre

Flying over the Sudan the captain announced that the aircraft had developed engine problems and we had to change course and head for Cairo in Egypt. An hour later there was a further announcement that another engine had failed. It was unnerving, but the captain did reassure us that the plane could fly on two engines and that we would land in Cairo before nightfall. I thought of the time we flew out to Kenya, when in my dream the fox men had said, 'Whoever passes here will never be the same again.' I now wondered if they had in fact meant 'Whoever enters here will never return again.' Not much I could do in a stricken aircraft except hope that the pilot was well-trained and kept a cool head. After hours of flying we eventually landed in Egypt. The airport gave the impression that we had landed in a war zone with military personnel everywhere. The UAR, United Arab Republic, consisting of Egypt, Syria and Yemen, had recently been dissolved. The Soviets were becoming well entrenched in Egypt, helping to build the Aswan High Dam, blocking the free flow of Nile water with all its sediment and thousands of broken-up floating papyrus islands from fertilising the Delta in the Nile's annual inundation. Lake Nasser was created to generate electrical power which Egypt needed to expand her industrial output and to supply power and light to an ever-increasing human whirlpool. From the airport we were promptly transferred to the most luxurious hotel I had ever seen. There were marble floors, bedrooms with lounges and of course, marvellous bathrooms. The bed headboard had a brass plate with buttons to push next to figures illustrating various requirements. One figure represented an Egyptian girl. I kept well away from the plate, having a vision of accidentally pushing the button and a whole harem of beautiful girls moving in with music and wine. I was too shy to handle that type of situation even under the banner of massage, relaxation or whatever. I went for a short walk with a middle-aged tea planter from Kericho. Only a few hundred metres away from the hotel I was approached by an Egyptian youngster who said that his sister had been educated in England and was very keen to better her English in conversation with an English-speaking tourist. 'You say yes,' he kept repeating insistently as we passed. Again I immediately saw the possible consequences such as myself running around Cairo naked, after criminals had relieved me of my passport, money and clothing and perhaps reported me to the police for having tried to rape their sister. I was adventurous, but not that stupid. The next day saw us in the Cairo museum with all its splendid displays of old historical artefacts. After hours studying, observing and listening I capitulated and went back to the hotel, suffering from information overload. There was simply too much to see. After a good rest evening arrived, and there was another walk amidst screaming policemen, middle-of-the-road traders mixed up with a traffic chaos that resembles an overturned ant-heap. Had I come back to civilisation? Early the next morning we went to see roses, who are always on the alert to give a scratch if one comes too close. They were grown for perfumes in fields irrigated from canals. The air was saturated with rose scent and the pink colours gave a beautiful contrast to the surrounding green palms. The extraction of the rose scent and perfume manufacturing was overshadowed by keen Egyptian salesmanship. Hundreds of small bottles filled with magic stood on shelves, keenly waiting to kindle the senses of lovely ladies and their admirers and transform their world momentarily into a place of gentleness and love. Who can be rough and cruel when submerged in rose-perfumed air?

Later the same day our unplanned stopover took about twenty of us to the pyramids at Giza, but only after our coach driver had stopped in an alleyway to have an hour-long argument in Arabic with our tour guide while we sat resigned in the coach. Giza, in those days, was well out of Cairo and not overrun by tourists, and no other groups were to be seen. The Great Pyramid was open. It was bigger than I had expected. I had a good look at the stone work and size of stones before entering. Being a practical farmer and work co-ordinator my intuition immediately rejected what I had been taught in childhood about the pyramid construction methods. No way could enough men get around these gigantic stones to move them, and if ropes had been used, the weight and thickness of the ropes would inhibit if not forbid progress. And finally, where would the working men be standing when a stone was moved outwards towards the edge – in the air? But that was not all. The stones forming the interior chambers were much, much bigger, spanning the chambers and weighing about forty tons. To move a stone, likened to a forty-ton container, over an open chamber on uneven ground, without pushing the underlying stones out of place beats me. How did the pyramid builders get the last stone up on the top? There is nowhere to stand! I felt almost angry that educated people could have taught us the rubbish they had, but obviously they just followed what they had been taught and had no choice but to relate the construction of these huge monuments to known construction methods. Man will invariably decipher the past according to his present understanding and unfortunately the evolution theory seems to forbid that highly evolved cultures, however different, may have existed thousands of years ago. A few thousand years here or there does not disturb the evolutionary march. It is only man's mind that becomes disturbed, especially when he finds out that greater and different understandings existed a long, long time ago. Man's ego tricks him into thinking that the greatest time is now. So a wrong account of the builders and their building methods will remain in place for ever or at least until an alternative historical account is formulated. In Kenya we had modern buildings with electrical systems receiving power from Uganda's hydroelectric system hundreds of kilometres away. Co-existing with this highly technical construction of the British, Africans were living happily in mud huts and giving their account to one another of the white man's industrious endeavours, not initially fully understanding and appreciating the knowledge transfer in such cultural hybrids. I would like to suggest that something similar existed in Egypt at the time of building the pyramids, but with a different outcome. The 'British' in Egypt packed up, left or died, possibly killed by the 'mud hut' dwellers. However, on the other hand their ability to transport, cut and lift those enormous stones indicates that they had followed a different technological avenue to our present one and therefore had a different thinking pattern of probably infinite possibilities and had simply dematerialised and vanished. They left the pyramids for the 'mud hut' dwellers and for us to marvel about. A statement in stone, a reminder of Jesus's words, 'What I can do you can do, and more' – if you follow the path that leads to wisdom. In the king's chamber I moved away from our little group and went up to a corner far away where only a little light penetrated. I sat down and closed my eyes, hoping that everybody else would go and leave me alone. As I closed my eyes a vision with a soundtrack came to my mental screen. There was thunder and rumbling, the light went out. Childhood fears of thunder almost paralysed me and I briefly opened my eyes to reassure myself. 'Have no fear, see where it takes you,' I instructed myself. Now a vision of an earth tremor. The light had gone because the tunnel had collapsed and tens of thousands of tons of stone had blocked the entrance. There was no escape. I was trapped here for ever. The body made some uncontrolled movement and then I saw a long tunnel, like an elevator shaft. I was sitting in the bottom of the shaft looking up. No roof covered the top and a round bright light shone into the shaft. Some invisible elevator transported me up the shaft to what appeared to be the top. The house in which the elevator operated was made of glass except for the foundation and the first floor, where a pyramid was standing in the middle of the floor. If the building was seen from ground level outside, no one would see anything except the first storey made of solid materials. I ascended to the floor just above the solids and looked out through the clear glass. A myriad of activities, a peculiar mixture, took place here. There was a war going on. It appeared that no one knew what he was fighting for, except that he felt that he had to fight for his belief. It was as though some old memory kept motivating most people here. A war, all against all, where the object appeared to be to steal energy from opponents. I shouted through the glass to someone nearby that he should try to use the elevator. He pretended not to hear me, perhaps he did not. Animals, snakes and strange-looking animal/man mongrels were also milling around. There was even a cloven-hoofed man with horns standing next to a chute where a sign said 'Waste Material for Recycling'. Not only was the activity strange, there seemed also to be some kind of urgency. People were scared that the light would go out or that they would run out of energy. There was no sun shining, just blended glowing light coming from no particular point. At one place there was a cluster of elevators going down. The queues here were long. Suddenly a wind blew through the place and like leaves in an autumn storm things and people changed position. The stage of activity blew away in the wind and the light changed like an aurora display. After a while creatures reappeared, popping out of thin air, humans formed and the war began again at the first scene with individuals trying to dominate one another. I realised that I was viewing man's negative-thought level.

The elevator took me higher up. Looking through the clear glass panels I saw fields, farmers' fields, factories producing consumer items, a world similar to the one we live in. It was the world of activity for physical survival, but all in a mental stage, before it unfolds and becomes manifest. Ideas were constantly weighed against one another, to produce and develop products most efficiently.

The next level hosted people debating system development. Controls, manipulation, religious belief systems, economic systems, communism versus capitalism and what system to impose, where, and on whom, were debated. The purpose of this desire to influence was not apparent. It just seemed that to influence the levels below with the introduction of functional patterns was paramount.

Further up. Here I saw people who had graduated from the levels below. They had learnt from life's varied exposures to interpret the evolutionary energy flow directly. They had a highly evolved nervous system that had become intuitive in relation to the world below them and could intercept the blueprint governing the lower levels. They could draw information from the original design system and modify it if they were prepared to take the long term consequences. They were the 'sons' of the God of our world, or 'Dynamic Man'.

I heard an echo of someone calling, which pulled my wandering, observing self back to the pyramid floor where the tour guide was about to pull me up from my sitting position. I took his hand, apologised and said something silly about tiredness from being in the sun when we had toured the rose fields.

We drove back to the hotel where we were told to be ready to leave for the airport in three hours' time. I went to my room, sat down and drew a sketch of my pyramid visions so I had easy recall for a later date. Whilst drawing I wondered whether I had travelled into a different level of the mind and had seen the creation of man's Higher Self, or is it the Higher Self that pulls man up and out of the material substances for unification? I felt that the round light I saw at the top of the shaft was in fact my Higher Self. The in-between stages were the astral and mental levels incorporated into life's activity to develop consciousness and mature the mind for unification with the Higher Self. At the time I had read nothing about astral planes, spirits, higher selves or mystical matters so was therefore not influenced by others' written thoughts or speech except Kariuki and other Africans, because up to now my association had been rather restricted by circumstances and I dared not introduce the subject when with other white people. I found that Kariuki's talks, my Nile visions and dreams all fitted the same pattern. I was now also of the opinion that the pyramids were not built as grave tombs, but rather as chambers for the living to experience out-of-body projection, to understand the mystical release of the soul after death. Later that idea became distorted by scholars, as we have seen in many other human rituals and activity, and the pyramids became a place for the dead to depart to the heavenly realm.

Diagram One

Formula for spiritual growth: Nature + Humans + Observation + Relating =

New Attitude

New attitude + New observation =

New knowledge

New knowledge + Past history + Deliberation =

Expanded Consciousness

Expanded Consciousness + Love =

New Dynamic Man = Sons of God

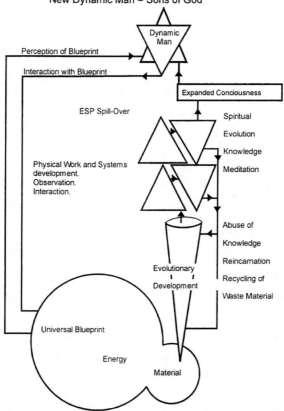

Early evening saw us in the airport. After boarding the plane at about eight o'clock, the take-off was aborted and we trooped back into the terminal building. Three hours later there was another unsuccessful attempt. This time problems arose upon starting the engines. There was another two-hour wait in the aircraft and then finally take-off. Our relief was short-lived. With the lights of Cairo still visible the captain announced, 'We can expect fire on board. We will fly over the desert to dump fuel and will be landing in Cairo again.' After circling for about twenty minutes the captain said that Cairo had no repair team and that we would head for Beirut in Lebanon. The atmosphere in the plane was tense and nervous, with an expectation of the worst. The air hostesses distributed ice to cool overheated heads and necks. Sitting in an aeroplane expecting it to turn into a fireball at any moment (it did indeed happen on another occasion) changes your brain waves. The observer self, as in the pyramids, becomes a master unto itself. The normal thinking self loses control to what I will describe as Higher Self influences. The diagram of the pyramid experiences dominated my mental activity and was seen in three-dimensional form from its foundation where life emerges from the matter/energy continuum. Alternation of life experiences stimulates soul awareness until eventually it obtains unification with the Higher Self. Then intuition becomes the new way of gaining information, by direct energy exchange. The question is, what carries or transmits intuitive information? My answer: When the eye sees an object, the image of the object is carried to the eye by waves at the speed of light and the brain converts impulses to a mental vision resembling the original object. In intuition a similar event takes place, but the interpretation is done directly by the observing self. 'Intuitive information storage', if one can call it that, is the original universal blueprint constantly modified by Universal Consciousness.

The information has to travel faster than the speed of light to be of value. Energy and matter, as we know, cannot be accelerated to a speed faster than the speed of light. But my intuition resolved that problem by introducing 'wave packets'. Existing outside of observable realities, these have always been and always will be traversing the universe at a speed exceeding light, in which information is held and transmitted. It is not a matter of known substances accelerating to the speed of light. Rather one of stating that the 'speed of light plus' exists in the universe and is the carrier of information. 'Viewed' from the 'wave packet', the known universe would shrink in size to where everything is interconnected and distance disappears somewhat, and the mind becomes universal. If we should manage physically to capture faster-than-light energy it would immediately change its status and turn into traditional 'stuff'. Mind travel, as I knew it, could be explained that way. I accepted that it was my philosophy, that it had value to me, but I also accepted that no one else might like or appreciate it. I could live with that.

At six o'clock in the morning we landed in Beirut and were surrounded by ambulances and the fire brigade. How it could have taken four hours from Cairo to Beirut I do not know. I suspect that the pilot was waiting for daylight before landing. Spare parts had to come out from England and the night was spent in the terminal building. The following day around eleven o'clock we were advised that the plane had now been repaired! Unanimously all passengers refused to board and asked for another plane. After much persuasion we eventually did board and were assured of a pleasant flight. Passing through a cloudless sky the captain flew low over the Alps and commented on the view. It was a thrilling, beautiful sight and somewhat compensated for the last twenty-four hours with no sleep. We landed in London four days late. I took the train to Denmark via Holland.

College in Denmark

November, 1962. Denmark had not changed much. 'Mejerholm' homestead, the neighbouring farm to my birthplace and the confirmation party venue, had burned down shortly after we had left for Kenya. The Rahbeck family had a lucky escape but lost all their possessions except the pyjamas they were wearing. A collection of our books which had been stored there also went up in smoke. A new modern house had been built and that is where I stayed until my school started, appreciating the Rahbeck's never failing open-hearted hospitality. I bought a small car, new suits and generally equipped myself sufficiently to feel comfortable.

The school was based on Gruntvig principles (a Danish philosopher), where students were supposed to discover life's spiritual meaning among other more practical studies. Lectures were given on philosophy, politics, psychology, comparative religion and history. Unfortunately too much emphasis was placed on great men like Freud, Darwin and Karl Marx. It was interesting, but I found it lacking. Carl Jung, whom I liked, was generally ignored. The school had a leftist leaning, which meant that most discussion was centred around distribution of wealth and other social inequalities. The school's original purpose had been distorted or forgotten. The practical subjects were of course beneficial. I found it fascinating in that I had to learn to explain my African experiences by first finding a common denominator so that my fellow students had something to relate to, and from there try to branch into the more abstract and mystical. I tried this and that way, using examples such as, 'Do you think it would be possible one day to transmit thought by machine to be reproduced on paper in America?' Or 'Surely it is logical to assume that we have Universal Consciousness since we originally came out of the same primordial soup?' But invariably discussion came back to society's ability or inability to organise itself for the lower to gain maximum benefit, for the able to produce more for the less fortunate. The idea that expression, creativity and new ways of doing things are the beginnings to new employment seemed to have missed them, so did intuition. When I said that desire and dislike influence productivity and that the underlying anger of communism was not charity and could destroy creativity and therefore society, eyes looked at me questioningly. Once I suggested that if a society was run by doctors only, we would likely all be sick. Concentrate on the negative and that is what will manifest! Praise the past for having educated us to this point, and project in thought a fabulous future. The ideas fell on deaf ears. The lowest must be the common denominator was an idea stated by a minister. Denmark as a nation has done well for its citizens materially and they have a very well-organised society, but at the time I felt that they had a 'very cold' connection to the universe. I was still not twenty-one years old, really, what did I know? I missed Africa, I missed Kariuki and his like, I missed the open spaces, the untamed wildness, a world where thoughts flowed freely where no conformity dictated. But a conflict had arisen. I rather fancied the Danish girls, and after all we had the same background!

Driving around the Danish countryside, never to feel threatened by your fellow man, also appealed to me. I visited my sisters who were studying and other families who were all fairly content and happy with their lot.

Prolific were the parties and dancing rituals that youngsters play, usually ending in love and mating, to be followed by responsibilities, mortgages, hard work to meet expectations, a sickly retirement and finally a box to be buried in which still had to be paid for, after years of taxes! Silken bonds of imprisonment! Time to flee!

Kitale – Uhuru – Mombassa and its History

I returned to Kitale in Kenya, kissed the ground and blessed my freedom. I loved the dry grass in the Rift Valley, the untended bush land, the warm sun and the fiery sunsets. My father had by now bought two farms and leased a third. I was asked by an acquaintance to supervise his ten-thousand-acre sisal estate while he and his wife went on holiday overseas. Keeping the huge decorticator machines running was problematic, but with the co-operation of other sisal estates' workshops we managed. I enjoyed my position, organising work, taking sick people to hospital, bookkeeping and seeing that one's involvement makes a difference.

Another acquaintance pleaded with me to farmsit while he went on holiday. It was a pig and cattle farm with a tame buck and two crested cranes, pets to be handled with love and understanding. The cranes were wonderful birds. I would feed them from my hand in the late afternoon, then they would do a short dancing performance silhouetted against the setting sun ending with a 'wau-wau, wau-wau' before they flew off for the night's rest. The owner later became a good friend. He married an African girl, but tragically appendicitis with complications beset him. He was transferred to Nairobi hospital where he died. Doctors were leaving Kenya and no new ones were coming out from Europe because of the uncertain future. No one really knew what would happen after the 12th December, 1963, independence day. Would Jomo Kenyatta be able to control potential troublemakers in the Kisumu area? How would the whites be treated in a long term? Did the white independent farmer have a future in Kenya at all?

Independence day arrived as all days do eventually. I had finished my temporary work and joined my father's enterprise on a neighbouring farm. Ulrich was on the other farm. The entire African labour forces of the two farms celebrated together. Games were arranged, meat for barbecues and *pombe*, African opaque beer, was provided for all. The African women and children sang and the atmosphere was excellent. UHURU had come, and Britain had managed to rid herself of a potential problem. Ulrich and I joined Erik, our transporter *Out of Africa* man, in Kitale Hotel for a drink in the evening – we could just as well join the celebrations in the new Kenya. Numerous Africans greeted us saying 'Long live multiracial Kenya with plenty of opportunities for all.'

My father's sister came out from Denmark for an extended visit and, not being English-speaking, invited me to join her on a tour to Kenya's main harbour town of Mombassa. It fitted in with work. My father could easily look after the two farms by himself for a while. He had good teams of foremen and of course Kariuki (Ulrich had gone to Denmark for a few months) not to mention my mother who was always there with a listening ear. She also possessed good intuitive insights. As on Bingley's farm and on Kipipiri she was the medicine lady, dispensing medicine to the frail, lame and drunk. Supervising that the children were properly looked after and fed correctly, she saw to it that they had their inoculations for diseases. She never complained even when her grown-up sons descended upon her with empty stomachs rather frequently.

Travelling by train to the Kenya coast was an adventure in itself. Two to a cabin with bunk beds made up in the evening and a dining-car with five-course meals. My aunt was a teacher in Denmark and had a great appreciation for modern art and literature. She lent me books for reading on the train in between our discussions and the prolonged silences when we were hypnotised by the beauty of the passing landscape. She had read Karen Blixen's book about coffee farming in the early days of Kenya, and her more convoluted material. In the train she was reading *Cry, the Beloved Country* by Allan Paton. She would fall into deep thoughts and after a while comment on the South African apartheid dilemma, realising that when man is born into a functional system anywhere in the world it is not easy suddenly to change the pattern history has laid down unless one is prepared for a bloody revolution, and then often the means become the end, instead of the end justifying the means. She had been a teacher in Greenland for many years and often referred its similarities to Kenya without expressing what she meant. Obviously it was not in temperature but more likely the yearning for answers stimulated by awe for the profound majesty and beauty of the natural unspoiled world. The empty ice fields, the open sea, the Rift Valley and high mountains, who was calling? She could not 'hear' the answers because her academic training in Denmark at the time stifled the inner quest. To dwell on the esoteric level of being was, sadly, not for a teacher to indulge in. Fortunately that handicap was not part of my world. I was responsible only to myself as far as thoughts were concerned although I had learnt discretion of expression. During the first night we passed through the forest area of Timbaroa where the line crosses the equator at two thousand seven hundred metres above sea level. In Nakuru we stopped long enough to take a taxi the ten kilometres to Lake Nakuru to see thousands of pink-feathered flamingos constantly taking off or landing as if they had an agreement that fifty percent should always be in the air to allow more space for those in the water. A number of pelicans were wading around in the shallow water, pretending to be owners of the lake. We sat in the shadow of a black-barked thorn tree and watched the display of comings and goings of the numerous varieties of birds, with the backdrop of Nakuru on the slopes of a once violent volcano. Concentrated observation of one thing shuts out other things, including time. For the mind time is non-existent but the body demands attention and linear time cannot be discarded. If we wanted to be on the train for Nairobi, our glimpse of eternity had to end. We said goodbye to the birds and knew that they had painted a picture on the mental screen to be appreciated by the lover of natural moving art. I was reminded that the mind is expanded by exposure to interwoven events. That is, layer upon layer of scenes carves a non-physical circuitry for the desirous. Only by desire is heaven yours. At Embaruk we went over the 'fox' viaduct and climbed for Gilgil. Here was a view over Lake Elementatia also hosting flamingos in its alkaline water. Acacia trees on the plains and larger yellow-stemmed fever trees graced the water courses and shoreline. Further afield steep hills dotted the floor of the Rift as if a child of a giant had been playing and emptied buckets of sand here and there. After Naivasha zebras and giraffe were in good supply. Zebras always look fat with an 'air mattress' under the skin to soften the blows of high-speed kicking hooves of high-spirited friends. The fleeing giraffe resembles the dog Pluto – long legs flying in all directions with a steady head above it all. I call it 'The Ballet of Savannah', with music by the never failing African doves. We reached Nairobi after the slow climb over the escarpment, up which for years the carriages were pulled up by cable. We booked into the New Stanley Hotel where personalities from all over the world were often to be seen. Nairobi in those days was clean, safe for evening walks and full of restaurants catering for all palates. The white population was about thirty thousand then. Trees, bright bougainvillaea, flowers and lawns occupied all spaces between houses and roads. It was like a gigantic well-kept park. Shops in Nairobi had merchandise from all over the world. Exotic smells of spices blended with incense swelled out of the Asian quarter, but on entering the *'dukas'* each had its own distinguishing smell. Muslim, Hindu and Christian traded side by side doing what they knew best, namely making a profit to improve their standard of living. The African market with fruits and vegetables enough to feed the growing population was a part of every town's layout. None in Kenya starved in those days. Unfortunately we had only one day in Nairobi, and then proceeded to Mombassa. But a few years later I came to know most of the night-clubs, restaurants and hotels in Nairobi very well. The long stretch to the coast took us through open grasslands, beautiful huge forests which later disappeared under the hands of unscrupulous charcoal burners, then the animal-rich Tsawo National Park, before finally reaching the wooded belt guarding the sea. A memory flashed of Bingley relating the building of the railway in the beginning of this century and the problems encountered with man-eating lions. Images of those noble big cats, the males wearing woollen jerseys draped over their necks, lazily reclining, waiting for the females to produce the meals, which could be a human snatched out of his tent while in dreamland, haunted me. Even male lions could go to that extreme if they were injured by lead lodged under their skin by humans, or became suffering invalids due to old age, thorns or porcupine quills in their paws.

Our hotel was south of Mombassa, a true tropical paradise with clear blue water, white sandy beaches protected by a coral reef and coconut palm trees along the beach waving their elegant fronds and providing shade. Shells and clams were strewn here and there. Drinks were served on the beach by polite African waiters. We had come to the place of true relaxation. But Mombassa had more. It had history to offer. Historical information prior to the politicised present era that forced rewriting of the past to give dignity to the present. As if that would change the credibility of dictators! It ignored the fact that 'by the fruits you shall know them'. Or was old history also written to serve the politicians of the day? It certainly appeared that the British came to establish peace, outlaw slavery, introduce trade and development. And how often does the one who holds control hand over to the majority without a fierce fight, retaliation and counter-retaliation? Would the Arabs have done that? At no time before has such a benevolent solution been made. In short, the British came into Africa and stopped ongoing wars, developed the colonies and protectorates and then handed them back to the original occupier. I cannot see how that act can be condemned by the sensible and responsible average human. Of course there will always be those who believe that rockets to the moon could have been built earlier had it not been for colonialism. My dear aunt shared my view, but only after seeing the whole picture, assisted by reading the history recorded below.

This is an extract from *The Red Book 1919*, a brief history of East Africa:

> Much reliable information about Equatorial Africa was possessed by the Greek geographers centuries before the beginning of the Christian era, their knowledge being chiefly obtained from the logs and stories of the ancient Phoenician mariners who had journeyed into the Indian Ocean. A detailed account of the coast, however, was not given before AD 150 when Ptolemy's writing and map were produced. A

more interesting and accurate description of East Africa littoral, which was called Azania, is to be found in the *Periplus of the Erythraean Sea*, the author and date of which are unknown. In this work under the heading, 'A Pilot's Guide to the Indian Ocean', by an Egyptian, mention is also made of the promontory of Zingis. The words Azania and Zingis are probably connected with the Arabic name for the coast Zanj or Zini, which is no doubt the same as the Persian *zang*, a Negro. '*Bara*' in Swahili means Coast and from those words we have the Arabic Zangibar, or Zanjibar, whence the Portuguese Zanzibar.

There has existed on the Coast of East Africa an ancient civilisation, which although sometimes spoken of as the Zang Empire, was never organised into a single state. From very early times there appears to have been regular migration of Himyarites from South Arabia to South Africa who worked gold mines, and built Zimbabwe and other ruins in Rhodesia, and it seems probable that such localities as the Lamu archipelago, Mombassa and Wasin, which offer obvious advantages as ports, were repeatedly occupied before the oldest colonisation of which we have many records. It is said that the first settlements were made by the Ammu Said from Oman, but there is no detailed information respecting this movement beyond the fact that the Chief of Oman, Said Suleiman, when defeated by the governor of Irak at the end of the seventh century, fled with his adherents to the land of Zanj. There is however a fair amount of tradition if not of accurate detail, respecting the colonisation of the coast in the tenth and following centuries and Arabic chronicles of Kilwa and Mombassa and other places ascribe the foundation of the Coast towns to Arabs and Persians. The presence of true Persians in East Africa which was formerly doubted, has been established by the discovery of Persian coins and inscriptions and the ruins of Persian architecture. Mogadiscio has the reputation of being the earliest settlement, having been built in AD 908. Then followed other towns and Mombassa in the year AD 1000... East Africa was also visited by the Chinese, and Chinese coins dating between AD 713 and 1163 have been found. The Famoa family at Lamu claim descent from some Chinese who were wrecked there... The traces of Egyptian influence are slight, but an Egyptian idol has been discovered at Mogadiscio and the royal house of Malindi assert that they are of Egyptian origin.

The Zanj coast towns apparently reached a considerable degree of prosperity and civilisation. Ibn Batuta, the Arabic geographer, who visited Mogadiscio, Mombassa and Kilwa in 1328, described Mombassa as a large place abounding in fruits and inhabited by a chaste, honest and religious race of the sect of Shaffia. It may be assumed from his narrative that the Wanyika had not then settled in the vicinity of the Coast. According to their own tradition, these people came from behind Shungwaya (Port Durnford), and probably trekked to the country which they now occupy at the end of the sixteenth century.

Although much information was possessed about the coast towns, but little was known of the interior except that it was believed to be inhabited by dwarfs and cannibals, and infested with wild beasts. The origin of the Nile, however, was always a source of interest to the Romans, Greeks and Arabs; and the greatness of the snow-capped peaks, called the Mountains of the Moon and Mount Olympus, was sung by various historians and poets.

The authentic history of East Africa can be said to commence in 1498 when the first Portuguese expedition, under Vasco da Gama, anchored off Mombassa on 7th April of that year. The city is described by Vasco da Gama as large and seated on an eminence washed by the sea. He also records the existence at the entrance to the port of a pillar and a low-lying fortress. After nearly suffering shipwreck while attempting to enter the harbour the Portuguese sailed to Malindi where they were hospitably received. 'The town' he wrote, 'lies in a bay and extends along the shore. Its houses are lofty and well white-washed, and have many windows. On the land side are palm groves and all around it maize and vegetables are being cultivated.' After remaining there for nine days the fleet proceeded to India. On the return voyage in the following year, Vasco da Gama again stopped at Malindi, and erected a stone pillar to the south of the town, which was dedicated to the Holy Ghost. This pillar, or a similar one built on the same site at a later date, is still in existence.

The next few years were spent by the Portuguese in establishing their supremacy along the whole East African Coast. All the principal towns and Sultanates, such as Zanzibar, Kilwa, Pemba, Brawa and Sofala fell before the invader, and on 15th August, 1505, a Portuguese fleet of sixteen sail, under Dom Francisco d'Almeida, who was afterwards Viceroy of India, stormed and sacked Mombassa. A year later the King of Lamu surrendered to the Portuguese and agreed to pay a yearly tribute of six hundred metikal of silver (three hundred pounds) in Venetian money.

In 1509 the appointment was made from Lisbon of a Governor of the provinces of Ethiopia and Arabia to reside at Malindi.

In the same year the dethroned Sultan of Kilwa, Jaji Husein, who had been defeated by the Portuguese General Vas de Goez, was deported to Mombassa with a number of his subjects. According to tradition, the Duruma – one of the Nyika tribes living immediately behind Mombassa – are to a great extent descended from the Makua and people of Kilwa who were brought to Mombassa by a certain Bwana Kigozi. It is possible that there is some connection between these two events.

The inhabitants of Mombassa were the people who gave the Portuguese the most trouble, and in November, 1528, Nunho da Cunha, with the help of the King of Malindi, stormed and burned this town for the second time. Nunho da Cunha remained in possession till March, 1529, when, after more than half his men had died of disease, the garrison was withdrawn. But the power of the inhabitants was broken, and Portugal was able for the next few years to claim undisputed sway over the whole coast from Brawa to Cape Corrientes. She ruled, however, with a rod of iron, and her pride and cruelty had their reward in the bitter hatred of the natives.

In 1585 a Turkish corsair named Mirale Beque (Ali Bey) visited the East African Coast, and claimed the sovereignty for his Sultan. He was well received by the Kings of Jumbo, Faz, Lamui and Mombassa, and after driving out the Portuguese from most of their settlements, he returned to the Red Sea in April, 1586, taking with him plunder to the value of about £600,000 and fifty Portuguese prisoners. The four towns which had aided the Turks were severely punished the following year, a punitive expedition being despatched against them from Goa.

From 1586 to 1589 the Zimbas, a tribe hailing from south of the Zambesi River (Zimbabwe/Rhodesia), overran East Africa. They captured Kilwa and massacred three thousand of the inhabitants, after which they pressed northward to Mombassa and besieged that town.

A second invasion of the Turks took place in 1588. After touching several of the towns on their way south, and exacting tribute, they landed at Mombassa and built a fort on Ras Serarii. On the same site the Portuguese afterwards erected a chapel, 'Nossa Senhora das Merces'. This building was turned into a fort by the Arabs in 1696, the ruins of which are now in a fair state of preservation.

On 5th March, 1589, Thomas de Souza Coutinho, with a fleet of twenty sail, anchored off Mombassa, and commenced to bombard the Turkish fort. The Zimbas, who had been encamped at Makupa on the mainland, also attacked the Turks and drove them into the sea. Many were killed, but over one hundred, including Mirale Beque, fell into the hands of the Portuguese. Thomas de Souza Coutinho then undertook a successful punitive expedition against the Kings of Kilifi, Lamu, Manda, Pate, Siu and Faza.

In June of the same year the truculent Zimbas attacked Malindi, but thanks to their allies, the Wasegeju, a wild tribe that had come from the interior in 1571, the Portuguese defeated them with great loss and completely broke their power.

In 1592 the Portuguese, with the help of the Wasegeju, captured the Kings of Kilifi and Mombassa and sacked both towns. For the former it was the death blow from which it never recovered. Recognising the great importance of Mombassa, the

Portuguese decided to make it the capital of their East African possessions and appointed the King of Malindi Sultan of Mombassa. The citadel of Mombassa, which was dedicated to God, and called Fort Jesus, was commenced in 1593 and was partially completed two years later. An inscription recording this event is to be seen inside the porch.

It was about this time that the first English and Dutch trading vessels visited the Indian Ocean. In 1591 the 'Edward Bonadventure' (Captain J. Lancaster), wintered at the north end of Zanzibar, and in 1595 a Dutch fleet was sent to India to trade with the natives. Owing to the advent of England and Holland upon the stage, and to the war of succession which broke out between Portugal and Spain in 1580, the supremacy of Portugal in the East gradually declined. In Africa they concentrated their forces as much as possible at Mozambique, Mombassa and Pate, and evacuated most of the other towns. Their future policy was chiefly directed towards the development of Mombassa.

In 1603 three blockhouses were built at Makupa to keep the Wanyika, who occasionally raided Mombassa, in check. The ruins of two are still in existence.

In 1612 the Sultan of Mombassa, Hasan bin Ahmed el-Malindi, quarrelled with the Portuguese Governor, who bombarded his palace. The Sultan retired to Kilifi, where he remained for eight months. He was then reinstated, but in 1614, being accused of high treason, he fled to Kabai. He was at first well-received, but was afterwards murdered by the natives, and his head sold to the Portuguese for two thousand pieces of cloth.

Sultan Hasan's son, Yusuf, was sent to Goa to be educated. He was baptised in 1627, when he was given the name Don Jeronymo Changoulia, and he married a Portuguese lady. In 1630 he was allowed to return to Mombassa, and was recognised as Sultan. A year later, on 16th August, 1631, all the Portuguese in Mombassa, numbering over one hundred, were murdered at his instigation, after which he took up his residence in the fort.

As soon as the news of the massacre reached India a fleet under Don Francisco de Moura was despatched from Goa to punish the rebel. Sultan Yusuf, however, succeeded in capturing two of the vessels; he then dismantled the fort, destroyed the town, and escaped to Arabia. During the next few years he caused the Portuguese much annoyance, attacking and looting their settlements in Madagascar, the Comoro Islands, and on the mainland. He was eventually killed at Jeddah on 26th November, 1638, in an affray with some Arabs. With him died the last of the Sultans of Mombassa.

In 1635 the new Governor of the Portuguese possessions in East Africa, Francisco de Seixas de Cabreira, repaired the fort. His valour and virtues are recorded in an inscription cut in the wall over the fort gate...

In 1660 the Arabs captured Faza and Malindi, and during the next five years repeatedly attacked Mombassa and other towns...

In 1678 the Portuguese undertook a punitive expedition against Pate, Siu, Lamu and Manda. They were aided by the people of Faza, and succeeded in capturing the kings of all four towns, whom they executed. They then built a fort at Pate and another near Faza, the ruins of both of which are to be seen to the present day. The next year, however, the Arabs forced them to retire to Mombassa and Mozambique.

The great siege of Mombassa, which was continued for thirty-three months, commenced on 15th March, 1696. On that day an Arab fleet of seven sail entered Kilindini harbour and bombarded Fort St Joseph. The entire population of the island consisting of fifty Europeans and two thousand five hundred natives, took refuge in and round the Fort Jesus, whilst the Arabs occupied the town Makupa, Fort St Joseph and the chapel Nossa Senhora das Merces. The Wanyika under the Chieftain of Chonyi and the Queen of Zanzibar attacked the Arabs on more than one occasion, but they were beaten off with heavy loss. Reinforcements and supplies were received from Muscat and Pate, and the Arabs were able to prevent four Portuguese ships that arrived from Goa on Christmas day from entering the Harbour. On 14th January, 1697, bubonic plague broke out amongst the garrison of the fort, with the result that on 23rd July there remained but the Commandant, two Portuguese children, the King of Faza, a few Wagunya, nine Swahili, and fifty native women. The Commandant, Antonio Mogo de Mello, died on 24th August, after which the King of Faza with his handful of men kept the Arabs at bay for three weeks. The relief, which had been so long delayed, arrived from Mozambique in September, and the garrison of the fort was strengthened by one hundred and fifty Portuguese and from two hundred to three hundred Indians and natives.

The siege was continued for fifteen months longer, and it was not until 12th December, 1698 that the Arabs effected an entrance into the Fort. The little garrison, reduced in number to eleven men and two native women, and worn out by continual fighting and watching, made but a feeble resistance, and were put to the sword.

Two days later a Portuguese fleet arrived from Goa, but the Admiral, seeing the Arab flag flying from the citadel, retired without attacking.

After the capture of Mombassa the Arabs pressed as far south as Kilwa, and occupied that town and the islands of Zanzibar and Pemba. Valis, or Governors, were appointed and the conquered places were garrisoned by troops from Muscat.

The loss of their East African possessions was a matter of great regret to the Portuguese. Expeditions were accordingly organised in Lisbon and Goa in the years 1699, 1703, and 1710, to retake Mombassa, but they met up with no success. At last, in 1727, a good opportunity presented itself. In that year the Valis of Mombassa and Zanzibar quarrelled, and the latter fled to Pate. The king of this town, however, having no wish to be mixed up in the broils of the Arabs, despatched a messenger to Goa and offered to place himself under the protection of Portugal. On 24th December, a fleet of six sail, under General Luiz de Mello Sampayo, set out from Goa to reconquer East Africa. But slight resistance was offered by the Arabs, who retired to Faza, and the Portuguese flag was hoisted at Pate and Sui. General Sampayo then sailed to Mombassa, and on 11th March, he bombarded Fort St Joseph and entered Kilindini Harbour. The next day the Arab Governor capitulated, and the Portuguese flag once again flew from the citadel. Within a few weeks of this event the whole of the East African coast from Brawa to Cape Corrientes was once more under Portuguese rule. But it fell again as quickly as it had risen. The men appointed as Governors were corrupt and incapable; their one idea was to become rich at the expense of their subjects by levying tribute and taxes, and they were brutal and arrogant in their behaviour towards the natives. In 1729 the people of Mombassa invited the Arabs to return, with the result that on 14th August of that year the Portuguese were driven from Pate, and on 29th November from Mombassa...

In 1739 the Imam of Oman appointed a certain Mahomed bin Athman Governor of Mombassa. He belonged to the Mazrui family, whose members have played an important role in the history for the last two centuries.

The tie which connected Mombassa with the distant Court of Muscat was very weak, and the supremacy of the Imam, as his name implied, was mainly spiritual. Preoccupied by their troubles with Persia, which ended in the overthrow of their power in 1741, when the Albusaidi chief usurped the throne of Oman, the Yorabi prince could give little attention to his remote African possessions. Matiomed bin Athman had, in consequence, no difficulty in throwing off his allegiance to his Sovereign and transforming himself from a Governor into an independent chieftain. He ruled in that capacity from Malindi in the north to Pangani in the south, as well as over the Island of Pemba.

His example was followed by the King of Pate, a member of the ancient Nabahan family, whose ancestors had ruled the whole adjacent coast for centuries before the advent of the Portuguese. During the next eighty years the Mazrui and the Nabahans were continually at war, striving for the supremacy of East Africa.

Wishing to take advantage of this state of affairs, the Governor of Mozambique despatched in July,

1769, two ships to recapture Mombassa. But the captain who was in command, fearing the disgrace of a defeat, returned to Mozambique without landing. This was the last attempt on the part of Portugal to regain possession of the territories that had cost her the lives of thousands of her sons.

In 1785 the Imam Ahmed bin Said, the real founder of the Albusaidi dynasty of Oman, compelled from the Masrui a temporary recognition of his overlordship; but it was not till after the accession, in 1809, of Said bin Sultan, the fifth Albusaidi Seyid, that the Court of Muscat conceived the design of re-annexing its old African possessions. In 1822, at the request of the people of Pate, who had been defeated by the Mazrui, Seyid Said seized Pate and Pemba, and threatened Mombassa itself. The Mazrui chief, Suliman bin Ali, invoked the protection of Great Britain which was refused him by Captain Vidal of HMS *Barracouta*, who was cruising at the time (December, 1823) on the East African coast. Notwithstanding this the Mazsrui hoisted the British flag on their own authority, and Captain Owen of HMS *Leven* finding it flying in February, 1824, established a provisional Protectorate, subject to the approval of the British Government. Lieutenant Reitz, R.N. (after whom Port Reitz was named), was appointed Resident, and on his death shortly afterwards he was succeeded by a midshipman named Phillips. The British Government, however, repudiated the Protectorate which was withdrawn two years later, and Salim bin Ahmed, who had deposed Suliman bin Ali, submitted in 1828 to Seyid Said, on condition of being retained as Hereditary Governor of the town, and sharing the revenue equally with the Sultan. The peace which was thus concluded was, however, only a truce, and after the Mazrui Arabs had twice unsuccessfully attempted to throw off the Muscat yoke, Seyid Said took Mombassa in 1837, and treacherously seized the reigning Mazrui, Rashid bin Salim, whom he sent with twenty-four of his adherents to the dungeons of Bunder Abbas to be starved to death.

The power of the Mazrui was thus broken. The unity of the State was split in two divisions, the elder branch migrating to Gazi, and the younger to Takaungu, where they governed as petty chiefs, though never formally acknowledged as such, until 1895.

In 1832, Seyid Said transferred the capital of his dominions from Muscat to Zanzibar, where, as at Lamu, an officer appointed from Arabia had governed since 1784. An account of the town was given in 1799 by Lieutenant Bissel, one of the officers of HMS *Leopard* under Admiral Blankett, who had been despatched to frustrate any attempt of Bonaparte's to reach India by way of the Red Sea. 'The town', Bissell wrote, 'is composed of some few houses, and the rest are huts of straw mat which are very neat.' From this it would appear that the wattle and daub style of architecture, now common, had not then been introduced into Zanzibar. The fort, which was originally built by the Portuguese, was repaired by one of the Valis or Hakims, an Abyssinian named Yakuti, about the year 1800. In the space of a few years Zanzibar was converted into the largest and most important city on the coast. The Americans established a trading consulate at the Seyid's Court in 1836, and being the first in the field, dispersed their cottons and hardware throughout Eastern Africa. Four years later Lieutenant-Colonel Hamerton was directed to make Zanzibar his headquarters as 'HBM Consul, and East

India Company's Agent in the dominions of his Highness the Imaum'. A French Consul took up his residence at Zanzibar in 1844, and Consuls were appointed for Portugal (1879), Italy, Belgium, and Germany (1885), and Austria-Hungary (1887).

Although the Americans were the first white people to exploit Zanzibar and East Africa commercially, the French, and in a less degree the Spanish and Portuguese, had since the eighteenth century looked upon both the island and the mainland as a happy hunting ground from which to draw their supplies of slaves, whom they and the Arabs shipped to Muscat, India, Mauritius and South America. It was estimated by Captain Smee, of the East India Company's ship *Ternato*, in 1811, that the export of slaves from Zanzibar numbered from six thousand to ten thousand per annum, whilst the import was about fifteen thousand.

It was for the prevention of the slave trade that England came to East Africa, her first agreement with the Zanzibar's Sultan being entered into in 1822. The task of abolishing slavery, which has been England's unaided, has taken eighty years to perform, but she may be proud of the fact that the slave markets of East Africa are now through her efforts closed, and that slavery has practically ceased to exist. Negroes are no longer torn from their homes and forced to face the horrors of a march from the interior to the coast or the terrors of a journey on a slave dhow.

Not only Zanzibar, but also Mombassa and Lamu developed into important seaport towns under Seyid Said's rule. Some time elapsed however, before the whole coast was subjugated and, amongst other towns, Sui, Pate and Faza caused him much trouble. Siu had in the seventeenth century suffered considerably from the aggression of the Nabahan prices of Pate, and in order to protect themselves, the inhabitants had appealed for help to the Somalis, who lived on the mainland opposite, offering, if they were successful in driving out the Nabahans, an equal share in the Government of the town. The Somalis agreed, and Siu was saved. A curious dual administration was then established, consisting of a Famao (a descendant of the early Asiatic colonists) and a Somali Sheikh. This system lasted till 1812, when the Famao Sheikh, by name Mataka, concentrated the whole power in his hands. The Somalis applied to Seyid Said, who attempted unsuccessfully to capture the town on 6th January, 1843. Operations were recommenced with no better success the next year, and it was not until 1865 after the death of both Mataka and Seyid Said, that the Sheikh of Siu acknowledged the supremacy of the Sultan of Zanzibar. The inhabitants of Pate threw in their lot with the people of Siu and retained their independence till 1866. Faza fell through the intrigues and treachery of Mzee bin Sef, who was afterwards appointed Governor of the town, and ruled as such until deposed by the agents of the Imperial British East Africa Company, when he was interned in Zanzibar till his death in 1896.

One of the most successful ideas conceived by Seyid Said was the erection of a line of trading stations from the mainland immediately opposite Zanzibar to far into what is now the Belgian Congo. Following close in the wake of the Arabs, European explorers journeyed into the interior of East Africa, and during the last half of the nineteenth century numerous expeditions were undertaken in all directions, thus opening up a country which till then had been practically unknown. Rebmann and Krapf discovered Mounts Kilimanjaro and Kenya in 1848 and 1849, Burton and Speke sailed on Lake Tanganyika in 1857, and the latter reached Lake Victoria a year later; Speke and Grant visited King Mtesa of Uganda and descended the Nile, on the banks of which they met Sir Samuel Baker in 1862; Cameron and Stanley crossed Africa, by different routes in the seventies; Fischer and Thomson penetrated into the Masai country in 1882 and 1883, and Count Teleki discovered Lakes Rudolf and Stephanie in 1887.

Seyid Said died at sea in October, 1856. His eldest surviving son Seyid Thwaini, became by the father's will Lord of Oman, whilst Seyid Majid, the next son, succeeded to the Government of Zanzibar and the East African Coast. The former, dissatisfied with his heritage, threatened, in 1859, an attack on Zanzibar, but was prevented by English cruisers. The dispute was referred to Lord Canning, then Viceroy of India, by whose award Zanzibar was declared independent of Oman, and the Imam was paid an annual subsidy by India. This payment placed Zanzibar in the position of a subsidised dependency of India. Seyid Majid died in 1870 and was succeeded by his brother Seyid Barghash.

During the last year of Ismail Pasha's reign over Egypt the Government of the Egyptian Soudan became very ambitious. It annexed a part of Somaliland and endeavoured to annex Abyssinia, whilst its officials were sent up the Nile as far as Uganda. In 1875, four Egyptian ships of war, under McKillop Pasha, steamed down the east coast of Africa, and attempted to seize the mainland ports. Anchor was cast off Kismayu in October, and a force of three hundred and fifty troops with horses and artillery was landed. The country at the mouth of the Juba was occupied until

22nd December, when, according to a proclamation of Sevid Barghash, 'It pleased the Almighty to bring about their departure', or in other words, they left in deference to orders received from the Khedive, to whom representations had been made by the British Government.

Between the years 1880 and 1885, the Germans became active in East Africa; their agents repeatedly visited the coast towns and made treaties with various chiefs in the interior. These treaties were unofficial till 17th February, 1885, when the German Emperor granted a charter of Protection to the Society of German Colonisation.

The dominions of the Sultan of Zanzibar were defined in 1886, when the boundaries were settled by an international convention. It was agreed that his possessions included the Islands of Zanzibar, Pemba, and the Lamu Archipelago, in addition to a ten mile belt along the coast from Tunghi Bay to Kipini Bay at the mouth of the Ozi River, and the ports of Kismayu, Brawa, Merka, Mogadiscio and Warsheikh. The territory behind the Sultan's ten mile strip was divided into two parts; the northern half was assigned to England, the southern to Germany.

On 25th May, 1887, Sevid Barghash granted a concession of his mainland possessions lying between the Umpa River and Kipini to the British East Africa Association, and in the following year his successor, Sevid Khalifa, made a similar concession of his territories south of the Umba River to Germany. The British Association was reconstituted as the Imperial British East Africa Company and received a Royal Charter on 3rd September, 1888.

In 1885 the Germans declared a Protectorate over the independent State of Witu, which had been founded by the Nababan refugees from Pate, and three years later they made a formal demand for the cession of the island of Lamu. The Sultan refused, and in August, 1889, offered to lease the whole of his territories between the mouth of the Ozi and Juba rivers to the British East Africa Company. Germany objected, and on 22nd October claimed a Protectorate over the country between Juba and Witu. The question was submitted to arbitration, but before a decision was arrived at a treaty was signed by England and Germany on 1st July, 1890, by which the latter resigned her claim to the territory north of the Tana, and to various other Protectorates, receiving in exchange the definite cession of the country held in lease from the Sultan of Zanzibar and the Island of Heligoland.

On 14th September, 1890, ten Germans were murdered at Witu, whereupon a Naval Brigade under Admiral Sir E. Freemantle was despatched to revenge the massacre. The town was burnt and the rebels withdrew into the forests, whence they long continued to harass the country. In 1893 the Company decided to abandon Witu, and the Government took over the administration of the Sultanate.

In 1892 Great Britain and Italy signed an agreement by which the latter was given administrative power of the Benadir Coast, from the mouth of the river Juba to Warsheik; and in 1905 all the sovereign and other rights of the Sultan of Zanzibar over these territories was completely ceded to Italy.

The Church Missionary Society, which had been established in Mombassa since 1844, sent its first party of missionaries to Uganda in 1877. They were soon followed by the Roman Catholics of the Order of the White Fathers of Algeria. The Europeans found that the Mohammedans had already preceded them and although they were at first well received, they had to suffer many indignities and persecutions at the hands of the King and his subjects. Before the arrival of the missionaries faction feuds had nearly caused the ruin of Uganda, and now that three new creeds had been introduced, the quarrels were intensified. For some years the country was involved in a religious war, the King favouring now one party, now another...

In February, 1895, a somewhat serious rebellion broke out at Takaungu. On the death of the Vali of that town, Salim bin Hamis of Mazrui, his son Rashid bin Salim was elected by the Company to succeed him. There was another claimant, who according to Mohammedan law had a better right to the Governorship, but as he was not well disposed towards the British, his claim was disregarded. He thereupon withdrew to Gonjoro and threatened armed resistance. A naval brigade was despatched against the rebel, who was defeated in an engagement and fled to Gazi. It was while affairs were in this unsettled condition that the rule of the Company came to an end. On 1st July, 1895, the establishment of the direct Foreign Office control over the East Africa Protectorate was effected by Mr (afterwards Sir) A. Hardinge, who was at the same time appointed HM Commissioner and Consul-General. In August the elder branch of the Mazrui decided to throw in their lot with their kinsmen, and the rebel forces were swelled by the natives of most of the coast towns from Kipini in the north to Vanga in the south. Mbaruk bin Rashid, the chieftain of Gazi, had already on three occasions rebelled against the Sultan of Zanzibar, and as he had never been properly punished, he doubtless thought he could defy the British authorities with impunity. But after sundry fights, seeing that the struggle was hopeless, he and his adherents crossed the frontier into German territory, and on 20th April, 1896, surrendered to the Governor of German East Africa.

The reports which were received concerning the future prospects of Uganda were so favourable that this country began to be regarded as a land of great commercial importance. The principal drawback, however, was the lack of transport. In order to remedy this, a railway from Mombassa to Victoria Nyanza was projected, and a preliminary survey made in 1892–3. The first rails of the Uganda Railway were laid in 1895, and although great difficulties had to be contended against a weekly train service from the Coast to the Lake was started at the end of 1901.

On 1st April, 1902, the Naivasha and Kisumu Provinces were transferred from Uganda to East Africa. The boundary between the two Protectorates is now a line drawn from the eastern shores of the Victoria Nyanza to Mount Elgon, and from thence up the Turkwell River to Lake Rudolf. Three years later on 1st April, 1905, the Administration of the two Protectorates was transferred from the Foreign to the Colonial Office.

Kenya was gazetted a province in 1905, and in the following year the Legislative and Executive Councils of the East Africa Protectorate were instituted by the 'East Africa Order-in-Council, 1906'. In 1907 the Anglo-Abyssian boundary was agreed upon, and a great part of Lake Rudolf was secured to the Protectorate.

Meanwhile new settlers were gradually coming into the country and 1908 saw an influx of Boers from South Africa, the majority of whom took up farms on the Uasin Gishu Plateau. In 1910, the steamship service of the Union Castle Line to and from Mombassa was inaugurated.

Considerable progress occurred during the ensuing years. The Convention of Associations, commonly known as the Settlers' Parliament, was instituted in 1910, and the following year saw the introduction of the non-Native Poll Tax. The Native Labour Commission was appointed in 1912, and the Nairobi Sanitation Commission in 1913. The Magadi Railway was completed on 24th May, 1913.

On the outbreak of war in August, 1914, martial law was proclaimed, and Defence Forces were formed at Mombassa, Nairobi, and Kisumu. Many restrictions were imposed on the people of the Protectorate, and the Compulsory Service Ordinance was introduced, but throughout the burdens were borne in a cheerful and loyal spirit.

The campaign in the adjoining territory was prosecuted with vigour and made further heavy demands on the Protectorate's Supplies. General Smuts assumed command in 1915, and during that year Kilimanjaro and Dar-es-Salaam were occupied by the British forces. General Sir J.L. Van Deventer succeeded General Smuts in 1917, and the German general, Von Lettow, finally capitulated after a prolonged but hopeless struggle on 14th November, 1918.

The conclusion of the victorious armistice on 11th November, 1918, was signalised by tremendous rejoicing throughout the country.

During the war numerous important commissions were appointed, including the Economic Commission and the Land Settlement Commission. These bodies made exhaustive enquiries into their various subjects and valuable evidence was secured and embodied in the reports.

The dawn of peace marked the opening of a new era for the Protectorate. Scientists are developing the natural resources of the Country, and planters and settlers are busy cultivating the rich soil of the lowlands and highlands, and the country looks forward to a period of progress and expansion.

The Red Book 1919
The 'Standard' British East Africa and Uganda Handbook and Directory
Printed and published by East Africa Standard Limited
Nairobi and Mombassa 1919

Regardless of the accuracy of *The Red Book 1919*, the fact remains that the British stopped the slavery trade and became the peacemakers of the time in an unimportant but nevertheless very tumultuous region of the world. Colonisation initiated a new era of stability and a process of political consciousness in the indigenous population, which would hopefully lead to individual consciousness and development of individual responsibility, moving away from the more traditional tribe consciousness or easily lead group spirit. It was not a question of divide and rule but the awakening of individual responsibility and awareness.

By reading Africa's old history, and about the race problems in South Africa, the future of Africa in general and Kenya in particular began to frighten me. Uhuru na Moja had come, and the law of Darwin was again in action. The violent history of the continent, the looking back to ancestors by the African masses for solutions, mixed up with the 'born sinner' and forgiveness attitude of the Christian church regardless of crime perpetrated (fighting in the name of Christ), and dictators with no accountability, were collectively a recipe for disaster. In discussion, my aunt saw a different evolutionary line. She saw, like most Westerners, that all Africans would become European-like in time. I accepted that I was influenced by Africa, black and whites living in Africa, and accept that my sudden lack of confidence was self-inflicted. Travelling back to Kitale from the coast after a wonderful and rewarding time, I began thinking seriously of going to Denmark to study and obtain some formal training. It was all very well to be able to manage farms, repair tractors, weld and make machinery, grow all sorts of crops, diagnose and inject cattle for disease, do bookkeeping and entertain a philosophy that only existed in my head, but these were only useful in Africa! Although Kariuki had said that I was an African, my skin was still white and Africa's future was as uncertain as ever.

Left Africa – Back in Kitale – Managing Maboonde Estate

Back in Kitale, after talking the problem over with my parents, we eventually agreed that it was probably best that I left for Denmark to get some formal training. Ulrich was of the same mind so we left together, leaving the management of the three farms to Chris and my father. I gave Kariuki a hug and asked him to look after my parents to the best of his ability, and he pressed my hand to seal the deal.

In Denmark I found factory work while waiting for a forestry training course to commence. Ulrich took up painting. The summer of 1964 was spent cutting down trees, cleaning the forest floor, painting signs and studying in the evenings, learning about the Danish fauna and flora in beautiful surroundings on one of the biggest estates. We worked hard and had excellent relations with our respective employers. We tried to fit in socially and to readapt to the conformist Danish way. Our multiple African experiences understandably were of no value, null and void, so we had no past! After many months of pain, despair, even silent tears in bed, not having developed any relationship with the Danish daily society or conversation, Ulrich one day said, 'I am leaving, going back to Kenya come what may. We do not belong here any more.' I agreed with him but being more stubborn resolved to persevere. Two months later I developed migraine headaches and was hospitalised for a short period while having tests. This culminated in an elderly nurse lecturing me on the need to meditate, the need of the mind to be emptied and relaxed for its energy to flow freely and not be blocked by frustration and negative emotions. I understood her very well. This was the first time I had met someone with whom I could relate and with whom I could discuss matters of the mind. Her talk made sense. Finally she said, 'If you do not meditate regularly, you will die young.' I knew that I had become too serious, a perfectionist, and was trying too hard to conform. I had to be kinder to myself and learn that life is not all work and spiritual philosophy, there must be a balance. But more importantly a senior nurse knew about stilling the mind in meditation and recommended it! I left the hospital and went back to my residence and work, and from then on practised meditation in the morning and evening as she had advised. The meditation, freeing the mind of daily related activity and stresses, gave rise to unhindered movement of mind not very different to what I knew from the pyramid and other experiences, but now with medical recommendation. My lonely life in the loftier world of mind had found a sympathiser. A week later Jacobsen, now ex-Kenya, phoned and asked if I would like to become manager on Maboonde in Kenya, a farm he had bought from the Elmers. He indicated the salary structure, an offer I could not refuse. It would be a commitment for at least three years. It suited me and I left for Africa again, feeling happy to be going back to my true home, even with the potential political turmoil in Kenya. I had become a detribalised Dane.

Maboonde Estate was bought by Jacobsen and Company when Mrs Elmer retired. Jacobsen had been General Manager here for years with Chris as Manager. I found it amazing now in January, 1965 to be living in the house where I had often visited Chris. The same place I had come to after the snake tumbled my motorbike over four years earlier. The manager I relieved stayed on for a month to assist, which was a great help. Many of the Africans who lived and worked on the farm were known to me from my Mitoni Mitatu days. The estate was a typical Kitale mixed farm, fairly flat lands with avenues of planted cypress and eucalyptus trees, a small stream being the northern border, a large coffee plantation gracing the homesteads which for a short time every year filled the air with a divine aromatic scent from the white flowers. Beside the coffee and grasslands for cattle, the lands were used for wattle trees, a yellow flowering mimosa, grown for tannin, and other crops such as maize, sunflower and small gardens for African cultivation. I had dairy and pig herds to supervise which required frequent visits. A school and clinic also had to be attended to, all in all enough to keep any manager occupied twelve hours a day leaving paperwork to be done after dark. Ulrich's farm was only half an hour away, and my parents were on a neighbouring farm to Ulrich. Chris was also only half an hour away in the opposite direction. I had a twenty-minute drive to Kitale, to clubs, cinema, hotel and Erik, so was well-situated.

Erik had achieved his ambition and owned one of the main transporting companies in Kitale. He had come to Kenya in the early fifties where his brother was already working for a friend. But as we often see Providence had other plans for he was killed in a car accident shortly after Erik's arrival. Initially Erik worked as farm manager but gradually, as a sideline, developed the transport business until it became a full-time occupation. He was an extremely hard worker, often loading and off-loading trucks himself, which motivated his drivers and other staff to follow suit. As his grandmother's sister's daughter, Karen Blixen, Erik had a mind of his own and did not follow the traditional convention and norms. If required he would work thirty-six hours flat out then have a good sleep. In the bars he consumed according to work performed, but never lost the ability to reason and give good advice to the shy, lonely and insecure. His cat Musungo had acquired the personality of its owner, strong willed and confident, preferring imported liver paté for dinner among other finer tastes. As in other places, Africa also had her sad work fatalities. I recall one terrible incident Erik had when cutting wood he supplied to the hotels and hospitals. The African who was helping to cut wood on the circular saw decided during lunch break to have a sleep in the warm sawdust underneath it. After lunch another workman started the saw which proved fatal for the sleeping person. As he rose his head was cut in two by the spinning saw blade. When things like that happened or even minor accidents occurred the immediate reaction was 'How could it have been avoided?' That in turn developed into an automatic warning system where all instructions were followed by, 'Before you start the machine please check that…' or to the tractor driver, 'Beware of other road users at all times…', which to an outsider could sound very paternal. The sisal estate I managed earlier had a similar tragic event, before my time.

Again during the lunch hour a worker had made use of the soft sisal in the press. He had fallen asleep and when the switch was turned 'on' the massive piston moved down with twenty tons of pressure. That accident was only discovered hours later when the blood-red bale was noticed. Chris had an unfortunate incident where a licensed tractor driver tipped the tractor over backwards because he released the clutch too fast on a hill. The driver escaped injury and realised what he had done wrong. After the tractor was repaired he did exactly the same thing at the same point but this time died under the tractor. The worst case I ever had was a driver who was pursued by an evil ghost, and in his frightened state exceeded a safe speed. He turned at an angle as if he was trying to escape from a charging rhino, which resulted in all four wheels spinning in the air. Fortunately the high speed had thrown him clear of the tractor. He later opted to become a manual labourer with a hoe.

Agricultural production increased on Maboonde Estate, but that was a general trend throughout Kenya after independence, to Erik's delight. In Trans Nzoia alone over one million bags of maize had to be transported annually plus large amounts of wheat, barley and sunflower. Dried wattle bark was taken to the tannin extraction plant in Eldoret. Thousands of tons of coffee and sisal were delivered to Nairobi for international markets. About fourteen rail trucks of pigs went to the bacon factory weekly. Butter, milk and cattle were also being exported from Trans Nzoia in large quantities. For a period a German scholar stayed on Maboonde in a camper van. His research was to record production output and potential output, crop types grown and other relevant agricultural information for a German university. As he said, 'One day, all that you have achieved may be forgotten. Then we will still have it on record in Germany.' Did he know something that I didn't know? Jomo Kenyatta kept on assuring whites that they had a long-term future in Kenya and that no dramatic change would take place. Tom Mboya, a younger modern dynamic politician, even predicted that the white population would increase, but he was unfortunately murdered. Politically the whites had no say because they were so few in numbers, so therefore were not more of a threat to the new establishment than dentists would be in any European country. Gradually the administration became Africanised. Farms were bought by African syndicates and individuals which everyone welcomed as that would help to develop a more economically balanced society.

With my father's consent I persuaded Kariuki to come, live and work for me on Maboonde. Again he was appointed senior askari. I had an excellent team, a foreman for each activity, who had a team of workers to supervise. After planting, while the crops were growing and with the help from Jacobsen's partner who farmed nearby, Chris and I visited America. We were interested to see hybrid maize production and agricultural machinery development, therefore spent some time at Ames University in Iowa. One of their professors spent time with us and during a conversation in a maize field expressed his feelings on pollution. He predicted that humans would drown themselves in muck. The mountains of humans' discarded material he saw piling up everywhere was generating an environment which one day Mother Nature would be unable to handle and many natural systems vital for human survival would collapse. I asked him how we could avoid or prevent disaster and without hesitation he said, 'Introduce worldwide measures to reduce the human population.' But he added, 'Not many politicians would dare suggest that, preferring to ignore such crucial problems in the hope that they will disappear by themselves. And eventually, when 'the shit hits the fan', politicians will withdraw from public life, blaming the catastrophe on consumer pollution. Really, what can they do with our runaway population growth? Okay, the next thirty to forty years will be manageable, but after that time God help us.' I had not been exposed to that type of thought before, but it stood to reason that if a country like Kenya, not to mention already overcrowded countries, doubled her population every seventeen years, catastrophe was only a matter of time. Being a biologist he knew that when living organisms, including man, lose living space, new stress factors disturb established balances resulting in diseases, and with all the best intentions no medical services would be able to handle the ever-increasing numbers of sick people – a brutal way for nature to rid herself of surplus! He would like to see a new spiritual dimension added to human values. Instead of quantity we need quality, he suggested. 'It is too stupid to imagine that our brain is able at present to understand all there is to understand in the universe. We must expand in consciousness beyond the known to find out what our options are.' I would have liked to enrol in 'his' university immediately to study a different consciousness and go where limitation is only a word. By now with daily meditation I was well over the fear that I suffered from schizophrenia or hallucinations due to a brain disorder! Thoughts that had occurred before my talk with the Danish nurse, because no one talked about those expanded or exalted conditions. My ability to change brain activity, or still it to zero, and thereby experience an indescribable surge of vibrating energy was what I believed to be a doorway to another consciousness. It is not a state of thinking because as soon as I tried to analyse the mystical state it disappeared. I often wondered what would happen if one were in that state for prolonged time. I believe that is exactly what saved my physical life years later in and after an air crash.

The same day on a lighter note we visited the university workshop were they had developed a strawberry picker and other weird and wonderful machinery. Despite the professor's negative predictions I loved travelling in America, meeting friendly and helpful people in New York, Niagara Falls, Chicago, Des Moines, Kansas City, Denver, Las Vegas and California. It was Roger and Hammerstein and Doris Day country, and we truly enjoyed ourselves. Flying from Sante Fe to Farmington in the Rocky Mountains our plane developed loss of air pressure and had ventilation problems, but this was only serious enough to cause a short delayed departure for Las Vegas – by now, I had really had enough of malfunctioning planes. Las Vegas made us laugh. Here hundreds of people constantly gambled and when some left the machines or tables others took their places like so many ants. I tried my luck on the roulette wheel and with a quickly developed system winnings were coming my way until a pretty girl with champagne disrupted my gambling focus. She was probably employed for that very purpose, but it was all in good fun. I saw everything American as wonderful, bigger and better, the land of free expression and new ideas, until fourteen years later after the air crash, when my wife was refused entry to the USA because she had been born in an undesirable geographical location. I know that it was not a reflection on or decision of the American people, but more a peculiar policy at the time of misguided politicians with their minds in a prehistoric cloud where revenge is taken on arbitrary individuals to punish a nation for political disputes.

I had a constant alertness towards the mystical and whenever I saw something that fitted the pattern of 'my philosophy' was swept by a feeling of recognition, almost like seeing the evidence on a road map when travelling and accepting that what is illustrated by symbols on the map also exists in reality. Why did the American dollar note have a pyramid with a large shining eye hovering above it? I could only reason that my pyramid experience was not unique and that others had had similar experiences, but why did no one discuss these fascinating topics? I had a feeling than whenever conversation strayed close to esoteric subjects (sometimes with a nudge from me), generally speaking people would think that a religious discussion was on the menu and became uncomfortable, unwilling to discuss their particular brand of religion or belief. I believe it to be a terrible shame that the established Christian churches and their dogma have managed to stifle the desires of individuals to discuss such matters outside church for mental stimulation or for fun, because it is fun to speculate and play with ideas. Why did Christian religion have to be presented as a final structured dogma to modern man, complete with heaven or hell but rejecting other plausible possibilities such as reincarnation? Surely an open-ended version would be much more desirable? On occasion I had challenged fundamentalist Christians and asked what they would do if the second coming of Christ did not comply with their expectations? The answer would usually be that 'He' would then not be the Christ. In other words, God's manifestation on earth would be deprived of freewill. He would have to behave according to historical manuscripts compiled by man over thousands of years and failing that would possibly be crucified again. Meanwhile the same Bible quoted Jesus as having said 'What I can do you can do and more', which can only mean that he did not reveal all earthly or heavenly secrets and directly challenged us to pursue and discover whatever we can find out about spiritual advancement. I was beginning to be convinced that sections of the Christian religion were busy killing spirituality and the concept of a spiritual God. 'God is Dead', the *Time* front cover read. I still accept that individual priests of any denomination can be spiritual, preach spirituality and the teachings of Christ, but I have seen too much in Kenya and other parts of the world to accept that the churches collectively are the representatives of God on earth. No wonder that the slogan 'God is dead' won the day! The Liberation Theology of the Seventies must have had its roots further back in the Fifties, going so far as to portray Jesus Christ with a AK-47 rifle in his hand fighting to 'liberate' Africans in Africa. An insane policy, that is comparable to liberating ants in an anthill. Yes, by all means changes of management policy can be a welcome development in any country, but what was beginning to unfold in Africa would not be of value to anyone. It was rather a design for eternal misery. My assumption that some churches had been and still were involved in teaching insurrection and bloody revolution in Africa had formed a groove in my brain, but I could not work out the hidden agenda and reason. The colonial powers had already complied with African leaders' wishes and demands or were presently actively engaged in negotiation. My private investigation continued...

On arrival home at Maboonde after my American visit I initiated the construction of a new farm school for children of the African workforce. Work on the farm had gone very well in my absence and I think the new school was a way of showing appreciation towards the employed personnel. The six-classroom building with green blackboards was designed by me and entirely financed by the farming partnership although we also accepted pupils from neighbouring farms. The school was taken over by the Kenya government in 1967; they then also became responsible for teachers' salaries and books which suited us, taking away the administrative burden. At the same time we also constructed numerous new houses for employees in the traditional African style and instituted a village committee, consisting of five elders and a chairman. They were to supervise hygiene and order. On one of my periodic inspections with the committee we found one house where straw had been pulled out of the thatched roof, a practice of the lazy to start fires in the morning, usually resulting in rain running down the walls and ruining the house. The occupier was reprimanded and told to repair the damage or stern measures would be taken. Two weeks later he had done nothing to indicate his intention to repair the building. An afternoon lightning storm set the house afire and it burned down completely with the occupier's belongings. After that no one transgressed the committee's housing rules, and rumour had it that I or one of the committee members was a witch-doctor able to call fire out of heaven. Not a bad reputation to have in Africa! My cook Joel shared his name with my great grandmother and knew his profession well. The kitchen was not connected to the main house and the only form of light in the evenings was a paraffin lamp shining on the black-smoked walls and the red light emanating from the cast-iron stove's gaping stoker hole. Joel had high standards and meals always consisted of more than two courses if I had remembered to acquire the groceries on his neatly presented list. He would starch shirts and shorts before ironing with an iron heated by internal charcoal fire. Suits and jackets were pressed with a damp cloth so they looked as fresh as from the dry-cleaner. In the evening while I washed he would select and arrange my clothes and shoes according to my intended activity, which could be staying home reading a book, in which case Joel would light the fire in the fireplace and pump up the paraffin pressure lamp, visiting my parents or going to a Kitale hotel or club, invariably meeting up with friends.

Kitale had a good selection of delightful characters. They were all moulded and coloured in their own special way according to experiences gained. All had a story to tell and put emphasis on what they perceived as being important, which could be the wind pattern in India, hunting, travelling or simply telling stories non-stop. These gatherings in bars were normally very amusing and drinks would flow freely but not so much that the vehicles could not take owners home. Clubs and bars were also the information exchange centres and genuine good advice could always be sourced. By now I had become more outgoing and would engage in dancing at clubs and parties but I also loved to watch and listen to the older generation.

On the way home in my Peugeot 403 pick-up I had an out-of-body experience – and not due to alcohol. Suddenly I heard a small click like the sound of a cracking whip, and from above I saw the vehicle being driven. Instead of darkness and shadows created by the car lights the whole landscape was light blue. I directed the car for a while from my new vantage position, fully aware of my body being the driver, but without 'seeing'. The eyes were with the 'above' self. That situation lasted for about five kilometres and then I was back in the body, looking out through the windscreen. I was mystified by the experience and tried many times to recreate it at will without much success, but it did happen again out of the blue. Once again it was sudden. This time it was while I was transporting pigs during the day. Seeing oneself driving with a load of pigs milling around in the back of a pick-up on a black strip of road is weird. The curvatures of the vehicle appeared very different because of the new fifty-metre-high observation point, but the event did not freak me out in any way. In fact it was similar to childhood out-of-body experiences, although distinctly different to the pyramid dimensional-change experience. I discussed the phenomena with my parents and they listened, but said that it was best not to dwell on such things. Years later they became very interested in the subject and I am sure that my father had out-of-body experiences before he finally sailed away in death with a sweet smile on his face. I believe that the fear of death can be overcome by the knowledge that individual awareness exists outside the body's parameters and that the brain is the physical link between the body and the Higher Self. It is well to remember that we are spirits who happen to be using bodies for this earthly experience, instead of bodies who happen to have spirits.

While stripping the husk from maize cobs during harvest in 1966 Kariuki's wife was bitten by a green snake. Fortunately I was in the field at the time and managed to rush her to hospital in less than half an hour. I led her through once well-kept gardens into the smelly green oil-painted waiting room at the casualty department where fifty or more people were waiting for attention. The new African attendant glanced at us, opened a door and disappeared, ignoring me when I said, 'Excuse me.' I knocked on the closed door – no response – so finally opened it to see a number of officials or doctors sitting around comfortably as if totally oblivious to the outside world. One was on the telephone discussing private matters, and it sounded like he was running a taxi service. I told them that I had brought in a woman who had been bitten by a snake. Still they ignored me. I raised my voice. 'For heaven's sake, wake up, someone out there is dying from a snake bite.' Annoyed, because I had disrupted an otherwise normal morning, they all looked at me as if I was mad, but after a few minutes the man seen outside earlier asked if he could have the patient's name, address and identity number. By now I was furious and tried in a controlled voice to say that I would wait and give all the required information as long as they would attend to her immediately. I ended by saying that she was from Maboonde and was called Wanjiko. 'How do you spell Maboonde?' he asked. I realised that I had lost and that nothing I did would make any impact here. After completing lengthy paper formalities he said, 'Now you can tell her to wait in the queue till her turn.' Leaving the office I saw that Wanjiko had passed out in the waiting room. Angrily I opened the door again and shouted that if that was how much Africans cared for one another, leaving a snake-bitten person to die, then UHURU had been granted to them too early! That seemed to work – they came and took her away. She died. I left the hospital and went home to find Kariuki, meeting him at the farm entrance. He had heard the news and was on the way to the hospital on his bicycle which we loaded on to the pick-up. We went back to the hospital where I left him. He returned to the farm in the evening looking very despondent. The body was brought back to the farm for burial. Kariuki became very insular and uncommunicative unless spoken directly to. He was suffering. He was aware of the hospital's neglect and informed me that doctors were often drunk on duty, and that the order of the colonial era had begun to erode. I could see that he was bitter, but life has its sorrow everywhere, I tried to explain. Kariuki had become a victim of what was beginning to unfold.

During 1966 police roadblocks became frequent obstacles to traffic and if the car was found to be in perfect order the officials would ask for income tax receipts for the last three years. If the document could not be produced on the spot, fines or arrest ensued. A number of whites were detained due to this ridiculous behaviour. The government also introduced stringent exchange control whereby it was impossible to use hard-earned money anywhere except Kenya. A small annual travel allowance was permitted and a lump sum of approximately five thousand pounds was granted if one emigrated from Kenya for good. Which my parents did. They handed the leased farm back to the owner who now lived in America. The farm was later sold to a syndicate of about thirty members. The beautiful garden my mother had cared for became a night holding pen for cattle and the interior courtyard was fouled by numerous goats and chickens. The order of most European farmers was very different to that required by the incoming African farmer, and the evidence of that was becoming more and more apparent. Hedges and garden trees soon turned into firewood, and flower beds and lawns became beds of rape. Grounds immediately surrounding houses were trampled to death and swept bare as a concrete floor. The expropriated farms had an even worse fate, often cut into small shambas without consideration of established contours, fences or water pipeline systems. Evolution does not really care if humans live on a dung-heap or in a garden of roses, but it is quite clear that if we accept the dung heap as a home we will have to live with the smell and whatever creatures normally prefer that environment. The two farms my father owned were managed by Chris and Ulrich respectively.

A British Commission had come out to Kenya to determine land compensation for expropriated farms for resettlement. This was an exercise Britain had undertaken to finance. The land issue was again becoming a priority in political slogans, not that there was a shortage of undeveloped land in Kenya but political UHURU was not enough. I discussed the matter with Kariuki who said that the churches were behind the demand for white-owned farmland. According to him, during Sunday church services (also held in our farm school buildings) priests were telling the people that Uhuru was a waste of time if they did not take over the properties of the whites. He emphasised that with this new teaching 'the people' now believed that they were poor because the whites were rich, and that only by destroying the rich would the poor be better off. I asked him if he believed this to be true. His hairline had receded and he looked like a professor even in his ex-army coat. In his wise confident manner he replied, 'If the poor destroy the wealth above them that means everybody will always be poor, so poor in fact that they will not carry over seed from one year to the next, because someone will demand the seed, believing it to be in excess of requirements. No, we must do the opposite. We must emulate the rich and see that the law makes it possible for many to reach what they aspire for. If the poor take over the land from the whites, what will happen to the businesses in town? Small African farmers will not buy machines and chemicals, so all these merchants, workshops and factories in Kitale and other towns would close down. African farmers will not grow the crops that can be sold overseas, so where will the government get money from? Poor farmers only think about hunger. They will always save on input and work, so will therefore always be poor. This new African socialism the churches talk about sounds wonderful to the young who have never done anything but gone to school. They do not understand the full picture, nor do their overseas-paid teachers. Poverty must be despised by everyone, not encouraged by jealousy. I have been to church meetings and listened, and I know that many preachers don't believe in their own social experiment, but they have taken over the preaching platform and their words are like sweets for the poor. Through repetition some preachers are beginning to think that what they preach must be right. The people are used to believing in the good word of the Bible, so these new priest-politicians can make them believe anything! They also say that everybody must work for the good of the state and serve Kenyatta. Bwana, have you seen that many of Kenyatta's ministers have bought farms for themselves? Those people tell us one thing and they themselves follow different ideas. Believe me, in three years time there will not be many white farmers left here. I know what is going on.'

'But Kariuki,' I interrupted, 'Kenyatta keeps saying that the whites must feel welcome and stay in Kenya.' 'Don't believe it Bwana. Kenyatta is either a chameleon, which I suspect he is, or he has lost control to his socialist bureaucrats. I believe he is a chameleon. His wife seems to be another power behind the scene. "They" say she has become head of the gangsters in the elephant ivory trade. Bwana, if I can advise, enjoy yourself, but make plans for the future. I am getting old and I would like to see Rhodesia. I have found out that from Nairobi I can get a lift on a truck to Zambia, and from there I will find a way to go into the 'White Bull', Ian Smith country, so if you don't mind I would like to resign. After my wife's death my life is over. I only have myself and I need adventure to free my spirit and forget my sorrow.' I was shocked, not wanting to lose one of my best friends, but for the same reason I could not stop him. He stayed on for another four months. Before his departure we shared a meal together with a few beers in the garden under a red flowering flamboyant tree. We sat in silence for long periods, the last of which he broke by saying, 'See your future in your head and it will come true, in that way you will create your own future life even in spirit life.' He stood up and said, '*Kwaheri.*' I replied '*Kwaheri Ndugu Yango,*' (Farewell my brother) and walked away to the house sadly.

A beautiful lonely soul in the world of turmoil was leaving, seeking new experiences, and perhaps would finally die far from friends or relatives in some strange country. I felt angry with local politicians and the political experimenters of the world. If the new Africa was designed by communists, socialists or new social gospel clergies, it was a recipe for disaster. It disregarded the individual, the 'system' being more important than people. Could it be that some of the above-mentioned parties were only tools for other more sinister agencies? I even had the horrible thought that a war was being fought in Africa between the superpowers. Not that America wanted to rule Africa or was interested in Africa. All they hoped for was that the Soviet Union would get so involved in African disputes that Africa would eventually drain the Soviet Union and possibly China of military hardware and financial resources. In that process the Communist block would become less of a threat to the West and might even collapse. Not an unrealistic plan. The Soviet's agenda was 'Through Africa shall we win the West', forgetting that Africa was not part of the classical history book and therefore difficult to assess. The cradle of evolution does not accept an imposed new order for long. The law demands retribution and offenders will soon come to grief. In retrospect the plan worked, if my hypothesis was correct. The Soviet Union fell for the trap and became so involved in Africa that they eventually lost the cold war and fell apart. China, after building the Tan Zam railway, gracefully pulled out of Africa, having found in record time that Africa is not just another continent. Higher living standards for its citizens is not really what African governments aspire for. Even Cuba, America's enemy number one, was dragged into the African conflicts. Did they really gain anything from such adventures? No, on the contrary, in their naiveté the communists had taken on more than they could chew, not realising that it would end with the results desired by the West, namely failed and collapsed communism without a hot war in Europe or America. So in that respect we will have to congratulate the political scientists behind the scenes because it worked! Though for the masses of people in Africa who were caught in the 'stampede' of communistic rhetoric and slogans, not always innocently, but in a gleeful desire to destroy the established order, it was a time of tribulation and turmoil and long-term irreversible damage causing total loss of faith in institutionalised government later. A sustainable level of development is now not obtainable on the African continent and the new states with changing names will not really be taken seriously by any government in the rest of the world in the future because of their willingness to use evil for temporary gain. The patching-up work conducted by some international organisations and governments is no more than self-indulgent penitence.

'Kings and Princes' of Uganda

In 1966, one Saturday, Ulrich and I visited Uganda with a friend who wanted to investigate whether a job offer by the Governor of Eastern Uganda was worth taking up. The Governor had advertised in a Kenya paper for a suitable person to manage his farm bordering the River Nile. Arriving on the farm some twenty kilometres north of Jinja, the town where the Owen Falls dam generates electricity for Uganda and Kenya, we found the 'King'. He lead us to his palace where dozens of slaves working on huge lawns bowed in respect for 'His Highness' as we passed. Our host remarked that the slaves were happy and at the moment were cleaning the lawn of weeds by hand. He apparently had more than one hundred slaves working on the farm whom he had collected from the prisons in Jinja. He explained that working with convicts was easy because they always obeyed instructions and worked hard. Then he laughed so his uncovered fat black stomach wobbled, implying that if any of the convicts misbehaved, he was a law unto himself. We entered his house after climbing ten large imposing steps with banisters. The hallway led to the reception room which was tiled like a bathroom in bright fancy designs. A few chairs were strewn here and there along the walls and the floor was polished red cement with loose scattered rugs. The 'King' clapped his hands after pointing at places for us to sit down, summoning four young girls who appeared with orange juice and roasted zimzim, a seed similar to sesame seed. He was adamant that we eat zimzim according to African tradition. It was, as far as I was concerned, one of those African traditions that are made up on the spur of the moment to impress visitors. He then proceeded to have a bath, or rather another bevy of girls came and washed him while we discussed the potential of the farm. He had been overseas and brought back ideas that would be difficult to implement due to lack of infrastructural support. He visualised a fish farm along the Nile from which surplus catches would be used for feeding pigs. Fruit and grain crops should be grown on the flatlands with waste material also being used for feeding pigs. He already had a well-established dairy herd and a modern milking parlour selling fresh milk and making butter. Thousands of acres of Indian-owned sugar fields bordered his land and he was convinced that they would help with whatever was required on the farm, because, as he said intimidatingly, 'It benefits everyone that I am looked after. You do understand that labour on sugar estates can be rather problematic, but here in eastern Uganda we have no problems because I am in charge of that department and we deal with troublemakers in the African way. I know that you Europeans are too soft and do not fully understand Africans and our hierarchy system.' He looked at our friend and said, 'If you come and manage this farm, any labour problems you leave to me, and I assure you that you will have no problems.' Regarding wages, he said that workers were paid according to needs and they did not need very much because they were supplied with maize flour and fish which they could obtain from the river themselves. We were then taken around the beautiful farm in his pick-up. It was not beautiful in layout and development, but in natural beauty – green grass, huge trees and the slow-moving River Nile. Before our departure we had a cup of tea and our friend promised to contact the 'King' within a month to let him know if he would take up the challenging position as farm manager. In the car going back to Jinja I advised him to forget the whole thing. 'The "King" is no more than a fat fool who utilises his temporary power for self glorification.' I felt that the way he treated his slave labour was disgusting, and simply by working for him one condoned it. Our friend agreed. We dropped him in Jinja where we had left his car earlier in the day and he drove back to family in Kenya. Ulrich and I proceeded to Kampala in my recently acquired Alfa Romeo for a night out. Sadly, our friend, for reasons best known to himself, committed suicide soon after the Uganda visit. Later that month the 'King' was removed from office by president Obote of Uganda, and never heard of again, most likely shot or killed in some unspeakable way. Uganda entered years of internal strife, culminating in the advent of the initially popular cannibal dictator General Idi Amin.

The relatively short distance to Kampala from Jinja took hours because the edges of the tarred road had broken off long ago, and hordes of humans were walking on the both sides, leaving only the middle section for cars and buses which jammed the road in front of us. Tall grasses and shrubs also seemed to be eager to take over the road. The road was a flowing river of humanity in all sizes and shapes and all carrying something. In Kampala, Ulrich and I checked in at the Queen Elizabeth Hotel. After a quick bath and a change into evening jackets we went to the cocktail bar for a drink before dinner. The barman served our brandy and ginger ale and asked if we had any objection to two girls from a nearby table joining us, or maybe we would like to join them? The two African girls were of the tall slim type with finely formed noses and attired in long, golden satin dresses, with long plaited hair. They joined us at the bar and introduced themselves as sisters, Lucy and Martha, daughters of the Kabaka, the King of Buganda. They spoke beautiful English, having attended private schools. Their brother was head of the Lukiko, the

Buganda government, at least that was the story. There must be hundreds of princesses in Uganda since the Kabakas had many wives and therefore multitudes of children. During conversation I asked them if the churches had an influence on Ugandans. Appearing shocked Lucy asked if we were priests, to which my answer was negative. Without reserve she asked whether we were homosexual as we had no female companions? That generated a bit of laughter and I explained that we were in fact brothers and had been to see the Governor of Eastern Uganda in connection with a job offer for a friend who had already gone back to Kenya. They found that interesting but warned us of forthcoming upheavals in Uganda, explaining that ever since Stanley encouraged missionaries to come to Uganda in 1877, the rule of the Kabaka had been undermined because the missionaries and church saw themselves as the lawgiver and standard setter. They accepted that the missionaries had given the people education and taught them the stories of the Bible, but Martha said, 'Do not forget that we had an established effective governmental system a long time before whites came to Uganda. Though, with the British here, the country has seen peace and the Kabaka have ruled as tradition demands. But now with democracies and feeble-minded people of low standing from the north having a say, what will that lead to? The people of Karamojo district are not civilised. They still kill people for Saturday fun. And maybe you do not know this, but many of the men educated by missionaries passed entrance exams to the mission schools by taking their trousers off in front of the fathers. What good can come out of young boys who have been spoiled by people pretending to be teachers and spiritual leaders? It is all too disgusting! Why can't these fathers marry women and stop this men-with-men nonsense!' She had anger in her voice. Lucy interrupted and asked if we would like to join them at the palace where they were having a party later in the evening. I looked a Ulrich and he nodded assent, so we accepted. But we excused ourselves from accompanying them immediately as we had already ordered dinner, and therefore would meet them in about two hours. They left saying that they would return to fetch us. We enjoyed our well-presented dinner and wondered what on earth we had let ourselves in for, but it could be quite fun to see if they did indeed come from the palace and how they conducted a party in that high society. We enquired of the African hotel manager if he knew the girls and he confirmed their words, saying that they were from Mengo Hill and of Kabaka family.

Around ten o'clock Lucy came into the bar and asked us to follow her. She had a VW taxi waiting outside. With Ulrich and I in the back and her in front, the driver zigzagged the road system to Mengo Hill. I had not seen a detailed map of Kampala but felt that we were on the eastern side of Kampala and too far away from the hotel to be able to walk back if necessary. When the taxi eventually stopped at a large house and Lucy got out I hastily tore a twenty shilling note in two, handed the taxi-driver one half and said, 'You wait here for the other half and I will pay you for the journey back to the hotel when we are ready to return.' He smiled and seemed happy with the deal. Inside a decorated reception room a well-organised party was in full swing, night-club style, with a live band playing modern music of the sixties. We sat down at a table and I scanned the hall, seeing only one other white person who appeared oblivious to his surroundings. Lucy brought drinks, brandy and ginger ales. After one 'twist' dance with Lucy, two medical students joined our table. Formal introductions completed, they asked where we came from. 'Kenya is our home, but we are originally from Denmark,' I answered in a mixture of English and Swahili. 'Oh, interesting,' he said, 'we have some Danish people working here in Kampala, we call them the quiet and confused people.' I asked why they had come to that conclusion. 'Well, quiet, because they say very little except what they are supposed to, so we do not know what they really think. These young Scandinavians come here and tell us that socialism is a good thing and the only way forward, and that we must all work together. They also say we must work hard to earn money to individually improve our standard of living. They do not seem to like the Soviets, champions of socialism and co-operative working, because of dictatorship, but at the same time they say we must have strong leadership! Your people tolerate Americans with reservation, mainly because they speak English, but criticise them for being hard on the poor and for fighting in Vietnam. In schools we are taught by Danes and other whites about Darwin, and that humans evolved from monkeys. Then on Sundays we go to church, some of us to the Lutheran church to which I believe the Danish state subscribes, and other Christian churches where it is taught that God created man in His image! Most Christian churches apparently believe in the resurrection of the body from the grave on Judgement Day, but then at the same time they speak of spirits of the departed in some angelic state awaiting judgement. Can't you see your people are totally confused and seem not to be able to make up their minds? We are also taught to have well-developed systems of law and order and tax systems, and at the same time we must have freedom for the individual and human rights. Whatever that is? Your people tell us confusing and contradictory things, at times by very arrogant youngsters, who themselves know nothing except the system they were born into, and have never even thought about all the contradictions. Here in Uganda, and that counts for other African countries as well, we have become more confused than ever because we listened to white man's wisdom. Now, we often wish that the English had stayed on as our protectors and mentors, or alternatively that the white man had left us alone right from the beginning. But we also know that time cannot be rolled back.' I saw lightning and heard thunder through the open veranda door and left the table to see if a rainstorm was approaching. Another light flash, a thump, and then I heard automatic rifle fire. Returning to our table, in Danish, I rapidly put Ulrich in the picture as to what was going on further up the hill. One of the students, noticing my concern, played it down by saying that President Obote and the army were trying to scare the Kabaka out of office. While we stood ready to depart he said, 'Look at our leaders, they are also totally confused, not knowing if they should be socialist, dictator or capitalist, so they eventually opt for them all.' We said thanks for the interesting discussions. I apologised on behalf of my countrymen's insensitive, arrogant behaviour and explained that we ourselves were detribalised Danes and had become half-African. They liked that, laughed and slapped us on the shoulders. We said '*Kwaheri*' to Lucy, Martha and the others and made a beeline for our taxi. The driver had not expected us back so early and was hemmed in by a car in front and one parked right up against his bumper at the back. He confirmed that he had heard four mortar bombs and sporadic bursts of machine-gun fire. With our plea to get us out of this 'war zone' he immediately proceeded to drive forward, forcing the car in front a foot forward, and then did the same to the car behind. Then a couple of harder pushes in both directions made the VW taxi a foot shorter, and, as requested, he managed to get us out and drove back to the hotel. We paid him his due, plus the other half of the torn twenty shilling note.

We breakfasted early Sunday morning and left Kampala for home, but this time decided to go via Mbale, the western passage around Mount Elgon into Kenya. We stopped here and there to view the wonderful landscape but saw no animals as the human population is dense in that region, and arrived at a Mbale hotel for lunch. Heavy rain clouds were falling over the rim of Mount Elgon like icing sugar on a cake and would soon cover most of the mountain. After driving about ten miles and passing a road sign indicating mountain caves, we reached a river in full flood, metre-deep water sweeping over the road. We got out of the car and marked the level of the floodwater. After some time it began receding and we decided to wait. Near the road was a little shelter for waiting bus passengers, I supposed, where an old man sat on a low bench. Two children aged about ten years were walking around watching us all warily. As the old man took some bread and a Fanta from his carrier bag, they leapt into the shelter, pushed him over, stole his food and ran off. We jumped out of the car to rescue the old man's possessions, but the little swines quickly disappeared into small coffee fields. The old man was not hurt but needless to say a bit shaken. He said in Swahili that when such young children become like hyenas, surely Armageddon was at hand. 'These children are not hungry. Look at the gardens here, we have plenty of food. They are nothing but young criminals who have lost all respect for other humans. This is not the first time children have attacked me. Sometimes I wonder if the spirit of these youngsters is not of evil crocodiles? I think they would also attack one another if one had what the other wanted. With the British gone law and order cannot be maintained because no one respects anyone anymore!' A bus came across the river, though the water was still too deep for us to cross. The old man boarded the bus headed towards Mbale, no doubt worrying about the spirit of evil crocodiles occupying the perpetrators of crime. We waited another two hours before crossing. Twenty kilometres further on, just as we entered the forest, the rain came down. It poured down in buckets and late afternoon turned into the darkest of night. The road was muddy, red and slimy, trees bending heavily over the road, accumulating water on their leaves which fell in big drops, splashing against the windscreen. With our headlights on it appeared we were driving in a tunnel heading for the dark womb of Africa, where no one asked questions, even of himself, for fear of the answers. We were driving into Bugishu territory, cannibal country, in the late afternoon in an outrageous rainstorm – and then we got stuck in the mud.

In no time, a whole gang of onlookers was standing around us. The car on the uphill had slid off the muddy road and was now stuck between some tall banana plants in a field. We nervously said 'Jambo' and tried to smile at our audience who, for all we knew, may have been contemplating our despatch into the cooking pot. We needed help to lift the car out of the bananas. Everyone had a solution and all ideas were aired simultaneously. After listening to numerous suggestions I detected one young man who appeared to have some influence. In Swahili I asked him if he could get six strong men to push us out and over the rise, about half a kilometre. We would pay them twenty shillings each for their assistance. That was equal to fifteen days pay for a farm worker. A debate between themselves carried on for about half an hour in the warm soaking rain before the six men were eventually selected. Negotiations over, with much heaving and grunting the car was soon back on the road smeared in mud, but with no traction. The wheels spun uselessly in the thick mud, so the six kept pushing till we reached the crest of the rise. Here we stopped to thank and pay them the one hundred and twenty shillings. Suddenly two of them blocked the front of the car demanding that amount each, before we could go further. The three other men with the leader had disappeared. Dismayed, Ulrich and I took stock of our situation. We did not have any more money on us. The remaining two began shouting, screaming and yelling into the forest. Ulrich got out of the car and tried to reason with them. It was still raining heavily and the road going downhill would be very slippery. Ulrich came back and said that they now demanded the spare wheel, so we decided to take a chance and go! The dreadful drums could be heard from all over the forest. The two jumped aside as the car moved. I speeded up, staring out through the mud-splattered windscreen into the dark rainy night, trying to control the car. For forty kilometres in almost trance-like concentration and many near standstill situations with wheels spinning in the butter-like mud, we eventually reached a more sandy stretch of road.

Our relief was brought to an abrupt end by men wielding AK-47 rifles.

'Go back and stop at the white line,' a tattily dressed gunmen shouted at us. I apologised for not seeing the white line, reversed and waited, but kept the car engine running with the headlamps on. It was not that I had not seen the white line in the dark, there was no visible white line. After about ten minutes two of them came staggering towards us. Through open windows they pointed rifles at us and asked what country we spied for. 'Are you spying for the communists or are you American agents? Speak up!' I responded to one who was looking at me with eyes bloodshot from marijuana and alcohol that we were farmers from Kitale just across the border in Kenya and that we were on the way home from a visit to the beautiful city of Kampala. 'Bring the car into my office,' he commanded. I drove forward again to where we had stopped in the first place, in front of a little shack office, and stopped outside as the door was not wide enough to bring the car inside as instructed. He busied himself trying to make some contact on a radio that produced nothing but static noise. He kept saying

'Over.' I thought, if nothing else, that at least the British had taught that man to say 'over' on a radio that does not work – not a bad achievement. But to supply that type of local savage with an AK-47 rifle defies any logical principle, unless the weapon manufacturer had lost control over production and simply gave rifles to anyone who asked, to make room for more at the factories. Suddenly he dropped the microphone, leaving it to dangle on the cable, as if he had lost interest in the radio for ever, and decided to shuffle some papers around in the dim paraffin light. The gunman on the other side could hardly walk and smelled of alcohol, but he insisted on searching the car. He too suddenly lost interest and walked away, disappointed at not finding a KGB *A to Z* or a CIA action plan. We were reprimanded and instructed never to travel at night in sensitive national security zones. We could have been shot because of our camouflaged Alfa Romeo car, painted green and smeared with red mud.

These people had Soviet KGB and CIA on the brain even in a drunken state – what was going on and why? We reached home just before six Monday morning, early enough for roll-call at seven.

That day my cook Joel resigned. He came into my office and said he had applied for a small farm in one of the resettlement areas and that one had been granted to him. He knew the officers dealing with the distribution of land and had therefore been on top of the list. He also informed me that he suspected that in a few years time I would leave the farm and go back to Denmark because Kenya would not be a place for white farmers, so therefore he had to look after himself. Kariuki had told him that before he had left for Rhodesia. I was a bit annoyed that he only gave two days notice, but fully understood his sentiment. He was kind enough to bring a substitute cook. I conferred with my two headmen. They did not know the new cook, but believed I should give him a try. They had also applied for resettlement farms but had so far been refused because they were employed. So Joel's contact had been worthwhile – he did admit that he had paid two hundred shillings to the officer friend.

A month after my new cook had taken over his duties, I asked him one evening to make soup from a Knorr packet as I was going out for my main meal. After my bath the soup was placed on the table. The soup powder had been mixed in cold water and served uncooked, full of lumps. I asked the cook if he had seen packet soup before, to which he answered that he had cooked thousands of plates of soup. Then the devil invaded him and he jumped towards the table, grabbing the bread knife. His eyes shone wildly. Perspiring and frothing he moved behind me with the knife raised and said 'Eat!' My automatic reaction took over and I turned my head and looked at him without making any sign of rising, and said in a studied calm voice, 'Well, because of some stupid cold soup you seem to be more upset than I. I do not really have to eat because, as I have already told you, I am going out. So if you like, you can look after the house and even have some soup.' I smelled marijuana and saw that he was shaking. I enquired where the dog was and whether he had been fed. Cook walked to the front door where the dog was sleeping on a mat outside. That gave me time enough to get up and exit through the other door saying 'I'm sure you will feel better tomorrow.' On the way to my car I met the farm foreman and told him that my new cook had gone mad and was in the lounge, sweating, with the bread knife in his hand. He said it had been a mistake to hire an unknown person. 'Leave it to me, somehow I will get him out of the house.' I called my dog, briefly remembering the burned dog on Kipipiri. Max often came with me to town, sleeping in the car while I saw a film, had a meal or visited friends. On my return at about midnight the cook had disappeared and I did not see him for four months, until one day in Kitale he approached and said that he was sorry. He did not know what had happened to him earlier, but was thankful that I had not reported him to the police because he already had a suspended sentence for manslaughter. He was sensible enough to say that he would not ask for a job although he was presently unemployed. I paid him money for the time he worked for me and we parted with no animosity. One of my main principles in life is never to leave unfinished business.

The 'Voice of Kenya' radio station announced that president Obote of Uganda had dismissed his prime minister and kings of the traditional kingdoms and that a new socialist constitution would be implemented. Our friends in Kampala had been right about coming instability. To know a little more of the early days in Uganda, referred to by Winston Churchill as 'The Pearl of Africa', I read with interest extracts from *The Red Book of 1919* and gleaned the following information.

A Brief History of Uganda

Native tradition must be relied upon for the history of the various countries comprised in the Ugandan Protectorate prior to the advent of the first Europeans.

At some period in the fairly remote past, the countries lying to the north and west of the Lake Victoria Nyanza were invaded by Hamitic people who came from the north-east, and established a dominion over the countries of Bunyoro, Buganda, Toro Ankole...

For a very long time Bunyoro, Buganda, Ankole and Toro were separate kingdoms. In each of these countries the Hamitite, or Hima type of native is frequent, this being especially the case in Bunyoro and Ankole, where the dominant caste approaches the pure Hamitic type. It is not nearly so marked in Buganda, and even in the reigning family, which traces its decent from the mythical founder of the conquering dynasty, the type has been partially lost owing to frequent inter-marriage with conquered people found in possession of the country...

The history of these countries during this long period is an almost continuous record of inter-tribal wars and internal rebellions, at one time Bunyoro power being in the ascendant and at other the Baganda. From the beginning of the nineteenth century the Baganda power increased greatly under a succession of powerful Kabakas (kings)...

Under them the Baganda established a partial suzerainty over the neighbouring countries and were feared all round the shores of Lake Victoria. It was during Suna's reign (1837–1860) that the first Arab traders penetrated to Uganda, travelling by the south end of the lake, and they returned to the coast with definite news of the great lakes, and also highly coloured reports of the civilisation and power of Buganda... The first approach of Europeans to Uganda was in 1858, when Speke reached the south end of the lake, which he named Victoria. In 1860 Speke, who had earlier discovered, with Burton, Lake Tanganyika, was sent with Grant to explore Lake Victoria Nyanza, and settle the question of the source of the Nile. They arrived at (Kabaka) Mtesa's court in 1862...

In 1875 Stanley, coming from the south, was much struck with the intelligence of Mtesa and with the commercial possibilities of the country, and sent a letter to the *Daily Telegraph*, calling for missionaries to Uganda, which was the first step towards bringing Buganda and the surrounding countries under British protection. This letter met with an enthusiastic response, and the first party of missionaries arrived in Buganda in June, 1877, ...and were joined soon after by another party who had made their way up the Nile from Khartoum....

In 1879 there arrived a party of French Roman Catholic missionaries. In the meantime the Arab traders had greatly increased in numbers and had been zealously preaching Mohammedanism...

In 1876 Gordon, then the Governor-General of the Egyptian Soudan, annexed the northern part of Bunoro...

Mtesa died in 1884 and was succeeded by Mwanga, a weak man of vicious and debauched tastes, whose conduct was such that, in spite of the reverence which the Baganda had always had for their kings, his Christian and Mohammedan subjects alike took offence...

In 1886 he started a systematic persecution of the Christians. He was also hostile to the Mohammedans. Christians and Mohammedans now joined hands and deposed Mwanga (1888), who fled without resistance to the south end of the lake, where he took refuge with some Catholic missionaries. Kiwewa, the eldest son of Mtesa, was put in his place, and a partition was made of the principal chieftainship between the leading men of both parties; but the Mohammedans were dissatisfied with their share, and attacked the Christians, killing a number of chiefs and sacking the missions...

The Mohammedans speedily tired of Kiwewa, who would not adopt their customs and also began a plot against them, and after he had been on the throne a few months he was attacked in his palace and fled, his younger brother Kalema being proclaimed king in his place. Kiwewa was soon afterwards caught and put to death. Kalema professed himself a devout Mohammedan and enforced Mohammedan rites, including that of circumcision...

There had been some difference of opinion between the leaders of the two Christian factions, during their stay in Ankole, but they at length agreed to invite Mwanga to return, promising to support him in regaining the throne...

Though Mwanga had been proclaimed king there was still some severe fighting before the Mohammedans were finally driven from the capital.

...a German, Dr Karl Peters had visited his camp with an armed force, and read his correspondence, from which he obtained information that decided him to enter Uganda. Immediately on his arrival he prepared a treaty which placed Uganda under German protection and persuaded Mwanga to sign it though the leading men of the Protestant party – or English party as is was called – would have nothing to do with it...

Meanwhile negotiations were proceeding at home between the British and German Governments; Peters's treaty was disavowed by the Germans, and by the Anglo-German Agreement of July, 1890. Uganda was definitely included in the British sphere. Shortly after this Captain (later Sir Frederick) Lugard, who was engaged in building a series of forts from the coast...

Fearing, from the news he had received, that the Europeans in Uganda were in danger of their lives, he marched with great speed, and breaking though the custom hitherto always observed of waiting for the king's permission to enter the country, he reached the capital at Mengo on 18th December, 1890. On the next day he presented to Mwanga for signature a treaty, giving the British right to intervene in the internal affairs of the country. This was at first strenuously resisted by the French, or Roman Catholic Party, but was finally signed on December 26th, though in the interval it had seemed almost certain that the excited feeling prevalent would have resulted in a collision between the two parties. The signing of the treaty did not, however, produce quiet.

Nobody appeared satisfied, and Lugard was assailed with complaints and objections from every quarter, while the French Missionaries openly threatened war if their demands were not granted...

The jealousies between the Protestant and Roman Catholic factions, temporarily composed by fear of their common enemy, had in the meanwhile again become pronounced, ...and a Catholic party had killed a Protestant... protests were treated with contempt, and soon after the Catholics prepared to attack Kampala, on which was Lugard's fort (January 1892). The attack was repulsed with heavy losses...

A new treaty was drawn up and signed, and agreements were also made with the Roman Catholic party and the Mohammedans, the former being given the County of Buddu to live in and some of the important chieftainships, while the latter obtained three small counties...

In August, 1894 Uganda was formally declared a British Protectorate and peace was established...

The railway from the coast to the lake had been spoken of for some years, and the preliminary survey had been completed in 1892, work was begun in 1896...

The lake was reached in 1902. The prolonged peace under a settled Administration caused a rapid advance in prosperity of the country.

Extract from *The Red Book 1919*
Published by East African Standard
Nairobi and Mombassa

The country prospered until 1966 when President Obote

changed the constitution and introduced socialism. Uganda was never a colony with white settlers, but had its roots formed by jealous missionaries.

Maboonde Estate – Visits to Lake Rudolf, Rhodesia, Kenya Coast and Goodbye to Kenya

By the end of 1966 most white farmers had realised that the future was slowly but surely disintegrating and that a long-term future could not be counted on. The Kenya government, in collaboration with the British government, had made the white Kenya farmer an endangered species – all four thousand of them. Farms were sold in ever greater numbers for resettlement, to African politicians or to the government for the purpose of maintaining seed and other specialised production. Farm dispersal sales became a regular event and what possessions great pioneers had brought out from England or India, frequently antique, or accumulated through hard work, were often sold to Africans who had no appreciation of the item's historic or monetary value, but were basically just after useful utensils and furniture. Being aware of their precarious situation, life for the white farmers changed and they learned to live for 'today' only because tomorrow was too complicated to contemplate. Since tomorrow is unavoidable, a new detached way of life developed for the next two years or so. Obviously a lot of future personal planning also took place, but that was mostly done on an individual or family basis and not openly discussed. It was, in some way, as though we were waiting for the unavoidable doomsday, as the clock ticked on. If not doomsday in the physical sense, then at least doomsday for what we had learned, loved and knew best, namely, producing food for the ever-increasing African population and world markets.

Whenever work on the farm permitted, I would go on sightseeing trips or adventures with Ulrich, Chris or friends to different parts of East Africa. During one such tour we went by car to Lake Rudolf (now Lake Turkana). On a Friday morning Chris and his girlfriend Jutta, a Danish bachelor of recent arrival in Kenya, and I departed in two VW beetles loaded with food, fuel and water for the remote Lake Rudolf area.

After descending from the highlands on small winding roads for about forty kilometres, the country became hot and dry, the only visible animals being goats, eating away what the sun had not yet browned or burned. Small thorn bushes with defensive spikes seemed to have objected to being the final prey of goats and survived, although the goats still had a go at them by standing on their hind legs to eat the green leaves. The local Suk tribesmen often walked around naked, with a stone tied to the penis in order to make it longer, a sight that confuses many when human aspiration and equality is debated, but for us who lived close by it was just another peculiarity which was accepted. After Kenya's independence it was recommended by the Kenya government that adult males should wear trousers. Horrible rumours about police shooting naked tribesmen could not be confirmed and remained rumours, although a traveller personally confirmed that he had witnessed such killings, and that the police justified it by saying that the naked tribesmen were wild. After driving another fifty kilometres we stopped for our picnic lunch in what looked like totally uninhabited country. But just as elsewhere in Africa, after a few minutes African children popped out of the ground (where else should they have come from?), and while we were still admiring and enjoying the open empty space and contrasting beauty, children's begging hands appeared. This begging, a geographically inherited habit and art that seems to be endemic in Africa from Cape to Cairo, I do not believe is caused by desperate need, but is rather a traditional habit, based on memory from past history perhaps, that travellers must pay locals in goods for passing through their area – a travel tax. An unwritten law that even Dr Livingstone had to obey in his African travels! Anyway, a can of baked beans and some sweets sent the children back to their point of emergence. As we approached the lake region the country turned sandy and desert-like with a few stony hills here and there. The locals of this land are Turkana, nomads who live mainly on milk from camels and drained blood from other animals. Unfortunately for the Turkanas they do not eat fish, of which Lake Rudolf has plenty, including the two-hundred-kilogram Nile perch. The Turkanas adhered to the tradition of cutting a hole just below the lower lip, and a swarm of flies could often be seen to frequent that area. During the heat of the day it is a good moisture supply for flies. I am told that the origin of that mutilation of the body stems from a lockjaw epidemic – the patient could be fed through the hole by relatives. Whether that is another white man's story to explain and make logical what he does not understand, or whether there is some truth in that explanation, I do not know. But I would guess that with the amount of flies hanging around the hole, if they were not already infected with some disease, the hole gave open invitation to all sorts of fly-carried diseases. Africa hardens its peoples and they seem to be immune to conditions that would kill other weaker versions of humanity. The flies were constantly attracted to our eyes for moisture, and stayed until they were flattened or removed by hand.

The night before our arrival ten centimetres of rain had fallen, that is, half the annual rainfall. It made the sand firm, which made it possible to drive off-road even in a VW Beetle. We left the road and drove eastward for about twenty kilometres to the shores of the lake. The only vegetation was a few ten centimetre-high thorn bushes which had to be avoided because of punctures. Here we put up camp, or rather, took out an old tarpaulin which we spread on the ground to prevent sand getting into the food boxes and sleeping-bags. The cars was parked at an angle, and after eating, sleeping arrangements were automatic. Jutta was next to the car, then Chris, followed by Ebbe and then me on the outside. Our roof was a beautiful view of the stars in a crystal clear heaven, disturbed only by fast moving fruit-bats coming from a nearby cluster of palm trees. The temperature was very comfortable and after a short discussion of the day's events, the stillness of the desert night filled me with a strange desire and longing to be alone. The feeling can be compared to the sensation one experiences when standing on a high cliff – something that pulls you towards the edge. The cliff, though, can kill in seconds if not respected, and the pulling sensation therefore must be counteracted and controlled. In the desert it is different. After everybody was asleep I sneaked away. I walked towards the pull of emptiness, then ran, and the pull moved with the horizon. The feeling of freedom in the warm, dark desert night was exhilarating and uplifted the spirit. I ran fast over the dunes and felt that I was dancing with the air. I ran further toward the nothingness and felt a joyful, overwhelming ecstasy, where Heaven and Earth seem to merge. I stopped and gazed at the stars. They all changed to brilliant rainbow circles and another surge of spiritual highs went through me. The desert became a gigantic house with glowing beings of energy. I lay down on a dune top, and at that moment saw a shining torch near our parked cars, some five hundred metres away. It was Ebbe, who had awoken and found me missing. He knew that lions could be prowling in the desert and now my absence placed him next on the menu! He was furious when he saw me approaching, smiling and as happy as a lark. He managed to make me feel a little guilty. I apologised and explained that I had had to go to the toilet, and as no plumber had seen fit to install a flush toilet nearby, I had to go well away from the camp. I could not, as so often before in similar circumstances, tell the truth. How could I tell him that I had been dancing with the wind under a colourfully decorated Heaven, with the Gods looking on, behaving like some wild demented person, running up and down sand-dunes in the middle of the night? My ego forbade me to tell the truth! We went back into our sleeping-bags. Before falling asleep I once more concluded that spiritual experiences cannot be shared, that they must remain very personal and that religion is essentially information and rituals put together originally by wise men to lead individuals to personal spiritual experience. As life had shown me, I realised that many triggers for altered states of consciousness existed, but I also came to the conclusion that desire, willingness and acceptance of the possibilities of such altered condition, are very important ingredients. Unfortunately the condition cannot be produced by intellectual processes or university studies. At some stage it is a matter of 'letting go'.

The following morning early we awoke to a glorious sunrise. Unfortunately one hour after sunrise the sun was already much too hot. After coffee Ebbe and I headed by foot for the lake shore and noticed something that looked like a small boatwreck. Getting closer it turned out to be the clean skeleton of a gigantic Nile perch. The scene stimulated feelings of the vulnerability of living creatures who endeavour to remove themselves from their designated environment, which I conveyed to Ebbe. He had no comment. We turned north, and walked along the water's edge for about thirty minutes, then turned west towards a slight rise in the middle of some sand-dunes to get a good view of the desert landscape. Standing on the rise, pointing out where we had walked and where the cars should be, we could not see the cars as they were hidden by other dunes. Ebbe suddenly threw a tantrum, as lightning from a blue sky. He accused me of dragging him into the desert to leave him to die and be eaten clean by vultures like the fish skeleton we had just seen. He started running in a north-westerly direction, quite the wrong direction if he wanted to get back to the cars, while shouting that he was not going to stay and dry out in the desert. He wanted to leave this God-forsaken sun-baked inferno immediately! I shouted back that if he continued in that direction he would most certainly get lost, baked, and possibly not see any human life before Libya. I slowly began to walk south eastwards. Admittedly, under the equator at ten thirty in the morning it is not easy to determine direction by looking at the sun unless you remember where it rose. After a while I saw Ebbe turn around and follow me, and in less than an hour we were back at our camp. The atmosphere was tense. Later that afternoon we decided to change the position of the cars to enable us to span the tarpaulin between the two vehicles for shade. I moved Ebbe's car to the new position and stupidly forgot to switch off the ignition key. I suppose the car had stalled in the sand, which resulted in a flat battery, to be discovered the following morning. Now Ebbe was convinced that the conspiracy of leaving him in the desert was engineered by us jointly and he ranted and raved. Telling him that the battery of one car could easily start two cars did not make sense to him. His battery was flat! Eventually I lifted up the rear wheel with the jack, and spun the wheel round backwards at high speed with the wheel spanner while Ebbe sat in the car with the clutch down. When I shouted, 'Release clutch,' the car started. Because of his peculiar behaviour I did not want to be in the car with him, but preferred to drive with Chris and Jutta. Of course that generated a new wave of fear in Ebbe, of being left alone to drive around lost in circles in the desert. Eventually I had to drive his car while he sat in the back-seat of Chris and Jutta's car. Getting closer to Kitale he returned to his normal pleasant confident self. We remained good friends till his return to Denmark a year later. But I must admit it is a strange feeling when a friend looks at you with total betrayal in his eyes, and will not listen to any form of reason. I surely and painfully learned that the environment can and does influence people's behaviour.

A few months after our Lake Rudolf expedition, when it was approaching harvesting time, I made arrangements with another Danish farmer, Paul, to go to Marakwet, a forest mountain area forty kilometres from Kitale to recruit labourers to pick maize – an annual event. We had sent a messenger ahead a week earlier to inform the local Chief, and to ensure that any recruits would be ready to board Erik's lorry that accompanied us. On our arrival, it was a Sunday, we were led into a round hut-cum-office by the guards to await the Chief's arrival. One hour later the Chief turned up with rifle-bearing soldiers. We said 'Jambo' and all the rest of traditional greeting ceremony, and were promptly handcuffed! Then we were accused by the Chief of neo-colonialism and of spreading communistic propaganda among his people. Rifles were pointed at our heads, at close range, and we were requested to confess our subversive intentions. Paul said, 'Do you not remember me from last year? Your people were paid a lot of money working on my farm. We sent a messenger to inform you of our coming.' The Chief told him to 'shut up', and not to interfere with justice and his administration. We were herded around, one minute made to sit down, the next to stand, while the Chief worked out what to do with us. I kept a cool head and said very little, trying to establish eye contact with the Chief and smile at him. There was no point in aggravating an already tense situation. After some hours Erik, fortunately for us, arrived in his Mercedes looking for his truck. The Chief happened to know Erik better than us and used Erik to defuse the situation he had created. He said, 'Jambo, my friend Erik, How are you? So you know these two white strangers, therefore I shall release them. You can go,' he said, pointing at us. We left with no workers, although over one hundred had gathered around our messenger and wanted to come. That year I hired a combine harvester to harvest maize. Paul did the same. How the Chief had got into his head that we could possibly be communist agents, I do not know. But obviously he had reason to believe that communist agents were infiltrating his area, or he simply had listened to the radio and could not figure out who was the enemy or was not the enemy.

Seven months later Paul was deported from Kenya with four other whites. They were picked up at night from their respective homes by armed GSU (General Service Unit, a special police unit) and driven to Nairobi airport without knowing why. Paul was one of the biggest pig producers in Kenya at the time and had at some point had an argument with the Uplands Bacon factory manager, who happened to be a relative of some high-ranking government official! Denmark later very decently compensated Paul for his beautiful lost farm.

On 4th June, 1967, I departed from Nairobi on a Kenya Farmer Co-op chartered BOAC plane for London, on holiday and planning to visit my parents who had now decided to resettle in Denmark. Around ten o'clock the next morning we landed in Benghazi Airport, Libya. The plane was immediately commandeered away from the terminal by gun-toting soldiers. After an hour or so we were permitted to disembark and walked into the terminal expecting to be able to purchase soft drinks or water. But with no success. The local officials were oblivious of our presence and airport loudspeakers screamed unintelligibly. It was impossible to penetrate their consciousness or get their attention long enough to make them understand that we had landed on a scheduled planned flight and were willing to pay US dollars for water and service. After much shouting and irrational behaviour on the part of the airport officials it became clear that something unusual was going on. I knew that Libya was independent, so it could not be another African independence celebration. Only after one of our own crew members told us that war had broken out between Israel and Egypt did we realise that our situation was somewhat precarious. The hypnotised stance of airport staff apparently stemmed from the loudspeakers' constant announcements of downed Israeli aircraft. When we left two hours later, sixteen planes had supposedly been shot down. Fortunately General Gadaffi saw no advantage in keeping a load of sunburned Kenya farmers as hostages and we arrived in London only a few hours late.

Before my planned holiday three young Danes had come out from Denmark to stay with me. They had come to Kenya on a student exchange system and temporarily helped to look after the farm during my absence. After my return two of them moved to other farms to gain experience and one stayed on with me. They were sincere, hardworking and full of idealism and saw no reason why Africa should not prosper with some outside help. Like many Peace Corps members and other volunteers from different parts of the world, they could not see that the white colonialist had been of great help to Africa's development.

Most of them had been brainwashed by their socialist sponsors and believed that individually white-owned business and farming in Africa was evil and had to be reversed. Prime Minister Harold Wilson of Great Britain contributed to the hatred of British overseas farmers and businessmen, and even managed to instil in the British public a feeling of guilt for the historical third world protection and assistance. He appeared to be a tool in the operation of the Marxist socialist world take-over. African socialists at the time portrayed England as a toothless, old, dying bulldog. I tried to advocate building on the existing foundation and expansion to everyone's benefit, but my influence, like most settlers', was very, very small and in the sixties the socialists and Marxists still believed that the Great Socialist Party had the answers to all evils, forgetting that it is individuals who make for new creative thinking and not a political party fossilised in its own rhetoric, slogans and history. I had many long and interesting discussions with those Danish youngsters covering politics, philosophy and farming. One of them later committed suicide for unknown reasons. Maybe at some point he realised that his idealism and hopes were unrealistic, and like other brainwashed youngsters of the time could not accept that their social dream also had bribery and corruption within it. It was not all purity, as the communist party had originally advocated and hoped for. The whole socialist/Marxist movement of the Sixties, in my opinion, should be classified as a religious cult, because it effectively attracted and produced non-thinking members. The average working African did not particularly like the Peace Corps type and considered them to be of lesser intelligence and of low standards. And their often know-it-all attitude irritated the adult African. We, Kenya white farmers, were often perceived by those socialist newcomers as the enemy and little interaction took place. But we did have admirers in other places from time to time.

I developed friendships with a number of girls during my Maboonde days. Some developed into pleasant evening discussions, others into 'going to parties', and one led to appreciation of classical music at home. And again others were friendships away from Kitale. Looking back, I see them all as wonderful girls, full of zest for life and good company. One was of Asiatic parenthood and Hindu by religion. She naturally believed in reincarnation, the law of karma, and knew about different levels of existence. My pyramid experience fitted that whole philosophy, and sometimes I felt overwhelmed by having been exposed to such experiences first, and only later finding out that other religions and people believe in things of a similar nature. Anita Amitabha loved the magic Dance of Siva and believed that Sakti, the creative female energy, was important to balance life in a western-oriented, materialistic, male-dominated world. She was a bit older than I and had been married, but could not reconcile herself to traditional Indian family lifestyle. Since she was living with her parents, our outings had to be discreet. One of her relatives who had accepted cross-race relationships became an ally. When her parents discovered what was going on they forbade her to go out at all. I do not believe I was the first European she had been friendly with, but to prevent her from developing further relationships her parents moved to Mombassa. It was accepted and acknowledged by both of us at the time that it was a friendship encounter, like meeting an alien from another planet, changing ideas, values and beliefs, adding spices to the journey we call Life. I enjoyed the secrecy of our relationship, with no one to criticise it, comment or form opinions of its rights or wrongs. We exchanged information and values and I learned to accept fully that all major religions have so much in common that they must have the same foundation. The *Bagavad Gita* makes that clear when Sri Krishna says, 'By Me, the Formless, all this world is pervaded; all beings have root in Me, I am not rooted in them.' And from Jesus: 'My Kingdom is not of this world.' The difference exists only in the minds of men and women and the way it is turned into dogma and rituals. Anita Amitabha's leaving was sad but accepted as the tide of the sea is.

During one of many trips to Nairobi on business and enjoyment I befriended the singer at Sombrero Night-club. She was from South Africa and later made a name for herself in that country. I remember her coming over to my table where I was eating a fried chicken with a bottle of wine. She asked if I had come from a strange place because that was what she could see. I answered in the affirmative and asked if everywhere was not strange. She was puzzled and that led to a conversation about Danes farming in Kitale, colonial race separateness and fairness, and the ridiculous South African institutionalised apartheid, where family in some instances could not see one another because of skin shade. An illustration of what may happen when bureaucrats take over the running of countries and formalise everything into law. By law, humans cannot be controlled, because evolution demands breaking of the law and confining boundaries. She sang well, and I enjoyed many evenings, often with Erik and other friends, in that establishment.

On one of those Nairobi trips one evening I met an American in the bar of the New Avenue Hotel. He had come from Rhodesia and highly recommended it as a place into which to immigrate. He believed that the British compensation of Kenya settler farmers would be finalised within a few years, according to the Stamp Commission recommendation. He was also of the opinion that Ian Smith, who had inherited an essentially British problem, was indirectly forced to declare UDI by the Wilson administration, so that England could wash her hands of one of her more complicated colonial possessions. 'England simply does not want to compensate the Rhodesians as they are the Kenyans. Wilson can't do it, he does not have the money. By indirectly forcing the Rhodesians to declare UDI Wilson felt that he could leave his naughty next of kin to the emerging Marxist-Leninist dictators, if need be, without losing too much ground at home, but he had to make the polite conservative English men and women of Rhodesia look wicked. In a way, to make it look as if the present Rhodesians were the original thieves of African land, conveniently forgetting that the present population of white Rhodesians are third generation, Wilson forced them into the camp of apartheid South Africa which of course suited his agenda.' Seeing it in retrospect that is what made Rhodesians look racialistic, and later the whole terrorist liberation war had reason to develop. All because British leaders of the time had lost the ability to negotiate with black and white Africans. Even in Kenya, with a little skill in negotiation by the British government, whites could have been part of and absorbed into the new system, but no, to grant Africa independence and remove the white population was the order of the day. Get rid of individual free thinkers and conservative capitalists to further the march of the new socialist order. America seemed to play along with the socialist Marxist take-over of Africa while they themselves were fighting communist terror in Vietnam. Their 'hidden' agenda was somehow to get the Soviet Union even more involved in Africa to drain Russian resources. The vacuum generated by British, French and Portuguese departure was ideal. The only way to destroy the Russian Socialist Marxist emerging empire, short of catastrophic nuclear war, was to bleed them to death financially. Give them the impossible task and hope they are stupid enough to fall for it. The Rhodesians, the Portuguese and South Africans were well suited to be pawns in that Superpower 'cold war' game. Unfortunately later I got caught up in that madness, both in Rhodesia and South Africa.

Some Kenya farmers did not appreciate the way they were to be compensated for a lifetime of effort and appealed to the British government to do better or renegotiate with the Kenyan government so they could stay on. Shortly after that objection was launched an outspoken local Kitale farmer was brutally murdered, which shocked us all and resulted in the small white community becoming lambs and accepting anything. We had to wind up and get out.

But we also had to keep on living as normally as possible until departure time, which included going to a party now and again. Coming home from a good old-fashioned Christmas party at Endebess, a club on the slopes of Mount Elgon set in a magnificent garden overlooking Trans Nzoia, a Kudo bull landed on my Alfa Romeo bonnet. It came out of the bush at high speed and tried to jump over the car, but landed on the bonnet. It quickly realised it had landed on something unusual, hopped down and disappeared back into the bush, appearing unhurt. Erik was with me and we inspected the damage. Since there was no frontal damage, we drove home after bending fenders away from wheels by hand. Feeling responsible, I kept on thinking that if I had only driven a bit faster or a bit slower, it would not have happened. For a time I felt I could reverse the accident if given a second chance, but unfortunately that is not how the physical world works. New parts were ordered to repair the vehicle. There were many promises, but still no parts. It transpired that the ordered spares for all Alfa Romeos were lying on the bottom of the now closed Suez Canal due to the seven-day war. I discussed the dilemma with the importers and they eventually agreed to deliver a new Alfa

Romeo sports car in London, on what was called 'overseas home holiday delivery'. I was to pay the price difference between the two cars and cede my insurance claim to them. I appreciated the concern and the manner in which the deal was concluded with the Alfa Romeo importer. But that was how Kenya worked. Everyone tried their best to accommodate and solve problems. Rhodesia, we discovered later, had the same quality.

In June, 1968, Chris and I travelled to Rhodesia via Malawi, there being no direct flight from Nairobi to Salisbury because of Mr Wilson's sanctions against Rhodesia, to see for ourselves if we could live and farm there. We were African farmers. We had, over the years, learned most East and Central African farming methods, problems and disease, types of crops grown and knew how to develop good working relations with the African population. Generally speaking, we considered ourselves good farmers and were not afraid to take on new challenges. On the political front I had grown to despise the devious leftist cult and their agencies who were engaged in driving Africa and the world into chaos. And the possibility of going back to live in the confines of Denmark filled me with horror. Rightly or wrongly, we felt like outsiders, and could not see how we could be reabsorbed into that system after being away for more than twelve years, apart from a brief high school experience and work in 1963–1964.

From that time I still recalled evening and class discussions where bright, intelligent teachers actively promoted rigid socialist party following, singing 'Internationale' and ridiculing individual creative thinking and imagination, calling it 'a mental disturbance of the idle rich'. Some academics wasted time on demonstrations, demanding banning the bomb in the West, but said nothing about banning the bomb in the East, condemning fascism in preference to communism. I failed to see the difference! I hear myself saying at the time, 'You cannot contain or ban the inquiring mind, you can only try to ensure that knowledge is not used for evil.' I had to live where I felt happy, and where my mind and spirit could be stimulated with the mystery of life and activity.

Our reception in Rhodesia was remarkable. The officialdom greeted us with typical British correctness but were overwhelmingly friendly and welcoming. We had meetings with the Land Bank, agricultural experts and farmers and fell in love with the country. Smiling faces were everywhere and race relations appeared excellent, especially considering the UDI declaration by Ian Smith's government three years earlier. We made up our minds that this should be our new home for however long it would last. Immigration papers were completed for our estimated arrival in early 1969. On the way out of Rhodesia we landed briefly in South Africa, but the 'vibes' of that country were inharmonious, which many years later I unfortunately had to experience in more ways than one. From Johannesburg, I flew to London to collect the new Alfa which I drove to Denmark, surprising my parents with a two-week visit. The Alfa was put in storage. I had a relaxing time and was told by my father, 'As for the future, do what you feel is intuitively right.' His wise words never failed me. I went back to Kenya to manage Maboonde for another season, but told Jacobsen and partner that I intended to vacate my employment by the end of April, 1968. Chris and Jutta were married and Chris sold the farm to an African gentleman, bringing their departure nearer. Ulrich was negotiating with a possible buyer for his farm. We were classified as aliens by the British and did not fall under their land buy-out scheme. Realising that we might not see our beautiful beloved Kenya again for a long time after our final departure, we decided to go to the coast for a few days together. We had to say farewell to all the things that had given us so much joy and fulfilment. The mountains, the plains, the trees, the variously coloured forever-flowering plants, the animals, the weather and the people, had all become part of our being. And now we were having a divorce, cutting off the very thing that had helped to form us. But we did not consider ourselves as sinners, doomed to failure. We are beings of Light, kin to the immortals, capable of royal conquests of soul if we but trust the whispering of our 'godselves' and live accordingly. Going to the coast was almost like a ritualistic baptism for the awaiting new, but we nearly ended up as food for sharks.

Driving to the coast we took a detour to Hells Gate, near Logonot. This is an appropriate name for a narrow, eerie, rumbling gorge where creatures from different dimensions seem to be on the brink of manifesting and woe to the one who sees them first. Madness is lurking for the unwary, unless the divine consciousness is present. Go and sleep there alone if you dare!

We stopped over in Nairobi, enjoying an evening out. Standards were still high in most hotels and restaurants and Nairobi was safe, even for the constantly increasing number of tourists and travellers, who had desires to quell their thirst under the midday tropical sun or wander around at night to find the 'right' night-club, of which Nairobi had many. Deterioration could be seen if one compared the city to six years earlier, but it was still a beautiful city, well spread out over forest areas with parks and open grasslands and flowering bougainvillaea and flame trees in abundance. The evidence of the expanding population was everywhere, a problem that eventually will send Kenya and Africa into the abyss of eternal despair unless curtailed in the most logical way – the people must stop having so many children! The alternative, ultimately, after destruction of the supporting environment, is death – if massive tribal wars can be withheld for that long! Masima Spring, where a whole river starts from a single hole, was our next stop, seeing numerous noble elephants on the way. We bypassed Mombassa town, heading north, and booked in at Driftwood Club near Malindi, just before dark. We had a few drinks in the tropical paradise before dinner, appreciating the waving palms, white sand and blue waters breaking on the distant coral reef. For the following day we made arrangements to go deep-sea fishing in a hired boat from a reputable company.

By eight in the morning I had caught my first thirty-seven-kilogram yellow tuna and another was caught a little later by Ulrich. Chris caught a king fish, and an accompanying friend a sailfish, when ten kilometres out on open sea the boat ran out of fuel. Our African skipper, beautifully dressed in white, had few words. 'Sorry Bwana, I forgot.' In a very short time our uncontrolled rolling in the waves attracted sharks, their dorsal fins clearly visible from the boat. Then there was the first direct hit. The two-metre-long monster sharks were deliberately thumping against the boat trying to sink us. We had to get help and quickly. The turbulent crashing of waves on the reef was also getting closer by the minute. On that front we had about an hour before we would be smashed to strands of fibre. Waving a T-shirt on a fishing rod to get the attention of another fishing boat made our skipper hysterical. He said that his employer would fire him if it was discovered that he had forgotten to put fuel on the boat, and it appeared that he preferred to be eaten by sharks after crashing on the reef than to be rescued! He physically tried to prevent Chris waving the shirt, so we had no choice, the skipper had to be neutralised. Without discussion Ulrich and I grabbed him, forced him into the cabin, and tied him up. Then he began to complain that he could not swim if his hands were tied back. I told him that the sharks would not care and it was time he got it into his head that he was no longer skipper and should stop whining or else. He looked out of the porthole and saw the proximity of the reef and began a pitiable garble, which we ignored. With the sharks methodically circling and hitting the boat we drifted very close to the reef before the other fishing vessel realised our distress. When they eventually pitched up, we had to be towed away from the reef before we could pour their excess fuel into our tank. As soon as the boat had engine power the sharks disappeared into the deep of the ocean. We sailed directly back to harbour with a very unhappy African in a white uniform. We were compensated by another day of fishing with the boat's owner as skipper.

At Driftwood Club I happened to share a cottage with another Danish farm manager from up country. We had drinks together and discussed many things, including leaving Kenya, fear of our uncertain future and about what meaning we could find in life. I recall him saying, 'I will keep on doing my best. No one can ask for more, and when I die, I hope to have no enemies. It is easier for the mind to reach the conclusion that you can't expect things to remain "the same" than for the heart not to want them to be.' The man had noble virtues, but again, for reasons best known to himself, he also committed suicide, possibly unable to reconcile his love for Kenya with the necessity of leaving.

Why do people commit suicide? Is it because of a firm belief in spiritual afterlife, or the opposite? 'When I am dead, I am dead, suffering is finished for ever, I cease to exist'? I believe both attitudes are held.

When a person has committed horrendous political or other crimes like killing, and his temporary institutional support net collapses, he tends to develop the convenient 'When I am dead I am dead' attitude, because he can't conceive of having to live with his guilty acts for ever. Therefore the only way out for him is death and darkness. Years after being shot down in a commercial airliner by a

Sam-7 missile, my wife and I were travelling through Botswana. In an art gallery in Gaborone we met a Russian agent who had been active in Zambia during the Rhodesian war. After being introduced, sundowners served and the usual Botswana complaints about dust and heat completed, I asked him if his attitude to life and death had changed since the collapse of the Soviet system. First he did not answer so I persevered. 'Maybe horror and suffering to you is no more than an academic abstract concept where feeling is totally absent?'

'What are you referring to? I do not understand,' he answered. Very briefly I told him of my view of Russia's contribution to Africa's 'liberation' and my own experience. I then asked him, now that the communist agenda is no more, if he, as an individual, could reconcile himself with what he had been promoting. That led to a one-hour discussion ending with me advising, 'Learn to meditate.' He committed suicide shortly after our meeting. I asked myself, was it too hard for him to think even of the possibility that awareness may not end with death? And therefore he had better get it over and done with before that nagging suspicion grows that life is more than the sum of the body parts? The Soviet dictatorship conveniently adopted a totally materialistic philosophy to enable some of its citizens to participate in murdering millions to keep the murdering machine in power. A meditating person who achieves glimpses of the world beyond knows that there is no escape from anything ever, that thought is synonymous with awareness and awareness is *you*.

Yet another acquaintance, an elderly gentleman who had come to Kitale in the early days of Kenya's development and had developed a number of important businesses and a beautiful farm, commented on the uncertain situation, 'I am getting on in age and have been fortunate enough to enjoy the opportunity to express myself in farming and other activities. I am too old to go anywhere else except where we will all have to go one day, so if I am pushed into a situation that I see will led to unhappiness, I will end my life in a car accident.' That is exactly the way he departed a few years later. The pain of leaving what you love is something politicians seldom take into consideration when they plan their 'New World Order'.

Driving back from the coast we had two punctures, the last near Mtito Andai in the Tsavo National park. I was elected to walk with the offending wheel three kilometres to the nearest service station for repair. Trudging along, I encountered a herd of elephants who had taken up play on the tarred road in front, but after a while the adults managed to herd the mischievous youngsters into the bush and they wandered off, allowing me to pass. The tyre was fixed and I managed to get a lift back to the car.

The next ten months were rather stressful. Work had to be attended to as if Maboonde was for ever. Painting and repair work, inoculating cattle and keeping records, spraying the coffee plantation, attending to the workers' numerous family and other problems continued. I told them that I was leaving Kenya for good. They responded with a typically polite African gesture, asking, 'Can we come with you?' My relatively new cook, inherited from Chris, concluded that life for white people was much easier than life for Africans. 'You see,' he said, 'now life in Kenya is getting difficult because our leaders have no knowledge of how to expand the economy to give us jobs, I must stay with little or no pay and accept it all, but you can just leave.' We accepted jointly that politicians do not provide good solutions, but what can we do?

I moved in with Ulrich on 1st April, 1969. He had just concluded his farm sale with a Pakistani Moslem called Alibhai, who called himself a criminal. His offence was coffee smuggling, although he was never charged. With the continued disintegration of the old colonial-organised trading methods in Uganda under the leadership of socialist Obote, and in Tanzania under the teacher, Julius Nyrere's socialistic Ujama, some Asians from Kenya stepped in and provided the services that these states could not offer their citizens, namely purchasing commodities produced by the working peasant. The state was supposed to be in that business, but with no accountability money shortage became the order of the day except in officials' pockets. A capitalistic system for the few within the socialist system for the many!

We temporarily shared the house with the new Islamic owners while official accounts and income tax returns were finalised. Kenya required by law a tax clearance certificate before air tickets to fly out could be bought. Strict exchange control regulations were in force and savings could not be transferred or taken with you, but overseas car delivery still existed. By that route we ended up with three cars in Denmark which were later shipped to Rhodesia, via Beira in Mozambique, but with hardly any cash money. Alibhai was one of those fine thinkers with whom I loved spending stimulating hours. He was, as far as I recall, a Mutazilites Moslem and a Sufi of a very tolerant and progressive order, and believed that we are all evolving spirits, temporarily occupying physical bodies. The Western Christian burden of guilt held no logic for him, except politically. Making a person feel like an unworthy worm could only serve to promote the power of already doubting, institutionalised, dogmatic non-thinking priests from the mainstream of Christianity. Alihai meditated regularly in a room that was set aside for that purpose only, and believed that by activating certain centres called *latifa* (*chakra* or energy centres), it was possible to see Light, transcend the physical, and float into different realms or dimensions. 'Grow as the flower grows, unconscious, but eagerly anxious to open its soul to the air,' he advised, 'and never become dogmatic. Kashmir is where you should live, the land where the pupil and master become one in spirit and the land reaches heaven with snow-white clean peaks.' I mentioned politics in some more general connection to which he answered, 'We had a game of chess last night. How many moves do you believe a good player must plan in advance, and also with each possible move work out the opponent's possibilities? That is politics – the distant important moves are all planned, often by unknown manipulators who hide behind lesser intelligent front politicians. And for the one who can't see far enough ahead, well, he will lose the game.' This was a rather upsetting way of looking at international politics and people's cherished democracies, accepting that we the population are no more than pawns in the international play for power and control, but it fitted my perception of the world we are destined to live in, while in physical bodies. I prefer the spiritual raiders of heaven who stop at nothing but the original source of knowledge and wisdom. The masters that go before science.

We helped Alihai on the farm for six weeks and whenever we referred to 'his' farm or car or whatever, he immediately corrected us and said, 'All that I have is yours and never think any other way.' We had been presented with a master, and appreciated it as long as it lasted, but yet again we had to say goodbye.

Erik took Ulrich and me to Nairobi where we had our last meal in a Chinese restaurant before boarding a plane for Denmark. Our final sad farewell to our beloved Kenya.

Rhodesia – Mazoe Valley and Gatooma

We arrived in Copenhagen the following morning, picked up the two cars and drove to our parents' home. My parents were by now quite happy in Denmark and I think they would have liked to see us all settled back there, but after thirteen years in Kenya we had become Africans and were too attracted to Africa. Sunshine, bush country, open spaces and the mystery that Africa contains, something intangible, were what we required to be content and happy. Rhodesia was to be our destination. We had no real idea what to do there, but hoped to find some farming-related occupation to begin with and maybe buy a farm later. Chris and Jutta had already gone with their new-born son and had rented a house near Glendale in the Mazoe valley. The cars were shipped off to the Port of Beira in Mozambique and while they were on the open sea Ulrich and I assisted my father to convert a barn into holiday accommodation, and appreciated my mother's excellent cooking for seven weeks.

In the loft in my parents' house I found a box full of books and documents. They were books Jutta had inherited from her mother who had recently died. The books were in English and had belonged to her father who had been a gold-miner in Klondike, Alaska, before the First World War. During the long, cold, dark nights at Klondike he had spent time studying Theosophy and the mysteries that confront the minds of those who have learned, often by necessity, to still all thinking and wandering thoughts, so as to experience the power of liberation. The first note I took out of the box read something like this: 'The great search of liberation and freedom is in reality the desire to bring forth the qualities and power of God, so that man may manifest them in himself, thus bringing forth himself as an ordered unit in the cosmic scheme, but man is bound in the flesh and knows only the physical aspect of himself. Yet man is more than a physical being, he is a mental and spiritual being. Because man is ignorant of the whole of himself, he is continually searching and he is unhappy. Because of his unhappiness and of his harassed searching, he sometimes does things to his detriment. Often he may turn to suicide, or he may turn to forms of vices, thinking to get liberation and freedom. A man drinks alcohol because it gives him a momentary sense of freedom from the mundane world. The real cure for man's woes is to find the God within himself and manifest the qualities and powers of God, so that he can say that he is one with God'. This is easier said than done, but it has to be done.

A new dawn had come. Reading some of the notes and books from the box I realised that my personal philosophy and exposure to mysteries was in fact not way-out or new, but rather common, and possibly as old as when the first human said, 'And who am I?' I suddenly felt that everything I had experienced so far had come in the right sequence, like going to university. I thanked my Guardian Angel and asked if the course was ongoing or if I could have a break. The answer was 'It never stops, just keep on pedalling, but realise that the manifested world is but an image in which to grow, and pure consciousness is the invisible from which all is governed.' Or at least that was the thought that immediately came to mind.

The 20th July was departure day. We said goodbye, which now had become part of our life. It suddenly occurred to me that there were too many goodbyes in our family! That inner joy of seeing family again and the unconditional love we all shared seemed always too short and interrupted with goodbyes. Being a close-knit family we somehow had learned to accept our geographical separateness and lifestyles, never knowing if and when we would see one another again. So, although painful, it was our choice.

As our aircraft crossed the mighty Zambezi river on the 21st July, 1969, our captain spoke on the intercom system announcing that the Americans had landed on the moon safely. Jubilation was heard all around the plane as if it was a success of a close family member. I suppose humanity is seen as a close family when you stand on a desolate, meteorite-bombarded moon, where no social security, pension system, or any other support system exists, especially if the rocket system fails to bring you back home to earth. There you are, totally dependent on man-made machines for survival, and the guidance system must work or else disaster can be predicted.

Part of the continent we were flying over in some ways illustrated that fine balance between systems that work or disaster. With the departing colonial order, and the introduction of some new untried social experiments sponsored by foreign agents, Africa was in turmoil. She was still trying to find a new alternative identity, and that unfortunately had to be, as a matter of principle, different to the former colonial powers to justify the fight for independence and liberation wars. If the astronauts on the moon had rejected the moon module and return system because they did not like its manufacturer, no uncertain criticism would have been levelled at them. And likewise, on our fishing boat before leaving Kenya someone else had to take control to avoid disaster. That was the Rhodesian situation in a nutshell in 1965. When Ian Smith had declared UDI

(Unilateral Declaration of Independence), a catastrophe was perceived to be developing. Harold Wilson seemed to have abandoned England's traditional colonial responsibilities and the white Rhodesians felt as though they were stranded on the moon and the mother country was prepared to abandon them there. With that insight we landed at Salisbury airport. We had arrived in Rhodesia.

Formalities were completed quickly by efficient officers. Chris met us at the airport, having driven forty kilometres from Glendale to fetch us. It was the dry season and the light brown grass and leafless Masasa trees were not what we were used to in our evergreen part of Kenya. We drove to the Miekles Hotel, historically the Rhodesian farmers' meeting point when in Salisbury on business, and admired the clean city with its smiling people. On arrival in Glendale Jutta was busy baking bread. Their little boy was sitting quietly in a chair, looking out on white cotton lands where African women were busy picking the white balls of fluff, and further afield huge citrus plantations were to be seen. On the other side of the tarred road lay green wheat fields and irrigation sprinklers ticking along made rainbows in the blue sky. Later in the afternoon we went for a short walk and noticed well-dressed Africans digging holes in a harvested maize field. On closer examination we found out that they were digging up mice which they explained shyly was a delicacy. The mice, after capture were dried in the sun for cooking at a later date. Why not? The French eat legs of frogs, and other slimy raw creatures are consumed with great gusto all over the world.

During the course of the following week we met local farmers, one of whom offered me temporary work as a farm manager while he and his family went overseas on holiday. I had done that type of work before. But first we had to go to Mozambique to collect our cars which were now awaiting collection in the Beira Harbour warehouse.

The Portuguese still controlled Mozambique and had a consulate in Salisbury from where we obtained the necessary visas. An overnight train journey took us to the coast. Beira was a typical Portuguese/African town. One felt like one was in Portugal with its pavement restaurants, coffee bars and flashing lights indicating night-clubs. And there were lots of people of all shades and hues sitting around in the warm breeze, waiting for Dr Livingstone's dream to come true I presume, namely, more trade with the rest of the world, to uplift the lives of Africans, blacks and whites. The cars were cleared by customs and filled with petrol, and we drove back to Rhodesia, most of the way through indigenous natural forest. Those beautiful forests have since disappeared under the hands of charcoal burners. We crossed the Forbes border post before entering Umtali, a magnificent little town nestling between mountains on three sides, and exited via Christmas Pass heading for Salisbury, arriving in Glendale late that night very tired. According to Rhodesian Customs law, immigrants were entitled to bring cars into the country without paying duty, as long as the cars were not sold within the first year. We needed money and with a relatively wealthy Asian population in Salisbury it only took us a few days to find someone to lend us money to the value of the two cars, the cars being the guarantee for the loan. And if the loan was not repaid within a year the cars would be ceded to the lender, a good and legal arrangement. In the meantime the cars were to be held, unused, in storage for a full year. The Alfa Romeo I kept, which turned out to be most unfortunate.

My temporary job was to manage cotton picking, oversee ploughing of lands for the following season, dip cattle, watch out for grass or bush fires and to construct a tennis court using ant-heap clay and sand. My team of African workers was very friendly and helpful and we developed good relations in a short time. On two occasions they spotted fire in the hills behind the house and were there before being called to assist beating the flames. In my spare time I built a five-ton farm trailer with the help of Chris and Ulrich. Chris was determined to buy a farm and had almost concluded a deal in Raffingora when it was arranged that I should come and view the farm. Ulrich and Chris had gone ahead. It was a beautiful farm with many indigenous trees and a river with a good water supply, on which a large new dam was to be constructed, but the seller had unfortunately not completed land preparation according to agreement and now wanted to back out of the deal. Driving back on a very dusty dirt road, where thick dust clouds hung for kilometres over the road in cool, unmoving afternoon air, following the passage of cars, I drove straight into the back of a stationary pick-up. Two farmers had stopped to talk in the middle of the road. I had been driving in the dense dust, wondering about Chris's farm purchase dilemma, and suddenly had to slam on the breaks, but it was too late. No one was hurt, the pick-up had sustained only minor damage to its number plate and rear lamps, as the rear-mounted spare wheel had cushioned the impact, but my Alfa Romeo was half a metre shorter and looked terrible. I was furious, and told the local farmers in no uncertain terms what I thought of them stopping in the middle of a dust-covered road – how dared they! The Banket Police Station was only a few kilometres away and the other farmer hastened there. I looked at my car again. What a wreck, curled up, twisted metal, the radiator pushed right into the engine. A policeman arrived and asked if he could be of help to get the car to a panel beater in Salisbury. I had expected instant judgement on the road, condemning drivers who stop to talk to neighbours! 'Mr Hansen,' the policeman continued, 'You are not allowed to drive faster than you can stop if a hindrance appears on the road. Imagine if it had been an African women with a child on her back crossing the road in the dust.' It was hard to accept the fact, but I also knew the law, and after standing around silently for about five minutes, feeling like a worm, the owner of the pick-up said that he would not sue for repair of his car. I had to accept my fault and eventually shook hands with all concerned, as if we had just ended some contest. The helpful police saw that the car was removed to Salisbury. It was four months before I had it back on the road. After the stipulated year I sold it to recover repair costs for it was not insured. A more practical pick-up was bought instead.

Chris eventually bought a cotton farm in the drier area near Gatooma, situated in the centre of Rhodesia. After completing my temporary job in Glendale, I joined Chris and Ulrich there, helping with the preparation and irrigation of the red dusty soil. During October, but before the first rain of the season, the indigenous trees flaunted new leaves of spectacular colours, displaying apricot, red, maroon and light green against a blue sky, and dry brown grass below, if not blackened by fires often started by honey seekers. Then, in the middle of October in searing heat, Thor, the anxiously awaited God of Thunder, migrated from the north to a more southerly latitude, angrily creating sparks from his iron-rimmed cart-wheels, and rumbles when turning or hitting the top of clouds, a display science has explained in other words. Then there were a few drops of rain. But the main downpour from Thor's overturned bucket fell to the ground on the other side the Gatooma hill. For days I watched that same spectacle culminating with rain on the other side the hill. I knew that if I should buy a farm it must be where those first showers gave the parched earth relief. Ulrich and I discussed the persistent phenomena and I silently enlisted the aid of divine forces to locate the desired land. Two days later a small advert appeared in the *Rhodesia Herald* that took my attention, announcing, 'Farm For Sale near Gatooma'. I phoned the agent and yes, the farm was just over the hill. After a quick walk around the fairly flat but neglected farm, with dyke-like hills on the eastern boundary, we drove the hundred and twenty kilometres to Salisbury, signed the purchase agreement and paid a ten per cent deposit. The estate agent, an elderly gentleman, Mr Mortimore, took a fatherly approach and went out of his way to be helpful, so typically Rhodesian. He introduced us to Land Bank officials and assisted us to fill in the required documents to apply for loans, which we were granted. He has since joined the ranks in Heaven and, no doubt, is thrilled with his new position. He deserves it. Twenty-four years later my wife and I met his (now middle-aged) daughter, who is very involved with matters of a spiritual nature and hosts a weekly television and radio talk show in the same country, now called Zimbabwe. I believe that she also investigated a more recent UFO landing near Harare (Salisbury). I told her about my UFO experience. We will come back to that later. Some remarkable people seem to have remarkable experiences, or is it as the Bible puts it, 'Ask and it shall be given' or 'Knock and the door shall be opened'. What door, many may question.

The farm Orange Grove which Ulrich and I had acquired in partnership was a deceased estate, with family members living in different parts of the world. The transfer of deeds could not take place before certain formalities had been completed which Mr Mortimore said could take six months to a year, but the law of Rhodesia states that the sower has the unhindered right to harvest and under that premise we commenced our new life. The farm boasted no house or improvements, and only one hundred hectares had been cultivated previously, so we had six hundred hectares of almost impenetrable thorn bush, shrubs mixed with poisonous Lantana, spear grass and nettle-like plants that gave bad burns. A haven for wild pigs, monkeys and snakes. It was a farm that used to supply firewood to the railway steam locomotives in the early days of Rhodesia's development, and it was just where I had wished to live when those early thunderstorms had produced rain. We bought a tractor and plough, and built a shack to live in and another smaller one to serve as a kitchen. Water was collected in two hundred litre drums in our pick-up from a dilapidated windmill, which we pulled down, installing a hand pump. We tried to hire some African workers, but experienced problems as we had no accommodation for them, although we were only three kilometres out of Gatooma. I built two huts with my own hands while Ulrich ploughed the land. Steven was hired to help build more huts and Samson became our first cook and house-helper. Firewood was used for cooking and heating water for bathing. The curtain for the bathroom was the natural veil of darkness after sunset, and evening light shone from burning candles. Beetles, of which millions appeared with the rain, loved their new shelter and shared our bunk-beds which were placed at one end of the wooden shack.

Two Persian carpets and a brass tray from Kenya were hung on the walls in the dining area, and shelves for pots and pans and papers divided the room. The carpets hanging on the wooden wall became food for termites and fell to the ground in shreds before we noticed that they had been eaten away. One day, after finding out that we had come from Kenya, Samson requested that an old man who was at the moment staying with him, and who spoke Swahili, help with cooking, making tea and washing, in order to give him more time to cut firewood, iron and remove beetles and termites. A well-thought-out work schedule. We consented and the old man called Joseph, with white curly hair and East African features, was to become our excellent cook. Joseph had apparently come from Kenya in the mid-Sixties, and had worked for the Rhodesian government as a land inspector. He had resigned a few months ago due to old age and now lived on a small pension. Upon meeting him I thought I recognised Kariuki from my Kenya time, but his words and gestures indicated otherwise. I was mystified. We talked about Kinangop, Kipipiri and Kitale, he knew them all, and he mentioned that he had been in Abyssinia and Burma during the big war with British officers. Could it be Kariuki? He was a bit shorter, and a lot older, but there was something familiar, the same eyes, a shine one seldom sees. I asked if he had been married in Kenya to which he answered curtly, 'They died.' I sensed that if he was Kariuki, he wanted to be Joseph now, and we should respect his wish to be anonymous. He looked after us as if we were kings in a mud hut. He shared our happiness when we laughed and also our sadness when our white kittens died after eating a snake. I could not get the Kariuki connection out of my head.

By the end of December, 1969 we had fields of cotton, soya bean and maize all growing well and looking beautiful. We had consulted the government agricultural advisers in Gatooma on how to grow cotton. Mr How was the name of our extension officer. He was extremely helpful and gave us an *A to Z* cotton booklet which we followed to the letter. A young man called Kenani was hired as tractor driver, working his way up over the years to become farm foreman. He was often in sole command of the farm during our absences, a very reliable man with that rare ability to know what we expected and wanted done before anything was said. So much so that when Ulrich and I, fourteen years after selling the farm, having had no contact with Kenani during that time, turned up unexpectedly at the now-derelict farm and asked for Kenani, we were told by a stranger that a determined Kenani had been sitting on a stone waiting for two white friends from long ago. He had left one hour before our arrival leaving the message that he was sorry to have missed us. Ulrich and I looked at each other in bewilderment and determined to find Kenani. We searched and asked around the district but eventually had to give up after driving more than eighty kilometres. It was one of those African experiences that makes your hair stand on end, confirming the interconnectedness between humans existing on an unseen level.

Our first season turned out to be a disaster. After the crops were knee-high the rain ceased and our beautiful-looking crops withered away, together with our belief that we had come to the right country. So far we had concentrated solely on farm work and planning the future development of the farm, not socialising at all except to meet some of the neighbours for tea. We saw Chris and Jutta on a regular basis and often debated the wisdom of having come to Rhodesia. Driving over to their farm on a back road one afternoon, Ulrich suddenly became very attentive, staring out of the car like a cat who has seen a bird nearby. He said, 'Stop, I have just seen a monkey herding a flock of sheep.' I reversed and sure enough a few metres into the bush land we saw the little monkey herding sheep, preventing them straying on to the road. How sweet and comical! We had met the owner of the farm before at a Cotton Research Station field day, but now, quite taken by the unusual monkey/sheep relationship, decided to pay him a visit. Charlie Conway was middle-aged and managing his brother's farm. The house was rustic and filled with artefacts, bones and stone tools from prehistoric times, displayed in cabinets like a museum. They had all been found in Rhodesia. In the heat of the afternoon we sat on the veranda for tea, Charlie barefoot, an old straw hat by his side and a dog lying at his feet, awaiting any gesture that might indicate the usual afternoon trip around the farm. We complained about the severe drought. 'What is it you want out of life?' he drawled. 'We have had droughts before and it will not be the last one either. Unfortunately it is your first year, but don't despair. Did you see the sunset last night, it was magnificent! Oh, there is my monkey shepherd. He will be coming for a sip of beer shortly. I live alone, my wife lives in Que Que. That is the way it is. I once farmed just to make money and I lost my farm, but now I have learned to enjoy farming, and in the quietness of the setting sun, sitting on my veranda, I experience more than a thousand books can tell me. I read books, they stimulate, but I prefer experience. You must have beautiful sunset from your hill. You have plenty of bird life on that farm. It used to belong to my uncle, you know that?' I knew that he was trying to talk about true values. We had lived like that in Kenya, although there I did not have the ultimate financial responsibilities. As if he could read my thoughts, he said that he of course did not know our financial position, but suggested that we go to the Land Bank and Commercial Bank to borrow money to make the farm beautiful. 'I am sure there will be no problems, people are talking about you two.' We shared his afternoon tour of the farm, and discussed Rhodesia's dispute about the Unilateral Declaration of Independence with England over a beer afterwards. Charlie believed that the Rhodesians were reasonable people, and if they were not pushed by the rest of the world into the South African camp, a solution would be found, and a more representative government of all the people of Rhodesia would only be a matter of time. He said, 'We already have a number of Africans in government, and that process just has to evolve. The Nationalist's freedom fighters consist of a small group of communist revolutionaries with little support among the African people.' He also gave us a brief history of Rhodesia's beginning:

'After Dr Livingstone's travels, traders and hunters reported that the land beyond the Limpopo was fertile and rich in gold, and should be opened up for agriculture, mining and trade for the betterment of all. In 1888 Cecil Rhodes sent representatives from Cape Town, then a British colony, to the king of the Matabele, Lobengula, to obtain a mineral concession for the territory. Lobengula, was the son of Mzilikatzi, who had migrated from Natal in South Africa with hordes of Zulu raiders and had finally settled just north of the Limpopo river. The territory north of Matabeleland was known as Monomatapa by early Portuguese traders and inhabited by groups of scattered Shona and Batonga people, who were retreating from the raiding Matabeles. Cecil Rhodes put a telegraph system in place. Roads and railway were built in record time. In a few years a thriving community was established and Africans were employed instead of sitting on hilltops waiting to fend off Matabele raiders.'

His account of colonisation corresponded with the following extract from 'Focus on the Rhodesian Settlement':

After the granting of the Rudd Concession, as it became known, Rhodes formed the British South Africa Company and in 1889 obtained a Royal Charter for the company to administer the country, although ownership still remained with Lobengula.

Rhodes immediately organised a pioneer column to occupy Mashonaland. It left Kimberly on 6th May, 1890, and consisted of one hundred and eighty men from the Cape and Natal, who were to provide the nucleus of a settler population and a force of five hundred men – the British South African police – to protect the column. The column reached its destination at the foot of Salisbury Kopje on 12th

September, 1890, and the pioneers spread out to begin mining and farming.

The British South African Company's Charter, originally granted for a twenty-five year period, was reviewed in 1914, and was extended for another ten years. After the end of World War One, the settlers began to press for an end to the Company's control, quoting the steady increase of their influence in the running of the country.

In a referendum in 1922, Rhodesians chose self-rule over union with South Africa and a year later Rhodesia became a self-governing colony of Great Britain. The British Government paid the Company £3,750,000 in settlement of all claims in respect of Southern and Northern Rhodesia. The Southern Rhodesian Government then paid £2,000,000 to the British Government for title to all unalienated land and public buildings.

The new Constitution provided for a Governor and a Legislature of thirty elected members. Britain had control only in matters concerning the constitution, external affairs and 'discriminatory laws'.

It was established by written convention that Britain would not legislate for Rhodesia on those matters within the competence of the Rhodesian Legislative Assemble, unless asked to do so.

In 1953, Rhodesia decided by referendum to become part of the Federation of Rhodesia and Nyasaland. Economically, the Federation was an enormous success for all member countries. Commercial undertakings, industrial development and projects like the Kariba Dam were achieved.

Politically, however, the Federation was not a success. This was largely due to the fact that Rhodesians were used to run their own affairs, whereas Northern

Rhodesia and Nyasaland (Malawi) were inexperienced. This was compounded by the British Government's change of heart over its African politics and the Monckton Commission report on the Federation's future.

With the impending dissolution of the Federation, a constitutional conference was held towards the end of 1960. It was attended by the Rhodesian and British Governments, by the Representative of the African Nationalists and by the Parliamentary opposition party. All but the opposition agreed to terms for a new Constitution, although the Nationalists later withdrew their consent.

The new terms were set out in two British White Papers and it was these terms which the electorate ratified in a referendum.

It was only when the actual Constitution was promulgated by the British Government that the Rhodesian Government discovered that an additional section, not mentioned in the White Papers, had been included. This gave the British Government unlimited power to intervene in the internal affairs of Rhodesia by means of Order-in-Council.

The British Government tried to explain away the inclusion of the extra section as being of theoretical importance only, but in fact it was a written authority for the British Government to interfere in Rhodesia's internal affairs.

The Federation officially ended on 31st December. Independence was granted to Zambia and Malawi, but not to Rhodesia, a territory which had been self-governing for more than forty years, while the other territories had never governed themselves. Mr Ian Smith, former Minister of the Treasury, became Prime Minister in April, 1964 after the resignation of Mr Winston Field. On 5th November, an independence referendum was held... of which eighty-nine per cent were in favour.

The British Minister of State for Foreign Affairs, Mr Gledwyn Hughes, arrived for talks in July, but subsequent negotiations broke down in London, because the British Government would not agree to Independence based on the 1961 constitution.

The patience of the Rhodesian Government was exhausted. They had made repeated efforts to negotiate but each time a settlement seemed near the British Government made more stringent demands. The Unilateral Declaration of Independence of 11th November, 1965, was the only alternative.

Recognition of de facto and then the de jure status of the Rhodesian Government was contained in judgements handed down by the judiciary. As a result of Britain's approach to the United Nations, comprehensive mandatory sanctions were imposed on Rhodesia on 30th May, 1968.

Proposals for a new constitution were announced by the Rhodesian Prime Minister. on 19th May, 1969. The subsequent referendum showed that the majority of Rhodesians voters were in favour of it... On 2nd March, 1970... Rhodesia became a republic.

Extract from 'Focus on the Rhodesian Settlement'
3rd March, 1978 Edition
Published by the Ministry of Information, Immigration and Tourism, Causeway, Rhodesia

Charlie's account was not unfamiliar to us, but it highlighted the historical problems the second and third generation Rhodesians had inherited, simply by being a product of British colonial history. And now Great Britain had handed her own problem over to the United Nations. Not a compassionate way of resolving next of kin dilemmas!

We found Charlie to be a kind, humble gentleman and took his advice to request further loans from the banks to develop the farm.

The local Land Bank manager appeared perplexed when I entered his office and told him that as far as I was concerned the Gatooma area was unfit for agriculture and should be handed back to elephants and other wild animals. 'How can you farm with only six weeks of rain in a year? I think it unfair to encourage young people or anybody else to farm here. We have lost our savings in the first year of farming, so what is the point of securing another loan and sowing another crop or developing the farm? With no harvests, how will we repay a development loan?' He left the office. Well, I thought, he probably sees you as an arrogant young foreigner with no perseverance. I had come with the intention of borrowing more money. Had my unplanned short outburst now jeopardised everything? I felt sorry for myself and was ready to leave the office when he reappeared with cups of tea. 'Let's have some tea and see if we have some common ground. Do you want to stay in Gatooma if possible?' I said, 'Yes' to that, and pulled out my proposed development plan and schedule of costs, which included opening up more land for cultivation, the building of African workers' houses, a community hall and school, a house on the hill for Ulrich and me, a new borehole for water and installation of water tank and pipes. On a different sheet I had requirements for seasonal loans for planting to the harvest of crops, wages, and our own living costs for a year. 'I see you have not included a holiday allowance, so we will add a bit on to your own living costs, because I believe you and your brother should go to Kariba for a well-deserved holiday. I consider the loan granted, but obviously it must be passed by the Board to be official. By the way, you should go and see your commercial bank. I am sure they will also give you a bit of credit for that little extra you may need.' I expressed thanks, and sped back to the farm to inform Ulrich of the outcome of my meeting. 'Well, are you ready to move?' He looked at me with dismay. 'I mean, we are going to have a holiday first and then we begin development. 'They have full faith in us, so we had better follow suit, and start enjoying our new country.' A big shift in outlook and attitude took place. I suppose we were also recovering from the cultural shock that always accompanies a move to another country, the leaving behind of the familiar support network and friends, a feeling of tearing and gnawing in the stomach which only disappears when the new becomes familiar, and with the gaining of friends to share thoughts, pain and joy. That all coincided with the banks granting us new loans. We felt accepted and welcome members of the Rhodesian community, and began to behave accordingly. With that, our view shifted. Beauty was seen and appreciated in small things in our daily work which helped us regain our 'free spirit' attitude. Fear had stepped aside, and the exhilarating feeling of creating beauty and working in harmony with our surroundings had returned strongly. We were gradually falling in love with our new environment and activity. A new reality was dawning.

Before going on holiday we cut a road through the dense bush to the eastern boundary of the farm where half-way up the hill a flat plateau protruded, large enough for a house and garden. A number of black mamba and cobra snakes had residence there and had to be evicted or eliminated before we could build our home. Some packed their bags and left voluntarily. We wanted to have wildlife around us, but not too many deadly snakes. Close to the site where the house was to be built a five-metre-long python had her nest in an ant-bear hole. She was adopted and admired, especially when her head was safely inside the hole. We referred to her as 'our snake'. Later that year she had babies, twenty-five of them! Africans believe that killing pythons can interfere with the weather pattern unless the right rituals are followed and the dead python buried in a river bed.

Our ten farm workers, with Kenani in charge, were given contract work, and Ulrich and I drove to Kariba for a four-day break to see the world's longest man-made lake. The countryside along the road to Kariba was dry with long yellow grass rippling under the leafless trees, protecting the dusty ground from wind and the first downpour of rain, except on some African farms and tribal land where goats had destroyed all vegetation. Roots had been pulled up and munched, exposing the earth to erosion and to the hot October sun which would kill any germinating seed after the first sporadic rain. Uncontrolled numbers of goats and cattle had transformed green savannahs into what is now Sahara desert, thereby changing the climate. The process is still ongoing, like a parasite slowly but steadily eating away its host. Man's very existence interferes with the 'natural order of things'. Unless we accept that man's destruction is part of 'the natural order', positive steps need to be taken to address the problems. Kariba Dam, its magnificent sunsets, over four thousand square kilometres of blue water filled with small kapenta and large tiger fish providing food for many, and animals gracing the shores, posing for tourist cameras, can only be an improvement to the otherwise scorching hot, dusty, inhospitable valley with 'rebel' Batonga tribesmen living in high-off-the-ground huts to survive the annual flood of the valley, mentioned by Dr Livingstone. Some of those Batonga are perhaps living proof of the evolution theory. They are born with two toes per foot only. If that genetic peculiarity is beneficial only time will tell.

We hired a boat and fished for tigers, the renowned Zambezi fighting fish, and caught many. We watched elephants bathing with their young, hippos playing hide and seek, diving and re-emerging in different places, and crocodiles pretending to be dead, only to explode suddenly into attack, often on their own kind. The penetrating call of fish eagles, hovering above, waiting to dive for their bit in the constant battle for food in the African paradise, is a sound that haunts one for ever.

Our hotel was covered in bright bougainvillaea. Bananas and palms grew in clumps around a garden full of happy, spirited, colourfully dressed freedom seekers from different parts of Rhodesia and the world. Crocodile tail and kapenta were on the menu, but I preferred the kariba bream, the 'St Peter' fish of Kariba. We played the roulette wheel and lost the money found under my mattress in the hotel room, left behind by an untraceable earlier visitor. One night after a long hot day of fishing, swimming and chatting to fellow Rhodesians over drinks about politics and 'the sick man of Europe', meaning Wilson's Britain, I had a dream which re-occurred years later and was interpreted by Charles M. de Beer of Umtentweni in South Africa, author of the books, *Dreams, Allegorical Stories of Mystic Import* and *Dreams, Mystic Stories, Volume 2*.

The dream: At the commencement of the dream I was aware that it had to be dreamt quickly because there was not much time.

Somewhere in East Africa I climbed into the enclosed compartment of an air balloon which was constructed of wood and leather, and flew over game parks, observing buffalo, elephants, etc., and was fascinated by the appearance of trees from above and by the animal track along rivers.

Late afternoon the balloon started losing height because of a drop in temperature. It landed on a watery mud-flat which was pleasant as it enabled me to observe animals drinking, but I was worried about safety. The wind started gently pushing the balloon and compartment along the ground and my worry for safety was unfounded. We were dragged along until we came to a tarred road where I disembarked. On the other side of the road were farms and a built-up area. A farmer said, 'What a box' in a disinterested manner.

At this time the compartment and balloon had separated and developed supporting cords between them.

Two boys were watching, fascinated and smiling, but said nothing. A third boy, separate from the group, remarked that the compartment defied gravity (because he had not noticed the balloon above). He asked how much weight the compartment could carry. I told him to get in and pushed the compartment. The child repeated his question. I explained that the balance was so fine that it could take any weight without changing height, and to demonstrate how to measure the balance, I positioned the compartment on the hands of a small clock, which took the weight without bending. End of dream.

Charles de Beer's interpretation:

> My reading of this very interesting dream would be as follows; The dream had to be dreamt quickly. As it is known that dreams are dreamt 'in a flash' and that even long, intricate dreams take but a few seconds to dream, I think the urgency refers to the interpretation of the dream and subsequent action on basis of its message. Time is our only raw material, while on earth, and we should not waste any of it. Let us be about our Father's business right throughout our life,

to make that 'daily advancement' the Freemasons speak of.

An air-balloon will fly away, high in the sky, and is round. Seen diagrammatically it is a circle. It can therefore symbolise the spirit, filled with the universal substance, the divine totality, universal, but also the individual, as symbolised by the enclosed compartment closely attached to it. It can therefore be seen as representing a specific spiritual-cum-physical entity, i.e. man in his composite nature of spirit embodied in, and hovering over, his physical body. Physical man, divine spirit, are closely intertwined in their 'at-one-ment', linking to form one unit, yet part of the whole, as the separate drop in the spray is yet part of the sea.

Africa is the 'dark continent' of earth, the most earthly. But East Africa is close to the rising sun, and this perhaps indicates spiritual awareness in earthly surroundings. Matter, but with a perception of Spirit that leavens it.

The dreamer, in this dream, in his spirit, up in the balloon, is shown the beauty of the ideal earth, as created by God 'who saw that it was good', Earth unsullied by man's creation.

The balloon coming down and landing can be interpreted as representing a new incarnation in the process of 'coming to pass'. At that stage the 'overself' and soul are still united. The exit from paradise has not yet taken place. The actual physical birth is still pending, and so 'the animals are seen to slake their thirst', that is, the soul is still fully nourished through its 'at-one-ment' with the spirit, symbolised by the flowing rivers.

But our sojourn on earth entails a plunge into duality, and the enclosed compartment is gently pushed and dragged to the tarred road, to man's road, where there are farms and also built-up areas, 'at the other side' of the virgin (paradisical) territory where spirit and (not yet incarnated) souls are still one.

Here, on earth, enclosed compartment and balloon seem no longer one single unit, but appear separate. Yet they are still connected by 'supporting cords'. A graphic description of man, on earth, who has lost contact with the Spirit, the overself, the divine part of his composite being. The dreamer has 'disembarked'. He now treads the physical earth, he is man incarnate whose goal it must be to unite again with the spirit.

To the unaware farmer, the tiller of the soil, working the earth, the body is but just that, a body. But to the three youngsters there is some awareness of wonder and mystery. They are more perceptive, keen to learn. The farmer represents 'the old man', man not yet reborn, whereas the three young boys stand for the spiritual trinity that will reign in man reborn.

To the youthful questioner, to seeking man, it is explained that the body will not be asked to carry more than it can cope with, that the Spirit protects, uplifts, keeps the balance.

The hands of the clock that bear the weight of the compartment, the body, point to duality in time/space, which are the restrictions man has to overcome with the assistance of his higher self; the balloon, with which he remains connected and which will help him, as aforesaid, to gain that equilibrium he requires for continued progress on the path.

The dreamer of this particular dream will be able further to interpret the symbolism in which this story has been given to him, and my reading, whilst, hopefully, of help in his musings, is not submitted as the only valid interpretation. There are always wheels within wheels, and truth has many facets.

Towards the end of drafting this dream-reading, still in the garden, two birds of prey, sailing majestically high in the sky, call to one another, thus drawing our attention. We watch their flight through binoculars, as – wings outspread – they ride the air currents. Finally they fly down the valley before us and disappear out of sight. Dark wings, pale underbody, they came not near enough to be identified further. Did they symbolise the spirit that does inhabit the earth? The light that shineth in the dark but that, so often, the darkness does not recognise? Is not that the reason for our dreams? Dreams that 'urgently' spur us on to tread the path to transcendence, to 'at-one-ment'? It is for each one of us to find his own answer, 'fascinated and smiling'. To hear the call, and to respond.

Waking in Kariba after the dream I felt that I had witnessed a very important revelation, a 'milestone' had been seen and balance was of importance. My interpretation at the time also saw the balloon as the Higher Self and the compartment as the physical incarnation. So, when years later I had the dream interpreted by the elderly mystic, Charles de Beer, in Umtentweni, RSA, whom I met by 'coincidence', if such a thing exists, I was reminded that dreams have messages in them if only we would take note, ponder and accept that they are a help back to 'at-one-ment', transcendence into pure consciousness, often using symbols from our daily working environment or memory patterns from the past. When I met Charles the very first time, he said, 'I have being expecting you.'

Driving back, we stopped for refreshment at Makuti where elephants were standing beside the road. Patches of dry grass here and there had been spared from the overnight bushfire inferno which had turned a huge area into a desolate, darkened desert with a few trees still smouldering and burning away. Others were protected by a thin layer of soil which termites had skilfully plastered on their trunks and had survived – a symbiotic relationship. The undulating horizon was blurred with haze and smoke suspended in the still morning air. The rain, that by its magic transforms even these dry areas into green park lands, was still months away. Elephants had to walk miles to fill their stomachs. The area between Kariba and Karoi, a one hundred and eighty kilometre stretch, feels as though it conceals mysteries. Maybe that is why the Karoi town emblem is a hooded witch flying on a broomstick. My future girlfriend and wife was born on a farm not far from Karoi. Her mother brought up children and ran a farm while her husband was defending the world against fascism and tyranny with many other Rhodesians in the early Forties. I did not know then that one day in the future with my wife I would be crawling around, a few kilometres from here, to escape brutal killers and molesters of the worst kind, after having survived the crash of our burning civilian passenger aircraft, shot down by 'freedom fighters'. Fortunately we can't see the future in detail, and fortunately we were invisible to the killers on the ground where we crashed.

Back on the farm things had gone well during our short absence except that Kenani had 'borrowed' the tractor and trailer and gone to a neighbouring farm to play football. On the return, he had pressed the clutch to reach high speed going downhill. Later he slowed down by releasing the clutch, which resulted in the engine being torn apart. Piston connection rods had smashed holes in the engine block and the sump was filled with broken metal. He apologised for having used the tractor, but could not understand why the engine had flown apart. We were not told about the downhill high speed bit until months later when Kenani reprimanded a fellow worker, who then out of spite enlightened us as to what exactly had happened. Somehow they had managed to push the tractor the two kilometres home. The tractor dealers were perplexed, they had never heard about such incident before, but as Brian Duly said, 'In Africa, even the impossible is possible.' With the courtesy of Duly's, and to our great appreciation, a new engine was fitted to our tractor, free of charge.

During the next few months our farm improvements progressed according to plan. A house was built on the hill, with views hovering above the treetops, facing west for perfect sunset worship. The ever-changing colour spectacle painted the sky to remind us that the only truth that exists is change. The forever unfolding physical phenomena were consigned to memory, kept in secret archives, to be reclaimed and reviewed by mind, years after the phenomena have ceased to be. A borehole was sunk, and water, millions of years old, extracted to irrigate gardens, plant nurseries and to boil for tea, the necessary ceremonial breaks in which to reflect and discuss work progress and priorities. A further one hundred hectares were cleared of bush, ploughed for cotton, and a number of houses built for African workers.

Our cook Joseph (or the reluctant Kariuki, as we called him between ourselves) had numerous days off work to visit friends, he said, which we had no problem with. He was becoming rather frail, and on occasion I asked him if he was eating properly. But always he said he was all right. One evening, before going home to his hut, he said that he had something to tell us, but we had to be alone where no one could hear or see us, not even his friend with whom he shared the hut.

A few days later in the car on the way to Gatooma he began talking about the forthcoming war in Rhodesia. I said very little but encouraged him to talk. In his opinion, the mission stations, as in East Africa, had slowly been infiltrated with social gospel preachers and many of the white Fathers had lost control over the missions to outspoken African preachers. Some mission stations openly sympathised with the Marxist-Leninist ideology. 'They do not believe in God's heaven anymore, but want to kill and intimidate people so that they can bring "their heaven" here to Rhodesia with leaders chosen by the Russians. I have heard that guns have been hidden on some mission stations to be used when the "time is right". Boss Bwana-Hansen, many people in the tribal area are scared and confused with all this talk. These people who have been trained in other countries say that one day the whites in Zimbabwe (which is their new name for Rhodesia) will be washing floors for the new black masters. They say that the Marxist-Leninists are winning all over the world over white colonial pigs, and that one day all who support them now will be rich and have motor cars. Schools and history books must be changed, they say, and we must rid ourselves of colonial influence and try to re-establish our perfect past where we all worked together on common land. The whites in Rhodesia are no more than bleating sheep to be got rid off. Tell me, how do the African peasant farmers in the tribal areas defend themselves against these people? Some school-leavers have already been recruited in to what they call the Liberation Army. I do not like what I hear, but I am old. These people with foreign ideas, they are not for freedom and liberation for the people. They want the spoils of war for themselves. I have seen Kenya, Tanzania and other places. I have seen enough, and I want to die before new upheavals engulf the place in which I live.'

I listened to the old African man with white hair who had gained insight and wisdom. Deep down I knew that he was right. I knew that the march of Marxist-Leninist Communism was, at the moment, an almost unstoppable evil and brutal force, and that the feeble-minded of lower intelligence would adopt that materialistic philosophy based on envy and hatred, with leaders who would be dictators for life. But I also knew that Rhodesia was my new home and we had to make the best of it. We also discussed the Mau-Mau in Kenya and how the family-oriented gentle African had the tendency to withdraw from public life if confronted with outrages and evil suggestions, leaving the gangsters and evildoers to run public office. 'Africa is where Darwin's law is carried out, the biggest gun wins, the masses blindly follow the few, the recognition of the law of consequence evaporates in the heat of shouted slogans, and compassion withdraws.' I had come across those thoughts before, back in Kenya, and now an old African was telling me the same thing. It was like reliving history, being in a room with mirrors on all walls and with no escape, forced to witness history. The earth is but a round ball in space where humans are taught to repeat history with little chance of escape. But by virtue of being born we have to be somewhere! It suddenly struck me that I also had the tendency and desire to withdraw from what I perceived as evil and unpleasant, and my escape existed in solitude where I could drift away in meditation. I was certainly never going to fight for or defend a political ideology or religion! That behaviour I would leave to kings, mullahs, popes, politicians and their henchmen.

Towards the end of the dry season and before we moved to the new house on the hill, Joseph became ill. He was bringing afternoon tea on a tray to our outdoor table, but left the tray in mid-air, half a metre short of the table, with the natural consequences. Teapot and cups lay broken on the cement floor. We stared at him aghast and speechless, while he knelt down to pick up the broken cups, but it was obvious that he could not see the pieces. I went to him. 'Joseph, stand up, leave the broken rubbish on the floor, don't worry about it. What is happening to you? What is your problem?' His gentle old face turned towards me with glassy eyes, tears running down his cheeks. 'My eyes have failed me, I only see a little white blur,' he uttered. He was distressed. 'Joseph, get into the car, we are going to the hospital in Gatooma immediately,' I instructed. Ulrich took the old man by the hand and led him to the car. In the car he explained that his sight had only deteriorated recently and that sometimes he saw well. He also suffered from headaches.

The attending doctor at Gatooma hospital gave him a bed for early examination the next morning. We drove back to the farm subdued and in silence. The following afternoon I called in at the hospital to see how he was getting on. His general condition had deteriorated and he said that without eyes he was better off dead, and 'that is what I will do.' He apologised for giving us problems, and added, 'You know me better that most, because you wanted to know. My watery eyes are failing, but my inner eye is about to open and the Grace of the Holy One to whom I am connected shall expose me to the glory of spiritual travel, where divine love will be a shining torch, and darkness is nothing but a word. I am going back to spirit after a lifetime of work and toil, but I am grateful, for my cup is full of invisible magic. My spirit is rejoicing because they know that I am coming.'

'Joseph, are you not Kariuki?' I asked softly. 'You speak like him!' 'Kariuki and Joseph are one in spirit, but so are all who understand the grace of appreciation, the illumination that comes from love and beauty, and from constantly striving for the highest ideal.' He answered in a voice that seemed to come from all directions. I felt sorry for the old man, but at the same time joy, for he was in no doubt as to where he was going. As I left his bedside he took my hand and said softly, *'Kwaheri Ndugu Yango.'* I quickly left the hospital with the pressure of tears behind my eyes. He died a few hours later, possibly by sheer willpower. His body was collected from the hospital, but I have no idea who buried him. He was not indoctrinated by imposed religion or church, but, as far as I am concerned, had followed the intuitive knowledge that we all have within us, and had used the key to ask 'Who am I to know that I am?' The answer had come to him, whoever he was, and created humility. I recall a section of the Bible that says: 'Except ye become as a little child ye shall not enter the Kingdom of Heaven'. I felt that that truth had been demonstrated to me through Joseph, alias Kariuki.

Strangely, Samson disappeared overnight after Joseph's death. Steven was then promoted to domestic manager.

Spring in Gatooma is when the Masasa and Mfuti trees don their gloriously coloured new leaves and a pleasant smell from flowering trees refreshes the hot, shimmering September air. Flying ants prepare to ascend from the depths of the earth, and chongololos (large black shiny centipedes) stampede the dusty ground with tiny feet, and African drums relentlessly disturb the heat-irritated sleeper, before the first drops of rain have fallen through the air.

The longed-for rains eventually came on the fourth of November with a full ceremonial introduction. Lightning and thunder announced the coming hours before the first drops wetted the thirsty soil where cotton seeds had carefully been sown by our home-made seed drill, waiting to sprout when rained upon. As the sun set in the west, the clouds became denser and blacker as they approached from the east. A wall of solid rain could be seen when the lightning lit the sky and thunder rumbled, echoing from the hills. We sat on our new veranda, in great expectation, overlooking the magnificent bushland below that shone with every flash of lightning, and further down lay bare red soil lands, potentially beautiful green cotton and maize fields. They were already perceived in the mind as healthily growing insect-free fields. The toads and frogs had emerged from underground caverns and taken their positions, sitting waiting for ponds to fill with water. They were still quiet, but as the rain began they joined in song, praising heaven for the liquid that makes life on earth possible. The drumming began on our flat tin roof, changing into a full symphony as the precipitation intensified, sounding like a thousand waterfalls. The smell of dampness was intoxicating. We took off our shirts and went outside to feel the rain and to defy the normal reaction to it. After an hour of steady heavy downpour we felt like Adam (before the dreadful apple), walking with God in our garden accompanied by a chorus of flowing, white-clad Light Angels, all ready to help growing plants if asked, loved and appreciated. At eleven o'clock and after the first hundred millimetres of water had fallen, we started the pick-up and drove down the hill to where the foreman, Kenani, lived. He was still awake – who can sleep to the beautiful sound of the first rain on a tin roof? He stood in the doorway with a big smile, silhouetted against the dim reddish glow from a paraffin lamp behind him. He shared our joy and we repeatedly shook hands, in spirit flying and somersaulting in the warm air among the falling water drops and singing the song that only silence understands. As dawn broke, with clouds hanging low over the hill and soft rain still falling, no work could be done in the sticky red soil. Everyone had a day off to celebrate. Beers were collected in Gatooma and African songs could be heard far afield.

We also celebrated by visiting Chris and Jutta from where we phoned Denmark to wish Mother 'Happy

Birthday'. Later in the afternoon drinks at Moores Motel were called for, where we met friends. One was Terry, a newcomer, also originally from Kenya. He had acquired a very picturesque piece of tree-filled land near the Gatooma water reservoirs, where he was developing a free-range chicken farm, a forever humorous subject of conversation. How free is a free-range chicken? Who is freer, you or the chicken? There were many silly questions and many silly answers with lot of laughter and great fun. Discussions about afterlife, mind over matter and UFOs were frequent in the motel, to the delight of travellers who often joined in. If our little circle of friends had not finished the philosophy of being and the locality of Heaven by eleven at night, the manager of the establishment would give us the key and instructions to help ourselves to the contents of the fridge and shelves, to look after other guests, and to settle the account by leaving cash or cheques in a glass, a trust that was never abused. The traffic in Gatooma after dark was minimal, and none of us were ever involved in an incident due to slight inebriation. The police generally kept a low profile and only on one occasion were we stopped after driving from Moores Motel on a punctured wheel to a local service station. The police, seeing the spark generated by the wheel's steel rim against the stones in the tarred road followed us to the service station. But when they saw the African attendant opening the workshop door and bringing out our spare wheel, left there earlier in the evening for repair, they just commented, 'It looks as if you chaps have things under control.' We said, 'Yes, yes, thank you,' but waited before using the jack and spanner till they had left so as not to show any clumsiness in getting that stupid little spanner on to obscure, very tight wheel nuts that suddenly seemed to have to be unscrewed the wrong way. That evening Ulrich drove home. By common consent, the most capable took over. That, by the way, was also how we shared work on the farm, and we never ever had any disagreement on how to divide the workload or over who did what.

The cotton germinated, then thinned to twenty-five centimetres apart and quickly grew into small bushes. With the help of the cotton research station, two young Africans were trained to scout for insects, and to record findings. Each type of insect was recorded on its own sheet and a graph drawn. If predator insect graphs were falling and an increase in ballworm eggs or other plant eaters were detected, we knew we had to spray. In a season the cotton was sprayed six to seven times, in those days, with DDT or organic phosphorous which the chemical companies claimed were safe. Cotton cannot be grown without spraying to kill insects, unless an insect-resistant cotton is developed. Our maize field was visited by kudus, wild pigs and monkeys, but according to our calculations they took less than five per cent, which was a fair price to pay to have wildlife on the farm. We accepted that.

We were blessed with a good rainy season and harvested more than average. Cotton pickers, mainly women in colourful dresses armed with cokes and sandwiches, were picked up in a hired bus from Gatooma's Rimuka township. A singer with guitar was engaged to entertain in the bus and while pickers waited to have their daily pick weighed before going home. A carnival atmosphere normally prevailed, and only on a few occasions did we weigh stones hidden in cotton bags. A committee of elders normally took care of the offender. We sold over one thousand five hundred bales of cotton to the Gatooma gin. We made a profit and further development could commence immediately. More African worker houses were built, another borehole sunk and irrigation pipes laid for a coffee plantation, and the nursery was already established. Also more land was cleared of bush for cultivation.

During the recently completed season we found that deep ploughed land yielded no more than very shallow ploughed land, and as ploughing red dry soil is difficult and expensive we decided not to plough at all, and opted for what is called minimum tillage, which means just enough loose soil, in a parallel strips ninety centimetres apart, to accommodate the planted seeds. It worked very well for the next five seasons till 1975, at which time the Danish Government appealed to us to quit Rhodesia, to make way for decay and destruction by an incompetent Marxist-Leninist dictator. They did not see it quite that way though, unless with the rest of the world they wished Africa down the drain, with all its megalomaniac despots who were supposedly democratically elected.

The western-educated mind cannot perceive the force of fear that controls large parts of Africa. There is intimidation, witchcraft, evoking of evil spirits, mysterious disappearances of those outspoken in opposition, mutilation of the living and the dead, and the constant abuse of all authority riddled with bribery and corruption. That is the history of darkest Africa. No traditional 'statecraft' experience was handed down through history except that of fighting an enemy for territorial conquest.

In other parts of the world law and order is a prerequisite for progress and development. For whatever reason, the destructive regressive forces of Africa not only had support from communists, but also had the sympathy and support of the western world, including the World Council of Churches and the United Nations in the Sixties and Seventies. Their adulterated agenda included KGB, CIA, International Finance and Third Forces – a new type of human behaviour was accepted. The perception of the archetypal man shifted downwards, closer to the abyss, and gangsterism became an alternative to civilised, negotiated order. I am not suggesting that the world was perfect before then, but individuals perceived that higher ideals were at least generally aimed for. I believe that forces of evil were boosted at that time by those various agencies, and that the present Islamic fundamentalism, drugs lords, planted refugees and terrorism, a few holding the many to ransom, are but children of that era. Wait for them to grow up!

Before receiving the letter from the Danish authorities asking us to examine whether our existence in Rhodesia was necessary and compatible with expected security, I had a dream that illustrated the pitiful world of man. Fortunately for me, as I saw it being drawn on a green board, it included an exit passage. But, unfortunately, it is clearly a lonely passage and can only be traversed individually. A helping hand on the way would be beneficial, and that should be the job of the churches. The vision is illustrated as I saw it.

For me, the diagram clearly illustrated a unified picture of the many components that dictate the human condition and burden. It appears that we are all weighed down by tradition, collective decisions or democracy in its diverse form. Our 'Big Brother', the ruling class, can decide to use a rightist or leftist system of control, but ultimately the dictation is finance, the brain or nerve circuitry system is money, be it state capitalism (communism) or conglomerate capitalism, and individual creative input and choice is largely curtailed. The educational system is determined by the finance system and 'hammered' into dogma by politicians who also dictate the codes of conduct of churches and science, generally speaking that is. Exposure to life and thought beyond the closed system is not in the interests of the ruling class and therefore often ridiculed. The political forces that wander off towards the abyss are left alone to do so, because they will invariably come back into the fold, after experiencing calamity – present day Africa? The escape is an individual experience and not an easy one. By

Diagram Two: Our Present World

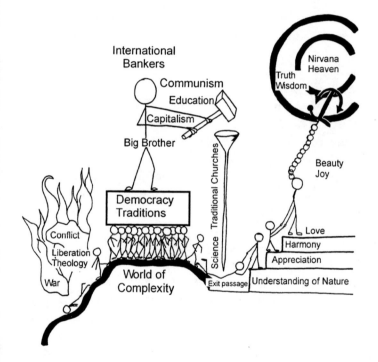

understanding the divine law of appreciation, beauty and love, the step leads to transcendence and the anchor to 'Heaven', 'Nirvana' or 'At-one-ment' can be achieved. Unfortunately the newly found freedom is not compatible with the closed human system of suffering, so presently death is the only permanent release. 'Be in the world but not of it', we are told.

A few weeks after the above dream, I heard a story about five blind men who had to identify an elephant. One was of the opinion that an elephant was a tree trunk. Another, who caught the tail, said elephants are like rope, and yet another said that it was like a fan, because he felt the air flow from the flapping ears, and so on. All perceived their little truth in front of them, but no one grasped the whole majestic elephant. The story sent a cold sensation down my back, because of my earlier holistic dream – seeing the whole elephant and not just a leg or an ear. We are not only components in a machine, existing so that the machine can keep on renewing itself. We have to resolve the riddle, and not only interpret convenient aspects, but try to understand the greater picture.

With that insight I realised that presently the change of government or of a money system would be like rearranging furniture in the same room, limited and with few options. And is that not exactly what international financial manipulators are aiming for? Capitalism for the few to control the many is a dangerous system that could lead to a new global 'French' revolution. I see society's control systems as genes with peaceful interaction and adaptation potential, but as in genetic material, diversity is essential for long-term survival. Lack of diversity can lead to a monstrous system with no ability to transform.

The 1971–1972 season started very well with good early rain, but on 2nd December a hail storm reduced our cotton plants to small stumps just protruding out of the soil. All the foliage was ripped off. Our sympathetic neighbour immediately offered tractors, planters and workers to re-sow the cotton, but after consulting with a specialist from the research station we concluded that is was too late to replant, and that there was a small chance that the cotton would re-grow. One of the experts suggested that we go to Beira on holiday while the cotton decided what to do! So as not to fall into despair over the unusual heavy hailstorm that had reduced green fields to bare lands, we left for Beira three days later on an Air Rhodesia Viscount plane.

We stayed at the Don Carlos Hotel, close to the lighthouse, a few kilometres north of Beira town. The sea was warm, drinks cheap, and the food excellent, especially the gigantic Beira prawns with peri-peri and garlic sauces. There was a real continental atmosphere, and no time to be bored or to dwell on invalid cotton plants at home. Beira hosted a number of night-clubs, including Moulin Rouge which had a reputation that drew guests from far afield. On entering at nine o'clock one evening we booked a table and ordered drinks and grilled prawns. Elisabeth, a young pretty Portuguese girl, joined us at the table. We watched the shows, danced, had more wine, and as the evening progressed became almost fluent in Portuguese conversing with Elisabeth. At some point I daringly held her hand under the table, or so I thought. Ulrich was doing exactly the same, so he thought. With no reaction from Elisabeth when I squeezed her hand, I could not resist a look under the table, and there I was holding Ulrich's hand! Elisabeth could not control her mirth, and delighted in telling her friends of our folly. For a short while we became the focal point and much laughter was heard from all directions. Later I was persuaded to participate in a show on the stage, but kept my eyes low in embarrassment. The morning broke to sad Fado songs vibrating in the cold morning air. Sad songs about the longing to return to Portugal on a sail ship after discovering America. We had egg and bacon with coffee then drifted back to the hotel for some hours of sleep before a swim. Beira was cosmopolitan and had flavours from all continents, and shops that offered merchandise from all over the world. There were tables on pavements and talkative people everywhere. They were a happy mixed lot who seemed to be living in an atmosphere of anticipation. Trouble was waiting though. Frelimo, the African Nationalist 'freedom fighters' of Mozambique, backed by communist Soviet Union (initially financed by the Ford Foundation, I was told), were slowly gaining control over the north and took over the country in 1975 after a change of government in Portugal. On a recent visit to Beira (1993) I saw devastation and can only feel sorry for the people of Mozambique. There were land-mine-mutilated one-legged mothers living in burned-out car wrecks, potholed dirty streets with unpainted dilapidated houses and beggars not old enough to walk, but still stretching out hands from their mothers' backs for crumbs to keep them alive in order to produce more humans in an already totally overcrowded environment. Is that what African freedom is all about? A return to pre-European involvement? Is that chaos and waste of human life what is referred to as sustainable development?

After landing in Salisbury and driving home, we could not believe our eyes as we entered the farm. The cotton had re-grown, shooting many branches from each little stem and the fields were green again. We later harvested a bumper crop.

Rhodesia was booming, and new industries were mushrooming up everywhere despite international sanctions. New townships were developed, large dams planned and built, rural roads tarred and numerous hospitals and schools built in tribal areas. A feeling of optimism prevailed. On the political front the Prime Minister Ian Smith was still negotiating with the British government and local African Nationalists and most believed that a settlement was just around the corner. Then a farmer was killed in the northeast of the country by insurgents planting land-mines on farm roads. A few weeks later another farmer was killed. After a lengthy debate and considering what Rhodesians from near and afar had done for us, Ulrich and I volunteered to join the Police Reservists, purely to help maintain security in our Gatooma region. We trained in rifle shooting at the local rifle range, participated in a few road checks and our social life broadened to include the Police Club.

At that time we had a number of dislocated visitors from other parts of Africa who had good reason to vacate their respective countries because of collapsed infrastructure, corruption, nationalisation or new laws that invalidated permits. One was Erik, the transporter from Kitale. His transport permit was in jeopardy so he sold the entire fleet to a Kenyan politician. He could not stay in Kenya any longer and intended to restart a transport business in Rhodesia. His story is, like numerous others, a sad one. He settled in Salisbury, involving himself in transport and truck repair work. During the bush war he broke his back. He recovered and married a girl of mixed race. She died of cancer. Years later he befriended an African girl who worked for one of the banks in the credit card division. During a holiday one year she fell sick and was rushed to hospital, but died. Erik, now an elderly philosophical man with experience to fill books, will be seen on Sunday afternoons at a Harare graveyard with two bouquets of flowers, having a quiet cry while the sun is setting, wondering what life is all about.

Another visitor was Ib with family from Tanzania where he had very successfully farmed sisal. He and many others could have been of great assistance to the Tanzanian state for many more years had it not been for that country having elected eternal poverty and mismanagement by design. He joined the Rhodesian Lands Department, inspecting contours and river-bed cultivation for a year, also readjusting after the traumatic upheaval of moving country and waiting until a suitable farm came on the market. Murra Purra, a farm thirty kilometres north of Gatooma, near Hartley, was purchased, with four shareholders, Ib, Chris, Ulrich and myself. It had sandy soils and had been used for tobacco growing for years, with fourteen flue-curing barns, but we intended to grow cotton and coffee. It was a picturesque farm, with large trees shading gardens scented by magnificent roses. The farmhouse was under thatch, built in different stages. Extensions had been added according to size of family of previous owners I suppose.

The eastern boundary was a permanently flowing river, and a tropical riverine forest with massive granite boulders, at one place forming a dam site where Ib later built a weir to hold back water for irrigation. The land was also decorated with huge boulders surrounded by large trees here and there, an attractive farm in an idyllic setting. Management of the farm was left entirely to Ib, so we had not created extra work for ourselves. We developed a close relationship with Ib and Birthe, and frequent visits were more on a social basis than business, although methods of farming were obviously discussed during walks around the farm – the way farmers love to exchange ideas. It was after such a happy get-together, driving back to Gatooma around ten o'clock at night, with Ulrich and his girlfriend Annette in the back seat of the car, when I suddenly saw an enormous orange light covering the entire road half a kilometre in front of us. Chris had left a little earlier so he had already passed the area. I slowed down but drove closer to see if the light came from an overturned petrol tanker, the only thing I could think of at that moment that could produce such an amount of light. I shouted to Ulrich and Annette to look out while keeping my eyes on the light. I could not identify the phenomenon. We were now only a hundred metres away from it, so I stopped and got out of the car. At that very moment it lifted and came towards us silently. Not a sound was heard except the usual crickets and frogs. I shouted, 'Hey, a UFO.' The light kept coming toward us while gaining height and moving a little to our right, changing colour to yellow, with a diameter of about twenty metres. After passing us it suddenly changed direction, a ninety degree left turn, and as we looked at it, now behind the car, it turned blue and disappeared through the cloud cover within seconds. It was truly a UFO, whatever that is. Anyone in such an object travelling at such speed would have to be uninfluenced by the 'G' force or the centrifugal laws. A human would have been flattened like a pancake, first on a wall or window and then later on the floor. It was only a light as far as I am concerned, but a very peculiar one. The following day Ulrich and I went to Chris and Jutta's for lunch. As I began to relate the story, Chris intervened to tell his part of the puzzle first. He had not seen any light, but closer to Gatooma than where we had seen the UFO he had stopped to investigate a car that had driven off the road and into a ditch. Chris had asked the driver if he could help. The panic-stricken driver explained that he had been totally blinded by a bright light hovering over the road and had therefore landed in the ditch, but could not elaborate on the nature of the light. Chris saw him safely back on the road and proceeded toward his nearby home. As he opened the homestead gates, he saw what looked like the shine from car lights turning in his farmyard only a few hundred metres away. Jutta and the children jumped out of the car and Chris drove to the yard where his African security guard was to be found, querying the origin of the light he had seen reflected on the tall trees. The security guard pointed at the sky with no special excitement and said, 'They often come from up there, sit here in the field for a while and then they are off again.' He appeared quite at ease with his explanation and probably felt that if his employer wanted to see for himself he only had to stay out in the open at night. Something unusual had been seen, but unfortunately for reasons of ridicule one keeps that type of information to oneself and close friends. Scientific authorities seem to have made up their minds that such phenomena do not exist except in the heads of the perceivers. That may be so, but then everything we see is in our head, and possibly is an illusion. Is the rumbling of the elephant's stomach not part of the elephant system? Cynthia Hind, a well known ufologist whom I have met feels that light of that nature could be extra-dimensional – a sudden slowdown of an unknown field stuff passing through our light wavebands. I, like many others who have seen something similar, can only speculate, but I think there is enough evidence to suggest that UFOs have intelligence behind them. Could it be faster-than-light emanation, something akin to reverse gravity pulses, from a black hole, slowing down around a field of intelligence, lighting up in the process and giving off an image? Who knows? With that experience and all the other exposure to mystical things, I became an avid reader of books on related subjects. Whenever I visited Salisbury I searched bookstores for books on psychology, mysticism, science and philosophy. I wanted to find out where my system begins and where it stops. In some way I felt that by reading and studying these subjects I was betraying what had come naturally to me through intuition and dreams, but I wanted to know more. A Transcendental Meditation course did not take me to areas of mind that were unknown to me, although I highly value that system. Ulrich, Terry and I volunteered as subjects for a hypnosis show in Gatooma, but on more than one occasion I was told that I was not a good subject, which annoyed me. I would have liked to have been hypnotised to experience death, to see if it corresponded with a meditation method I often used, in which I instructed myself to shut down all brain activity, thereby realising that we are more than a body with a brain. This is a practical system of escape if disaster is coming your way.

A young professional gamekeeper trainee from Denmark was another visitor. He had been visiting Zambia where he intended to go hunting on private property. After days of bureaucratic juggling to have his rifle released, he eventually gave up the nightmare, flew to Malawi and then on to Rhodesia. His long-term goal was to become a white hunter in Africa, an ambition he had developed very early in life – a carry-over from some previous existence? Perhaps he had been an explorer a hundred years earlier in a previous life, when Africa was visualised by most white people as a hot, hostile hell full of cannibals and poisonous snakes. He had the crazy idea of shooting a buffalo and asked if I would like to join him. We would fly in a small aircraft to a hunting camp on the shores of Lake Kariba with a professional hunter. I went along with the idea not to hunt or carry a gun, but so as to get an aerial view of our farm, which was close to the Gatooma airstrip, and to enjoy a break from everyday activities. We landed, after flying over magnificent bushland with dried-out sandy river beds appearing like a reverse delta, on a small airstrip that had a mound in the middle, causing a double landing. In the camp we were shown to our 'house' built of local poles, a wooden floor and reed walls half-way up to the thatch roof for good ventilation. We drank our sundowners in silence, watching the splendid red sun setting over the water, while quealea birds flew past, hippos snorted in the lake and weaver birds in tall thorn trees loudly debated where to build their nests. I noticed that just behind our hut meat from a previous hunt had been hung on lines for drying into biltong. After sunset darkness follows quickly and a light meal was consumed under paraffin lamps which attracted hordes of mosquitoes and other insects. So bed was an alternative and the lamps were doused. Holger intended to start his buffalo hunt very early in the morning so a good rest was called for. An hour later a noisy performance of some sort could be heard outside, and after ascertaining that Holger was not sleeping, I jokingly asked him if he could hear the lions plucking meat from the drying lines. He promptly leapt out of bed and pushed a small sofa in front of the open entrance. Puzzled, I asked why he was doing that. 'Well it is nice to know when they come for us.' He loaded his rifle. Next morning we found out that the lions had indeed eaten all the meat from the drying lines. A leopard had also left paw marks in the sand. The campfire was lit early and cups of steaming coffee were waiting. There is magic in an early morning campfire and a cup of coffee, a ritual I loved and greatly appreciated. The Land-Rover was packed with all that is necessary for a buffalo hunt, including drinks, sandwiches, winches and ropes, and off we drove on small tracks along the Zambezi valley. At some point the professional hunter decided it was time to walk and parked the Land-Rover under shady trees in the middle of nowhere. We walked for hours in long dry grass and in hellish temperatures. The doors to hell had been left open for the wicked to enter. I wondered about the sanity of the participants who had willingly paid for such adventure, but I did enjoy it when we eventually saw a herd of buffalo and were told to crawl like lions towards them. Apparently buffalo pretend not to see lions, so as long as we played lion we were safe. We crawled to within thirty metres of mainly cows and young bulls. Not good enough for Holger, who was after a trophy of record size. We crawled back behind some bushes before we could stand up again. The afternoon, after a short lunch break, was spent walking around in circles, searching for elusive buffalo and to give the client value for money in my estimation. Just before nightfall we got back to the Land-Rover and noticed that a herd of elephants had stampeded the ground while trying to get oranges out of the vehicle. The next day I refused to participate in the buffalo hunt. I preferred a quieter day of fishing, cruising on the lake and appreciating its beauty. By mid-morning I was relaxing in the boat chatting with two Africans accompanying me, after catching enough fish for dinner, when we heard sounds that were just too different to hippo snorting. The skipper was quick to start the outboard engine and shouted, 'We are being shot at with automatic AKs, get to the bottom of the boat.' I could see the splashes where bullets hit the water. They came from Zambian soil, probably fired by over-enthusiastic drunk soldiers. My two boat fellows were ready to go over to the Zambian side to clean up the unruly Zambian army, but we agreed it was better not to lower ourselves to that primitive level. In the evening we all shared dinner around the campfire, eating my eleven talapia. The next morning I joined Holger's hunt again, but armed only with an eight-millimetre camera. On a plateau under shady trees, a herd was seen, and so as not to disrupt the hunt I dropped behind and remained at an ant-heap where a fallen tree had partly covered an ant-bear hole. I heard two shots and the next moment saw stampeding buffaloes by the dozen coming my way. With my feet, legs and half of my body squeezed into the ant-bear hole and my head under the fallen tree, I was not visible to the confused buffaloes and had them jumping right over my head with their hooves only centimetres away. I knew I was safe as long as the beasts continued running away, which they did, including the animal that had been hit. When the dust had settled and I dared to surface, Holger and the professional hunter were already walking off in the direction of the injured animal. When I caught up with them they were about to walk straight into a female elephant with a little calf. Having nothing else to say than 'Elephant!' I commenced filming the encounter. Fortunately the elephant decided to be friendly and walked away. The hit buffalo was found dead a little further on. It was then skinned and cut up, loaded on the Land-Rover and taken to camp. The horns were cleaned and eventually despatched to Denmark, where years later they fell off Holger's wall, nearly killing him. Poetic Justice? The meat of the animal was salted, peppered and dried into biltong strips, a way of preserving meat that goes back many decades, to when Prince Albert of England slaughtered hundreds of animals on a Sunday afternoon hunt for fun.

During the evening, in the light of the campfire, Holger told of Danish-African project assistance to other parts of Africa. How taxpayers' money often and at best ended up in unworkable projects mainly designed to impress TV viewers of the donor country, and at worst enriched African politicians. The socialist and the western world gave the impression that by introducing a few projects here and there, the thousands of projects that white Africans controlled became dispensable, including the farming sector. At least that is how the new African politicians perceived it. This was totally forgetting Africa's fundamentals, that very few Africans think in terms of nationhood, and who can blame them when African politicians are concerned with self-enrichment and glory only, but the problem goes even deeper. Traditionally, the African village system is controlled by a Chief, who executes the law according to his interpretation. That is the traditional, fundamental control unit of east and central Africa. Beggars in the street are controlled by a Godfather (Chief). Street children have a Chief. Criminals have a Chief. Farm workers have a Chief, whether the owner of the farm is aware of it or not is irrelevant. The new African states have a 'Chief' as head of government (and often run the state accordingly). The Chief is all powerful and does not tolerate opposition. His welfare is of interest to his subordinates and his displeasure is feared. The Chiefs bear allegiance only to a king, if a king exists, but may co-operate with other Chiefs, if a common purpose and gain can be established. The Chiefs keep position by having powerful ancestral spirits at their disposal, and visits to mediums in flashy cars are common practice even by so-called Christians. Unfortunately they now also use land-mines and AKs to maintain their position.

The free-thinking Africans, of which there are many, have no chance to change society because the 'Chief' system is too entrenched, but from early to present times, they preferred to work for the European-organised administration of state (including police and army), private companies or on white-owned farms. Some even left their motherland. To introduce true democracy in Africa is like asking Dr Livingstone to rediscover Africa. Many times I have heard Africans saying, 'We have to vote for "him" otherwise we will die.' And that is true. They will die or disappear into correction centres, often financed by foreign aid, from where a return ticket is seldom issued. It is well known that fear and anxiety drain people's energy, destroy visions and make life meaningless, but they also inflate the 'devil's' ego and often fools think that the 'devils' are the only safe leaders to follow.

The following day we sailed to Binga to collect fuel for the camp and to my amusement the great buffalo hunter was as seasick as you can be, feeding the fish with his breakfast. Holger maintained that the waves were taller than in the North Sea, and that troughs made the boat scrape the bottom of the lake, but later he did admit that holding a glass of water in his hand and looking at the ripples could produce the same results – no wonder he stuck to coke! Our flight back to Gatooma in the midday turbulent air also turned Holger's empty stomach upside down and his face green. But he got what he wanted, and his single-minded pursuit of becoming a hunter in Africa paid off. Today he brings hundreds of tourists to Southern Africa to photograph the outstanding beauty and to give clients an African experience that he himself was fortunate enough to enjoy years earlier.

Ulrich and his fiancée Annette were married in 1974 and we had the great pleasure of seeing my parents in Rhodesia for that occasion. They adored our farm and were captivated by the way we ran it, like a commune or kibbutz, where most of the profits were utilised to improve life for everyone. We toured Rhodesia with them, first to the spectacular Matopo Hills near Bulawayo where thousands of granite boulders, some as high as skyscrapers, stand as silent sentinels in the bright sunlight. Their multi-coloured lichen rock faces, thousands of years earlier, enticed wandering bushmen artists to add their decorations and impressions for us to see and appreciate. Between the trees and boulders in that natural cathedral, the Matabele ancestral spirits mingle with that of Cecil John Rhodes, whose grave is carved into solid rock and who loved the hills with passion. The spirit of the Matabeles and Rhodes are in the same 'well', if one likes it or not, and only when the past colonial era is appreciated, with its failures too, and its memory cherished, will strong decent men re-emerge in that region. Finland never criticises its former colonial masters, but expresses gratitude. 'We are great because of our past', I have heard it said. 'Input from others can make us even greater.' Wise words for Africa and the churches to ponder on. Greatness is to acknowledge that fossilised dogma is unsustainable and that new input is essential for growth. Humans are not born sinners as the Christian church would like us to believe. We are born ignorant of spiritual laws in varying degrees, therefore are not born equal. To acknowledge wrongdoing does not automatically merit pardon or the blotting out of past wickedness, but by learning from wickedness it can become an instrument for progress towards greater understanding and ultimately 'Heaven' for the individual, and no revenge is called for. A perceived enemy can be the instrument to greatness.

My parents loved Bulawayo with its tree-lined streets wide enough to turn a span of oxen, beautiful colonial buildings, a museum second to none and an extensive glorious park in Selborne Avenue where a police orchestra played during tea, which was served with scones and jam on the lawn. It was a city from where the railway line would have branched off to Cairo via the Victoria Falls Bridge, had Rhodes's dream come true. The road to Victoria Falls winds its way through forests of Rhodesian teak and African villages, over the 'stone that burns', the first name for the Wankie coal fields, then passes through an eroded hilly area where aeons ago water from an interior lake made its way. A night was spent in the gracious Victoria Falls Hotel and early the next morning, before too many other tourists came on the scene, we went and stood next to the statue of Dr Livingstone. It overlooked that long magnificent falling flow also called 'The Smoke That Thunders', Mosi oa Tunya 'which must have been gazed upon by Angels in their flight', that flung aside the veil to the divine. The mind became still, and in the rainbow

Angels sang an ode to beauty. Dr Livingstone is not alone! We experienced what I believe is union with the divine, that awesome feeling no human words seem able to describe.

My relationship with my parents expanded and we discussed life, death and mystical things as if we were talking about planting potatoes. They loved the discussions, the speculation, and the thoughts that try to formulate the unknown. At times they became youthful and full of enthusiasm for all the fun that the afterlife may offer. The ultimate journey is our certainty, and should be viewed as life's joyous fulfilment and left to unfold, that is, if we do not burden ourselves with preconceived ideas and unfinished business before departure. 'As you sow, so you reap.' It would be great if we all could die with the love and appreciation I saw in my parents when they finally rode the wave to their new macrocosmic home.

Ulrich's marriage brought about the building of another house on the hill, which was completed in 1974. I designed it in typical African style with round rooms, a thatched roof, no ceiling and a veranda with excellent views over the lands and coffee plantation below, which by now was ready to produce. After the first year of frustration the cotton and maize farming had turned out to be very successful, and now the coffee was promising. The scent of flowers, earth and growing things mingled with the wafting music of Mozart, Handel and Beethoven, vibrating in the same space as the light from the twinkling stars of the clear Rhodesian night. We were close to having the ideal farming enterprise in an idyllic setting and a way of life we enjoyed. I met a girl and her little boy through a friend. They came out from Salisbury to visit the farm one Sunday. Meeting Diana, I somehow instantaneously felt that I had met my other self or soul mate, but unfortunately Diana was going through a difficult time with a separation and probable divorce at a later date. She, in her own wisdom, preferred not to visit or see me again, but wanted space to sort out her dilemma in her own time, which I could only respect, although her image had etched itself into the deepest part of my being, there to stay, as an eternal companion. If I never saw her again I could live with that, but in some mysterious way I felt that if I did not see her again, my whole philosophy of life's interconnectedness beyond the physical, and spiritual purpose, was in jeopardy. I had no idea how I should meet her again or if I was even waiting at all. My cottage on the hill was completed while I served my first stint in the police reserve outside our own Gatooma area.

Mr Ian Smith's negotiations had not produced positive results although nearly all whites and ninety-six per cent of the Asian population had accepted the latest British Lord Pearce agreement proposal for majority rule within ten years. That would have given the African politicians ample time to slide into the democratic process. But the 'freedom fighters' said, 'It is not a question of taking over government. It is not a racial conflict either, the whole system must change. We do not want to inherit a colonial western system, we want Marxism-Leninism.' The Lord Pearce plan failed because the Commission was able to contact only six per cent of African adults, mainly through mass meetings. It was on that basis that the Commission found the proposals were not acceptable to the people of Rhodesia and therefore not implemented. Displaying typical African behaviour, the masses of ordinary people stayed away from the Commission's meetings, simply disinterested or intimidated by insurgents. The communist insurgents gained wind in their sails. The Soviets poured arms into Africa, and military training camps for volunteers and forced recruits sprang up in many countries. The Soviets had not hesitated to proclaim their policy goals. As long ago as in 1957 in his book, Maj. Gen. Lagovakje of the USSR drew attention to the fact that the US has almost no chrome of its own and that the material is essential for the production of alloys for jet engines, gas turbines and armour-piercing projectiles. This, he said, was the weak link of the US and one which the USSR should exploit. Rhodesia had chrome.

The USSR believed that by controlling Africa they could cut off supplies to the US and strangle them into submission, failing to realise that they were pursuing decoys of entrapment. Vietnam had shown and taught the US that superpowers cannot win a battle with sophisticated weapons against guerrillas, who melt into the hills and bush, blending with the local population. It is too expensive to use fast-moving aircraft and missiles to try to kill one guerrilla hiding in a grass hut which he can rebuild the next day. This was the US attitude: Let the Russians get into Africa under the banner of Africa's final liberators, the liberation movements seem to welcome them anyway. Then when the Soviets, after establishing their puppet regimes, can't deliver better life to the African masses, the US will finance and establish a relatively cheap guerrilla uprising against the USSR-sponsored regimes to drain USSR resources to the point where the socialist Soviet goal of world domination will not only destroy the participating countries, but the motherland itself. We now know the outcome. It worked with disastrous consequences for Africa, and the Soviet 'empire' did indeed collapse. Europe and America had no fatalities, nuclear war was avoided and the threat of global war reduced. As my Muslim friend in Kenya had said, 'Politics is like a chess game, the pawns fall first.' In the early Seventies the USSR increased its spending on arms phenomenally, while US strategic spending fell by eight per cent per year. Rhodesia was among those to be sacrificed. The CIA built a huge airport near Gatooma with underground shelters and hangers. What for?

We were no longer in the cold war conflict zone. It had escalated to a hot war with land-mines indiscriminately planted on country roads. After five peaceful years, Ulrich and I were now called upon to help protect contractors installing an electric fence along the northern border to prevent communist insurgents entering Rhodesia and planting land-mines, burning schools down and terrorising the local African population, capturing by force new recruits. In the long term, therefore, this protected our own area too. My first call up was for fourteen days in Mukumbura to guard the fence workers. We flew there in an old DC 3, low enough to make treetops bend and local Africans and chickens run for shelter. That was apparently done because intelligence knew that heat-seeking missiles had been brought into the area, and by flying low we would be out of sight before a missile could be fired. The camp itself was very desirable, had it not been for the purpose we were there. It was what tourists would pay many hundreds of dollar a day for. It was an uninhabited river valley with plenty of elephants and other game. There were superb meals, good comradeship, good discussions and plenty of time to read books, and no obvious indication of war. But that is what guerrilla warfare is all about, until suddenly bullets are flying from all directions. My second stint with five other farmers was in the Sanyanti bridge area, forty kilometres west of Gatooma but within our area. Our mission was to stop road traffic and search vehicles for weapons. Here we had no permanent camp, and slept between the trees and cooked in a pot hanging on a wire from a tree branch. We took it in turns to be on the road while others rested or walked around. On one of my walks I went under the Sanyati bridge. No water was flowing in the river at the time and one could walk in the sand from side to side under the five-metre-high bridge between concrete pillars. It was here my memory rolled back to

Kipipiri, and history repeating itself, because the pillars had been used as blackboards inscribed with Bible related messages. They had probably been composed by learned men from a nearby Catholic mission station. 'Jesus is waiting for his second coming. He cannot come before scriptures are fulfilled, therefore rebel against authority and against your parents as the Bible requests you to do, to fulfil prophesy. Everything, all evil has to be broken down. Christ in his wisdom will rebuild society for the people, the young, who will survive, live and rule when all of old has gone into eternal fire of brimstones.' What an abhorrent distorted message! On the other side there was more of the same nonsense. 'You must hate your brother, sister, father and mother. All individually must serve the new kingdom, and none must have allegiance to family. The new state is your family and the new leader will represent Christ on earth. Schools will be restructured. Teachers are wanted, learn to teach and be between the elect. Takawira.' 'Takawira' was a powerful African spirit entity.

I got hold of Roy, our team leader, and showed the writings to him and also told him about how the Mau-Mau had utilised biblical scriptures for political propaganda. It was obvious that the message on the pillars was written by a well-educated person who was a believer in communism. Roy did not share my concern and reckoned that the writer had just diverted slightly from the biblical message and in his opinion it was not a communist revolutionary recruitment placard. Most Rhodesians were of strong traditional Christian background and somewhat naive – naive as babes in the wood – and would not accept that the church could possibly be involved in subversive activity, preaching liberation theology in the physical sense. At my request we drove to the nearby Mission station and were promptly told by a white priest to move on. We excused ourselves by saying that we were investigating a murder case and believed that a reliable witness was to be found in their hospital wing. He asked for a court order. We left, but knew that they were hostile to us. Young Africans passed from one building to another without casting an eye in our direction. This was very unusual behaviour and enough to tell us that something untoward was going on. But our job was specific, not to interfere with or disturb public life or investigate possibles and maybes. We lived in a free country where freedom of association was protected by law. As the bush war escalated further, it became apparent which missions were teaching the biblical, spiritual messages of love and compassion, and which were in cahoots with the murderers. Many great upright priests, white and black, were butchered and killed in cold blood by 'freedom fighters' because they rejected violence and communism as an extension of Christ's message. The World Council of Churches gave religious respectability to the whole terror movement by calling it the 'Programme to Combat Racism'. Before the programme's inception in 1970 it was unthinkable that prominent church leaders should support murder and mayhem to overthrow the social order, whether 'just' or not. Today it is taken for granted that the 'armed struggle' (bayoneting babies and raping women) is a legitimate and sometimes unavoidable method of securing 'liberation'. The first African president of Zimbabwe (the new name for Rhodesia), Reverend Banana, proved the point when he was asked, 'Would Christ support the liberation struggles in the world today?' He replied 'When I look at a guerrilla I see Jesus Christ... The guerrilla dies that we may have life.' This quotation is from *The Herald* 2nd November, 1980. Did not Solzhenitzyn warn us 'that foremost among their gravediggers will be deluded Christians in the West?' And now in 1997 the world asks, 'What has gone wrong in Africa?' A huge part of the Christian church was hijacked and acted as an organ for communism, and as Solzhenitzen predicted deluded Christians of the West paid for the destruction of Africa. I am a firm believer in all religions that promote the principle of love, compassion and spirituality, and I see that in most religions, where no distorted interpretation by man in his desire to rule has occurred. But I also firmly believe in the karmic law of cause and effect which implies that we as individuals have to live with 'what we have sown'. I wish no damnation on anyone, but I think it is overdue time for all who gleefully saw Africa destroyed and helped to finance the mayhem, to go there now and help in its reconstruction. Congo, Rwanda, Mozambique, Angola, just to mention a few, need help. The alternative, ghastly to contemplate, is a reincarnated life in a black body in one of those countries with oppression, torture, poverty and AIDS rampant. Maybe it will take more than one lifetime to compensate for the suffering many socialists and deluded Christians wilfully supported and contributed to. Do not worry about time, a million years here and there makes no difference to the Universe, and black bodies are not in short supply, but remember the road to hell is paved with good intentions.

After the Sanyati police patrol I discussed the church implication in the recruitment of 'freedom fighters' with Kenani, our farm foreman, who had by now also joined the police reservists without even telling us. He had not been to the Sanyati area, but he had heard rumours that recruitment was taking place. Being quick-thinking he sent his nephew, named Witness, to Sanyati the following day by bus. Witness returned overwhelmed by what he had found out, basically confirming what I had suspected and more. He said that many boys and girls had been promised money, higher education and high positions in the new Zimbabwe Marxist government if they joined the 'freedom fighters', and many others had been kidnapped by gangs during night raids on homes and carted of to Zambia, not to be heard from again, to the distress of their parents. That information was passed on to the Gatooma police intelligence unit who undertook not to come and interview Witness. Nevertheless, the following day a police car turned up in our farm village and asked for Witness. Being a sincere young African he repeated the whole story. That was not the right way to conduct an investigation in Africa and the investigating officer should have known better. I was worried and annoyed by their blatant method. Witness was later run over by a fast-moving car and died. The killers did not stop and not much could be done about it.

As the insurgents infiltrated more areas, the call-ups became more frequent. One of us, Kenani, Ulrich or I, was constantly away on duty. I did eighteen stints of fourteen days each with many days of training in between. One camp was protecting African road workers retarring a road. Another time we were supposed to block an infiltration route. In that camp a lone African came towards the camp at midnight carrying a bundle on his head. The person was requested by one of our African police mates to stop or return to where he or she had come from, but the black shadow kept on moving towards the camp. Was it a suicide bomber? Or a decoy with AK-carrying snipers in the bush following him? Impossible to tell. We were given instructions to stop him, but not to make any approach. A few minutes later another radio message instructed us to shoot him in the leg. That was done. We then approached the area from two different directions and found a scared old African woman kneeling on the path with a round bullet hole in her leg below the knee. A Land-Rover was summoned to the scene. I helped her into the vehicle and drove with our commander to a Mission station fairly close by for initial treatment. The commander gave me a warning. 'This is probably what the "terrorists" are expecting, that we will take her to the mission station, and a land-mine is waiting in the road for us. Most likely they forced her to walk towards the police camp.' The old wrinkled African woman, crying with pain, managed to tell us that she had indeed been forced by 'soldiers' to walk towards the police camp in the dark, knowing full well that she may get shot. At the mission station, the white German superior, very annoyed and hostile, did eventually agree to assist while arrangements were made to have her flown by helicopter to Salisbury the following day for further treatment. It was a ridiculous affair. An old women had been injured, for what? Anger took the better of me. I can't exactly say who I was angry with, but I felt that something had to be done. At the Mission station before we departed the police officer asked for a volunteer to travel with us back to camp – a way of avoiding land-mines, he explained. 'These guys here know what is up, and having one of them in the Land-Rover makes our journey safe. If he refuses, we stay put.' Driving back in the dark, with occasional lightning from a far-off thunderstorm to be seen, thoughts raced through my head. A mixture of anger, resentment and frustration. 'God so loved the world, that he left, so men could become beasts and killers', passed through my head. 'Let evil kill evil, and get out of the way. If Africans want to murder one another why don't we just let them get on with it?' Then I remembered stories about Germany from the Second World War. Sweden, at some point having been requested to investigate the rumour of genocide, sent a delegation to Germany, who were wined and dined and reported back that Germany was a very law-abiding country and not involved in mass murder at all! The world observers only see what they want to see. If I announced that one sole African elderly women had nearly died – been shot in the leg because of etc., etc., who would care? Madness had infiltrated an inspiring land of great potential, where solutions could easily have been found to fairly straightforward problems, if it had been left to the people of the country to find the solutions. But outsiders had started a chaos that would be very difficult to stop. The early morning patrol was getting ready to go out when we got back to camp. I was supposed to have driven with the V-shaped truck, but because of my late arrival jumped into the back of a normal truck that followed the land-mine-proofed vehicle. Two kilometres from camp, the V-shaped vehicle driving fifty metres in front of us hit a land-mine and blew up. A front wheel with part of the front axle and part of the engine flew high in the air, and the truck stopped one metre short of plunging into a ravine. There was chaos all around, with police reservists from diverse backgrounds trying desperately to remember what to do in that situation. I stayed in the back of my truck, lying flat between the sandbags waiting for bullets to fly, but the expected ambush did not follow. Some of the reservists suffered burst eardrums but there was no other injury. A letter was found near to the mine crater, reading, 'Thanks for shooting our mother in the leg'. I asked myself how the hell did the land-mine planters know that the old woman was shot in the leg? Only from the Mission station!

I had had enough and took a holiday to Denmark, intending to stop over for a week in Israel where I arrived during Yom Kippur holidays exactly a year after a war there. I hired a taxi with a Christian Arab chauffeur and saw all the historical places from Tel Aviv to Jerico, and swam in the salty Dead Sea in record time. Two days were spent wandering around the Old City. But I had become hypersensitive and saw ruins of war and catastrophe in nearly all directions. I picked up mental pictures of battle upon battle in the same places, like many war films being shown on a TV screen simultaneously. In the garden of Gethsemene during an evangelistic meeting, the stage collapsed, and having some form of weird bird's-eye view of the setting I found it pathetic. During early evening I found a heap of rubble shaded by an old olive tree near a corner of the Old City wall overlooking the Mount of Olives. There I sat and cried by myself for myself, for Rhodesia... The next morning I changed my ticket and flew to Denmark where I had a serene holiday with my parents for four weeks.

In my absence Ulrich had made more improvements on the farm. Electricity and telephones had been installed. The lands had all been prepared for the new season. The coffee had flowered and a very good crop was expected. The African farm village had a new water pipeline put in for irrigation of their vegetable gardens in the dry season. We had other visitors from overseas who were enraptured by the beauty and the friendly atmosphere that prevailed in Rhodesia, despite the war that was taking place in the border areas. But the war spread further, to include ambushes on tourists travelling on the main roads, the first one near the Lion and Elephant Hotel, Bubye River. Police-escorted convoys had to be introduced. And farmers, cattle ranchers in the south of the country, had to have protection, because after Mozambique had been taken over by communists, insurgents began to infiltrate from the south-east. The army was short of manpower to seek out infiltrators. We were called upon to report to the army because they had decided that we were young enough to serve in that capacity. That was where we put the limit. Ulrich and I took off our Police Reserve uniforms and said 'goodbye', ready to accept the consequences. We were called back, to explain that we were Danish citizens with Rhodesian residence permits, and that army service would put us in the category of mercenaries, which was totally out of the question, whereas Police Reserve duty to maintain law and order was acceptable. The army officers stared at one another and with no other fuss handed us back our various papers and said, 'Okay, go home.'

'Brightlighting' was the name for protecting cattle farmers. This means that the serving police member had come from Salisbury, from the bright lights. It consisted of protecting farmers, mainly cattle ranchers, in the border area with South Africa. A crazy idea. Sometimes we left our farms vulnerable to protect part-time farmers who lived in South Africa and came to Rhodesia now and again to count their cattle. In between their visits African employees took care of the farms. On one such stint the farmer had a heart attack, and I was called in to the enormous house from the horse stables where my food was served – fortunately I love horses! I was to protect the family, but not to upset the daily routine of the farmer, his wife and two teenage daughters. He recovered. But I must admit my heart was not with that family. I was sickened by their attitude. Once at another farm I guarded, after the departure of the husband to South Africa for the day, his wife screamed blue murder that she had burned herself on the stove and needed to be bandaged. Her hand was a burnt mess, she maintained, but my eyes saw nothing of the sort. I bandaged her hand and quickly disappeared between the many trees of the lowveld farm and talked to the cattle. On yet another farm in the area, the owners decided to spend a weekend in Messina, South Africa. After packing the vehicle they asked me to escort them and open two gates out to the main road where they would join the southbound convoy. No one considered who should escort me back to the farm, and cover me when I had to stop to open and close farm gates, or who should help protect the farm in case of an attack in their absence. I withdrew my concern, and left the rifle in the Land-Rover when opening gates, and for the night I found a clump of trees well away from the homestead where I slept. Had anyone attacked the farm, they could have done so with no retaliation from my side. Some of the people I had dealings with here were of a strange breed and not what I referred to as Rhodesians. During that time the rail traffic to and from South Africa ceased. Rumour had it that South Africa was putting pressure on the Rhodesian government to opt for a South African-sponsored solution to the political stalemate. Ian Smith subsequently travelled to Pretoria to meet the South African head of state, Vorster. That was in September, 1975. 'South Africa is taking revenge on English-speaking Rhodesia – remember Rhode's raid on Pretoria, and the Boer War concentration camps' was whispered in the 'dark', and Rhodesians became wary. At police briefings we were constantly told that 'We are here to maintain law and order until the politicians find a solution.'

Who could find solutions when one side had no intention of participating in discussions, but was determined to take the country by bloody revolution? The revolutionary leaders did not only want the white-dominated government out, they also preferred an escalation of war enabling them to tyrannise the African masses into submission, so as to make them obey the Marxist system later with absolutely no opposition. With the ongoing war property prices were falling rapidly and the new masters would get what they wanted for a song. With that scenario in mind I crept into my sleeping-bag under a clump of trees on a strange farm wondering if the time had not come to change location, to quit Rhodesia, but to where? I prayed, asking questions of higher powers who seemed to be totally disinterested in man's phoney power game, manipulation and greed. I asked for meaning in existence. I meditated, fell asleep and drifted away to the land beyond conundrum where drawings talk. And here is what I saw on the board for 'Gods in the making'.

Reducing the unfolding of man's purpose to one drawing on a board during the night was like expanding the mind to encompass the entire universe. What was going on?

Was the dream vision supposed to explain everything? Was it some sort of 'theory of everything'? My memory of the drawing was clear and while having morning coffee in my solitary situation I drew the vision on paper and some days later sent a copy to my parents in Denmark. As illustrated we are spirits inhabiting bodies, but the spirits have to gain experience and 'grow' through all the growing mediums that exist, crystals, plants, animals and then humans. Presently we have become preoccupied with our mechanical brain and its manipulative ability and thereby have separated ourselves from our spiritual self, and communication can really only take place when the brain ceases to roam and wander. We should remember that the brain is merely a tool for the Higher Self. Intuition is communication with the Higher Self. In the build-up of human society, a suppressive system has emerged where each institution protects its subjects by restricting the desired inclusiveness, and things become fragmented. The parts become formalised and fossilised. The Higher Self loses energy and becomes semi-dormant. Only through 'cultivation' of the Higher Self by surrounding it with love can we re-establish sufficient contact so that at some point consciousness shifts to the Higher Self. When that happens the 'sting of death will be known no more' and the spirit entity can go through the 'ring of no return' and be among the Gods. In the meantime the law of cause and effect is in place, Karma and compensation drive the learning process, and rebirth is as sure as, Amen, in the church.

I have since used the diagram in evening meetings with friends where we discussed the growth of consciousness. My contribution was named: 'Emphasis on Variation of Consciousness'.

One day a learned man went out to sea in a little boat.

He asked the boatman, 'Tell me, my good man, do you know anything about astronomy?'

'No Sir,' replied the boatman.

'Ah, what a pity. One quarter of your life lost! But perhaps you know something about physics?'

'No Sir,' repeated the boatman.

'My poor man,' exclaimed the scholar. 'One half of your life gone to waste. But perhaps you know something about chemistry?'

'Never heard of it,' said the boatman.

'Oh, what ignorance,' lamented the scholar, 'Three quarters of your life completely lost!'

While this conversation was taking place, the boat was moving further and further out to sea, and soon a storm arose with heavy waves and high winds.

'Sir,' shouted the boatman. 'Do you know how to swim?'

'No,' screamed the scholar.

'Then, Sir,' said the boatman, 'You are about to lose four quarters of your life!'

There are many trees, yet not all of them bear fruits.

There are many fruits, yet not all of them may be eaten.

Many, too, are the kinds of knowledge, yet not all of them are of value to men.

We have many ways and possibilities of viewing reality. Pick any, look around, and evidence can be found to support your claim. That is how varied creation is.

Early man and primitive thinking man lived or are living in fear of a revengeful God, believing that whatever happens is due to the approval or disapproval of God. They have *religious consciousness*. Orthodox religion hammered down that belief system and man forgot his origin, his own divinity and his purpose.

Along came the modern technological and scientific age and everything is explained theoretically in separated fragments. We developed *mechanistic consciousness*. We have by now 'forgotten that we forgot' and scientists are trying to

Diagram Three: The Theory of Everything

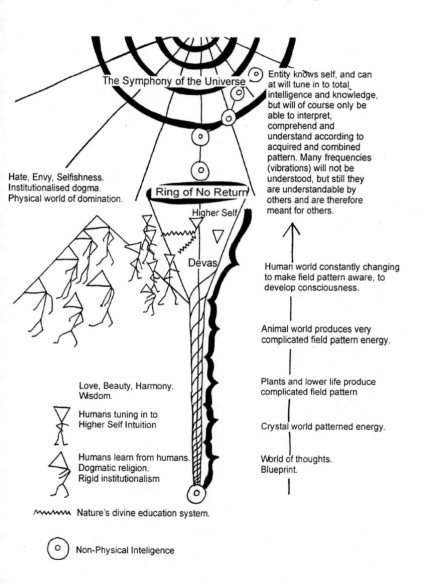

compose a unity out of fragments. Remember the blind men and elephant story. Over time this led to the worship of objective knowledge, the increasing quantification of all phenomena, the narrowing of the focus of our vision and our inquiry, and to a large extent the elimination of the sacred.

Power politics and the establishment of new models of a world society are a form of game politicians play. They are political scientists. In the East the system was called State Capitalism, and in the West, a cobweb of High Finance is the controlling factor. The system can be based on a computer model where the circuit is international finance. Individual humans have little meaning in the system. The model finds that the masses do not know what is best for themselves. Education is mainly geared to make us cope with and obey the system. Computer intelligence can predict the future according to information given to it.

The computer was asked, 'Does God Exist?' and the reply was 'Yes, now He does!' (Psycho Cybernetics).

One can only wonder what will happen in a 'storm'. Can we swim?

The 'storm' is here for all to see. We are *all* standing on the threshold of total ecological disaster because of our fragmented knowledge and of our desires to transform nature to suit our demands. The human population now far exceeds long-term carrying capacity and this will be aggravated by pollution and diminishing clean water. And as the triangle in the dream indicates, many of our traditional systems have become too rigid to allow nature's creative thrust to change them. Selfish forces dominate, and selfishness has the tendency to contract and to lock itself into static positions. We need, in meditation, to communicate with the 'Higher Self' and thereby follow the path to higher evolution. We need a shift in consciousness, a new *ecological consciousness* – and it will come, if we like it or not!

The life-force is one force and must be treated so. The whole is more than the sum of its parts. If we keep on unscrupulously destroying nature, soil life, forests and animals, we are in fact destroying our own spiritual composition. We have a shared foundation with all things, and remember, 'All mankind is born for perfection and each shall attain it will he but follow his nature's duty.' If we assume that the universe is spiritually alive and that we are spiritual agents, and if we act on this assumption, we shall find ample evidence that the universe is transphysical and transbiological – or simply spiritual.

To the divine mind the cosmos is divine. To the crass mind the cosmos is crass. To the monkey mind the cosmos is monkey-like. We have to rediscover our true nature, our Higher Self, the Divine Light that is connected to *all* life – omnipresent. When that is realised, we can live in harmony with all, and death is buried. The accumulated pattern of knowledge/wisdom/love will come to know Itself independently of the physical body.

We now enter the next stage – *cosmic consciousness*.

The universe is neither big nor small; neither beautiful nor ugly; the glow of mind fills the void and makes its space divine.

Mainly due to the constant call ups in the Police Reserve, and taking precautions against a future that seemed to head towards a Marxist dictatorship, Ulrich and I decided to put our beloved farm on the market for sale, to leave us free to leave Rhodesia should it become necessary. We still hoped however that some political settlement could be achieved with more moderate participants. Putting the farm on the market coincided with the letter from the Danish authorities suggesting departure was overdue. Selling something we had built from scratch, having employed thirty people who had become dependent on the farm's future, felt like a betrayal of trust and a betrayal of what is fundamentally right. On acquisition the farm was only a small piece of overgrown uncared-for land on planet Earth – on our floating ball in space. But some politicians had decided that certain geographical locations on that ball belonged exclusively to one group of people, or at least they used that to justify the killing of the 'uninvited visitor'. I saw the picture differently. We probably all have our origins in Africa. Maybe the reason that most Europeans who come to Africa melt and mix into the earth of Africa is that they are blending with their own past selves. Anyway millions of years ago small groups of people wandered away because of persistent overpopulation in relation to food available. These groups, over time, were exposed to different circumstances, seas and deserts, and the natural selection and elimination process eventually produced 'Adam', whose nervous system at times resonated and vibrated in tune with the universal creative force. God had been perceived and religion was born. The rest of the story is well-known. In 1956 when my parents emigrated to Africa and I met up with my distant relations, my ancient forgotten roots, the feeling of 'Here I can contribute', was overwhelming, and interaction commenced. But as it turned out, our African family at large preferred to do everything themselves. For a short time in human history that will be possible, but in the long term the human race has no choice but to join hands in a long line from the lowest all the way to merge with 'Heaven'.

Territorial rights and nationalism must eventually give way to the evolutionary doorway through which man can enter the cosmic realms. We all now have 'Adam's' nervous system. A dual type system. When seen from the physical side it is one system, but when the 'critical mass' is reached it changes to resonate in tune with The Universal Creative Force. With that initiation a new insight opens and the new system redirects the flow of energy, a reprogramming, and a reborn man emerges. Man and God will again walk together in the 'Garden of Eden'.

The sale of the farm was concluded in 1976 and we moved to Salisbury where we bought a house. Kenani left his employment and wandered off into the sunlight, feeling disillusioned and betrayed. He is now to be found in beer halls telling the tales of 'long ago when we…'

Ulrich and I intended to remain uncommitted until the end of the bush war, although we were called up for some light duties in Salisbury. He and Annette went overseas for an extended holiday and after a medical examination I was excused from carrying and firing a rifle due to a hearing problem which was aggravated by loud noise. I got used to my inactive life and in a way enjoyed it. I read the newspaper in the morning while having tea, boiled eggs, avocado pears and toast. Then I visited friends, often Erik, where others would participate in discussions asking what to do next, and 'Why can't we just have a normal change of government and a gradual change? Why must we have a Marxist dictatorship imposed on us? If the British committed a crime by allowing Rhodes to invite settlers to the country, surely that was not our crime? Since when do you punish sons and daughters for crimes grandfathers committed?'

To have something to do after Ulrich's return from Denmark we bought some old tractors which we rebuilt in Erik's yard and sold on open auction. We also looked at a number of farms for sale in case the war stopped and the political dilemma was sorted out, but for the time being preferred just to wait. In mid 1977 I left for Denmark, determined to locate another home somewhere. I went to Spain and looked at small holdings there, but although we had money in Rhodesia it could not be transferred due to strict exchange control, so I eventually offered our house to the Danish government who declined the offer.

While in Denmark I had a letter from Diana. My parents noticed that my opening of the letter was not 'normal' and asked questions that I could not answer. I had not read the letter yet. After three and a half years a letter, wow! She wrote that she was still in Salisbury, and that she had had a dream about me, in which I had lost my legs. Which in a sense was true. By selling the farm I *had* lost my legs, metaphorically speaking. She included her address.

I wasted no time, explained the situation to my parents, who were thrilled on my behalf, said goodbye, and took the first plane back to Salisbury. Back at home in Salisbury I saw Diana nearly every day. We had long afternoon walks in the gorgeous Botanical Garden. We sat under the trees and discussed philosophy, psychology, religion, mysticism and life in general while her little boy Bruno played on the lawn. A new life was in store for us. We decided to unite forces and get married. I phoned the news to my parents and Chris and Jutta only a few hours before signing the marriage documents in the magistrate's office. A few days before that an advert had appeared in *The Herald* advertising a commercial fishing business for sale in Kariba. A relatively small amount of money was involved, so while awaiting the outcome of the Rhodesian political and war dilemma we thought why not live in Kariba, where Chris had recently bought a house we could rent. The purchase of the fishing business was concluded the day after Diana and I got married.

Moving to Kariba

Commercial fishing for the small kapenta on Lake Kariba was relatively new when Ulrich and I bought Sea Farmers Ltd. The pontoon boat *Huhu*, acquired with the business, was the first experimental fishing pontoon on the lake. Before the massive Kariba dam wall was built, spanning the narrow gorge at Kariba, the Zambezi river would come down in flood for a few months of the year, inundating low-lying plains, but with the erection of the wall, water permanently flooded the entire valley, creating a lake more than three hundred kilometres long. Thousands of animals and humans of the Batonga tribe had to be relocated to make place for water and fish. The main reason for the dam, though, was electric power generation for industrial development in Salisbury and Bulawayo. The new environment was very different to the old flood or drought situation, but in a fairly short time plants, humans and animals adapted to the new ecological system, and for the newcomer it is difficult to visualise the valley without water. Trees along the water's edge have grown bigger and are green all year except in September/October when new red or light green coloured leaf pushes old overworked leaves off. The small kapenta fish, a freshwater sardine, was not indigenous to Zambezi river system, but was introduced from Lake Tanganyika. They adapted well and within a few years of prolific breeding were to be found everywhere in the lake and fishing could commence. The first commercial fishermen and the Fishery Research

Station worked in close co-operation to monitor replacement of stock, habits of the fish and methods of catching them. It was soon found that fish quantity was related to nutrient levels in the water so there was no real reason to restrict catches. Our coming to Kariba was not to make money but to be constructive while awaiting the outcome of the Rhodesian bush war. Rhodesia was still a well-functioning society, although we had to put up with the stresses and annoyances such as driving in convoys, and shortly after arriving in Kariba being bombarded by mortar bombs from the Zambian side. Most homes had bomb shelters for those occasions, constructed of old railway sleepers and sandbags. The mortar bombs appeared not to be aimed at any particular target but just stuffed into a tube and sent off. Five of us sheltering in a two-by-two-metre bomb shelter with the neighbour's shivering sweaty dog was not pleasant. Bruno's seven-year-old friend, Sebastian, who had been exposed to a similar bombardment before, dived into the nearest house on the way home from school after hearing the first bang, and commanded the occupants, who were newcomers, a women and daughter, to take refuge under the dining-room table with bed mattresses placed on top. This is an illustration of how quickly children learn to accept and react to situations to which most, fortunately, never get exposed. That particular bombardment of a dozen bombs only caused minor damage to our neighbour's harbour site and a transport vehicle. The company, Sea Farmers Ltd., consisted of a piece of land with a few drying tables at Andora harbour, a tin shack and old pontoon boat with a net and a small service boat with an outboard engine. Eight employees were keen to carry on working for the company's new owners, so they were hired.

Our house, No. 3, fifteen steps up from Muchurara Road, was a small shoebox-type house with two bedrooms, a lounge, bathroom and kitchen. Prefabricated under asbestos roof, nearly all the houses were identical and built on the slopes and the top of the hill for Italian workers during the construction of the dam wall. They were meant to have been demolished after the dam's completion, but instead were sold off to individuals for vacation or full-time homes. Ulrich and Annette rented a similar house on Syringa Road. Furniture was brought up from Salisbury and Diana established a small garden with a huge flowering bougainvillaea creeping up a tree as the main feature. The house faced east, with splendid views over bush land where lions, baboons, elephants and giraffes could be heard or seen on a daily basis. Leopards also hid in the bush but were seldom seen. Their desire for dog and cat meat meant that only those kept indoors at night survived. Baboons at times roamed between the houses but never on Sundays when the males of the human species would be around. For some reason baboons do not fear females. One day Diana sensed a visitor in the lounge and, emerging from the kitchen, saw an enormous baboon investigating the seating arrangement. Diana greeted him with a surprised 'Hah!' He responded with a similar grunt and walked leisurely out with his tail in the air, had a look around and descended the stairs. They were normally not aggressive but could be a nuisance if they decided to search the dustbin for leftovers. Since they would be convinced that the item at the bottom of the bin was the choicest, this resulted in a very messy back garden with papers flying in the wind. Many houses had dustbins in wire cages to prevent our cousins helping themselves. Bruno went to the local junior school which had a fantastic view over the lake.

Ulrich and I joined our boat crew eager to learn the fishing business. All was quite simple as long as the boat and equipment were in good order. We sailed out into deep waters at about six o'clock in the evening. When the echo sounder found what appeared to be a school of kapenta, we threw the anchor, and lowered the net through the centre of the pontoon where a four-by-five-metre hole allowed the net to hang down from four cranes, like a big bag. That was lowered to about fifteen metres below water level, and an electric lamp followed down to a position just above the rim of the net. A diesel-powered generator would run all night, supplying sufficient light for under the water and above. After the net and lamp had been lowered everyone would settle down for a cup of tea or a meal. After three hours of enjoying the clear night sky beneath millions of twinkling stars and at times a bright moon, it was time to lift the net. Four men would winch up the net with the lamp remaining in the net to which the kapenta had been attracted like thousands of moths around a candle. The net was then pulled up on deck and the fish crated with salt. That would take less than an hour and the net would go down again. If the school was large we would stay in the same place all night. Early in the morning the boat would enter the harbour with about six hundred kilograms of fish weighing a few grams each, which were distributed thinly on the drying tables. They would normally dry in one day in sweltering temperatures and were bagged in the late afternoon to make room for the next day's catch. The fish were sold to wholesalers in Salisbury who repackaged them for the retail market. Because of their long shelf-life and since they were a good source of protein they were sought after by an expanding market. During the day in baking heat we would do repair work to boat and net, and as far as possible avoid touching the bilharzia-riddled lake water.

Rhodesia's political problems drifted to a background compartment of our minds and we did not worry too much about them. We knew that Ian Smith had held meetings with Dr Kissinger of the USA on more than one occasion, and that 'one man one vote' and majority rule had been agreed upon and were to be introduced within a year or two. But sadly, the Nationalist Marxist movement, with its guerrilla fighters in the bush, did not want a negotiated arrangement. They wanted a revolutionary take-over. On 3rd March, 1978, Ian Smith signed an agreement with internal Nationalist leaders including the Reverend Sithole who at one time was the main militant leader, but had now fallen out with the other lot. That agreement entailed an election, a 'one man one vote' election. Needless to say, the external leaders refused to take part, so the result was a foregone conclusion, although the vast majority of voters opted for the new dispensation. We participated in the supervision and collection of ballot boxes, and as far as I am concerned the election was as free and fair as any election in Africa has ever been. But the Soviets, Cubans and their agencies were not going to give in to internal rearrangement. The USA saw fit to support and back dictator Mabuto Seko Seko of Zaire from where they supplied arms to anti-Communist guerrillas in African countries already controlled by the Soviets and Cubans, to keep the pressure up. The Soviets, though, were clever enough to stay clear of a possible jungle war in Zaire. Little Rhodesia, with a terrorised African population and a weary white population ready to accept Russians, Cubans, anyone who could stop the laying of land-mines in roads, had few options. I recall Prime Minister Ian Smith saying on one occasion, 'I don't want anyone to fight and die for an ideology,' but Ian Smith was a cattle farmer. What did he know of devious international politics and a 'cold war' with millions of land-mines planted indiscriminately? His views and values belonged to a different era. He was not a Churchill, although he had served in the war of all wars. He did not have a quick fix solution for Rhodesia or Africa – who has 'quick fix' solutions for Africa with its dictators, military coups and warlords, where in many places life has reverted to conditions not even imaginable to Western minds? I think we had accepted our fate and that was to stay in Kariba come hell or high water. At last change was coming to Rhodesia, and the land was to be called Rhodesia Zimbabwe.

Sea Farmers Ltd. was doing very well, and leaving it in the very capable hands of Ulrich, Diana and I decided to take a short holiday to South Africa, to swim in the salty Indian ocean, and to see Peter, ex-Kenya, his British-born wife Juliet and their five beautiful young daughters. I was godfather to the youngest. We bought our ticket for departure from Kariba on 3rd September, 1978. Bruno was to remain behind in the care of Ulrich and Annette.

The Aircrash

The red afternoon sun was about to set over the water of Lake Kariba. We stood waiting to board the plane, somewhat subdued and reluctant. We should have been happy and vibrant – were we not going on holiday? I put our foreboding down to the fact that we had left Bruno behind, but cancelled that thought, knowing he was in good hands. It was not school holidays and we would only be away for ten days. Apprehensively we stood there at the small airport looking at the setting sun while passengers of different races and nationalities, mostly holiday-makers, boarded, until an Air Rhodesian hostess asked, 'Aren't you travelling?' We could delay no longer and boarded flight 827 last. It was a four-engine Viscount named 'Hunyani', and we had to take the available seats which were in the back of the plane on the left side. We buckled up. There were no elephants to be herded off the runway so we had a normal take-off. Gaining height revealed the glittering sunlight reflected in the water. But we flew east towards Salisbury away from the lake, and were soon over dry bush country where smoke from bushfires could be seen here and there. The air hostess served drinks and I commented to Diana, 'We are flying over where you were born, we must be near Karoi.' I had just said 'Karoi' when the plane shook and a loud explosion was heard as fire poured out from the inner starboard engine. A surge of vibrating energy came over me, somewhat neutralising fear. On the intercom the captain announced 'Mayday Mayday.' No one screamed or panicked. An elderly person emerged from his seat asking for the fire extinguisher. No one answered him, but it was quite a sensible request. Diana took my hand and we sat still. Everything seemed to be very still and silent. Quietly my mind formulated, God I have not found out everything I want to know, I am not ready to die. The captain broke the silence by saying the plane was under control and we would shortly make a crash landing. 'Empty your pockets, take shoes off and hold your ankles.' The flames extended the length of the plane to the tail fin, like a gigantic acetylene welding flame. I wondered if it was possible with such heat to land the aircraft before the wing melted and fell off. We turned in a full circle while descending sharply. I whispered to Diana, 'Pray,' and another surge of energy went through my body, and my observing self somehow split up in two. I saw the ill-fated plane rushing down toward the impact point – but from the outside. I also saw myself sitting next to Diana with her hand folded in mine. Then there was an echo, like sound underwater, the captain saying, 'Brace for impact, heads down!' I automatically obeyed and squeezed Diana's hand, but somehow I also saw the tree branches passing the window, and then things turned black. Although black, I could hear what sounded like waterfalls, and had no knowledge of my own body. Then a white light formed in what appeared to be the end of a long black tunnel, and the waterfall sound changed to howling wind while I zoomed up the tunnel. About halfway up the tunnel I slowed down and the noise again increased. I reversed in the tunnel. It all seemed to happen in slow motion with no hurry or emotional attachment. Coming back to what appeared to be the beginning of the tunnel I started coughing. I had sand in my mouth. I tried to stand up, but some force held me down. I felt tired and wanted to sleep. A commanding voice said, 'Loosen your seat belt,' and the realisation that the plane had crashed and was now lying still, but burning, hit me. I saw some legs but my brain refused to register the horrible implications. My emotions were numbed. One women's red hair was being consumed by flames and others were on fire with folded hands over their heads lamenting 'Oh God, oh God', still strapped to their seats which had broken loose from the railing in the floor. I had no way of getting to them because of the heat and flames. Lying on my back, trying to push out or smash a window with my feet proved futile although I had not taken my shoes off. Glancing around I saw no instrument with which to break the window. I looked at myself – no injury or torn clothes – then I noticed a little crack in the fuselage and tried to open it. A man came to my assistance and together we managed to rip open a hole big enough to get out. By now my normal self was back, and I shouted through the hole, 'Loosen your seatbelts and get out.' I managed to lift a little girl out, reaching her from the outside of the hole. After putting her down, I went back to the hole and there was another child waiting, then another. Tony, the man who had helped enlarge the hole, started to take injured passengers away from the aircraft. The old man who had asked for the fire extinguisher emerged and collapsed down on the broken-off wing lying parallel to the fuselage. I asked him to move away because of the fire and possible explosion. He answered, 'Please leave me alone and let me die. What is left for me?' I rushed over, lifted him up and deposited him thirty metres away where others were standing. Then, realising that I had not seen Diana, the first feeling of panic came over me. I rushed back to the hole and shouted, 'Diana' and there she was standing just inside the hole with yet another child in her arms. A quick 'Thank you, God', and the pressure of tears was strong behind my eyes. Diana came out. Her skirt had caught fire and she had ripped it off, but she was not injured in any way. She said, 'It is too late for the rest, they are all on fire, get away from here.' She used my shirt to wrap around herself. We lifted and carried the air hostess away. She had a crushed leg and was drifting in and out of consciousness, but did manage to ask on two occasions, 'Did we get all the passengers out?' We put her down on a small patch of unburned grass, a hundred metres away from the crash site. Diana stroked her forehead, telling her not to worry and 'to float with the clouds'. She became very still and silent. I urged everybody to move further away because of the danger of explosion. A few minutes later, as predicted, the wing exploded in a mushroom fire-ball. The thought that we had been shot down entered my mind. It was still light, but would rescue manage to come before nightfall? I knew that the Rhodesian helicopters could not navigate without a visible horizon. September nights can get very chilly. With the group of thirteen now together, Diana suggested that we try to locate bandages and something to wrap around the air hostess who was shivering from cold and shock. We had seen suitcases on the ground near the crash site, but did not know if they had burned with the wing explosion. We left the group of survivors. A young teenage girl followed us a few paces behind, explaining that she now could not pay her taxes because her income tax returns had gone up in smoke. It was obvious that she was suffering from shock. Close to the still-burning fuselage we saw a pretty little Asian girl dead on the ground. Her face like a doll, she must have been thrown out during the crash. We passed suitcases and walked a bit further. I wanted to see if the area on the other side the burning fuselage was large enough for a rescue helicopter to land. We also noticed that the tail section of the plane had broken off behind the toilets lying separately some fifty metres away. I heard faint voices, and in a split second saw shadows moving behind long, burned, bamboo-like grass, about seventy metres away in the opposite direction to the survivors. Very briefly the possibility that communist-trained bush fighters could be in the area entered my mind, but I brushed the thought away. Knowing and having seen what these killers had done to many Africans and Europeans before, I think the thought was too terrible to contemplate and therefore the brain refused to entertain the possibility. We had just begun walking back when a burst of machine-gun fire opened up on us and in the direction of the surviving passengers. The same surge of energy went through my body as in the plane on the way down and no fear was registered. After running a few paces we dropped flat on the ground, and in the dusk a bluish hue seemed to encompass us. Bursts of an automatic AK-47 rifle firing with tracer bullets continued and came closer. The air was criss-crossed with red streaks. The killers passed us at about ten metres, storming toward the small group of crash survivors. After passing us they stopped firing indiscriminately, but still let off single shots while shouting. One off them yelled in English, 'We are your friends, but you have stolen our land, we will kill you.' They also shouted, 'Give us your valuables.' An elderly lady pleaded for the children, but to no avail. All were shot in a hail of bullets. Nice friends to have! I whispered to Diana, 'I think I can just as well stand up and try to reason with them.' She held me down and said that at the moment no reasoning would help. She had formerly worked for a firm in Salisbury responsible for defending captured insurgents on behalf of Amnesty International. She knew what to expect and she asked me to take her rings off so that the terrorists would not cut her fingers off in the process of stealing the rings. It was getting dark, silence had fallen over the area, but the bluish light was still to be seen. After about half an hour we decided to crawl away from where we had lain flat and very exposed on bare ground near the crash site. Slowly we crawled towards the grass patch where we had left the air hostess. Maybe we could get under it and be covered by the grass? Would the killers come back? We crawled past the corpses of the passengers, and close to the air hostess where we found a thirty-centimetre-deep ditch into which we could just fit with a little grass cover. I was nearly exploding and had to urinate, which I managed without getting my trousers wet. We stayed there for about an hour, after which numerous women, men and children came and raided the crash site for whatever they could find. It sounded as though someone was giving orders, possibly forcing the locals to cart away what they could carry – a typical insurgent tactic – to get locals implicated before the Rhodesian security forces arrived. The villagers left and stillness eventually settled over the area. While lying there, thoughts of how and why raced through my mind. I was amazed that I felt less anger towards the brutal killers, who had just shot and killed all the surviving passengers after a horrifying air crash, than towards my own fellow citizens of Denmark, Norway, Sweden and others who gleefully supported the communist revolutionaries with material and financial assistance. When will these people realise that Marxist-Leninist doctrine always turns out to be totalitarian and brutal and will resemble any other Marxist-Leninist state around the world? – one despairs that left-wingers beyond high school level cannot understand that. You cannot change a system or government for the better by giving it to terrorists. These were thoughts that came of themselves. A surge of energy again rushed through all my being and I relaxed and vowed, 'If we get out of this I will never waste my time on hatred or on negativity and become like one of "them", but I want to see true justice done even if it takes a thousand years.' At that very moment Diana whispered, 'Do you believe in reincarnation?' Whispering back, I answered, 'It is not a question of believing, I know, and I also know that God is on the side of life, otherwise life as we know it would not exist.' We heard footsteps. Then there was more movement in the burnt bushes and so we kept quiet and still for a long, long time. It must have been around midnight when four or five rifle-carrying men returned talking loudly and accommodated themselves very near us, where the air hostess was lying. We heard a lot of commotion and rattling and at one time a man came so close that I could see his legs and boots in the dark. They hung around for about an hour, gang-raped the dead body of the air hostess (we learned later) and then disappeared again. During that time I was constantly filled with what I keep on referring to as surges of energy. It was a type of meditation where the brain stops analysing and emotion and fear cease. Much later, believing ourselves to be the only ones alive, we decided to find a better place to hide, as we had no guarantee that rescue would come in the morning. After daybreak other curious wanderers could enter the scene. First we tried the tail section of the plane to see if we could crawl into the fin, but it was too noisy, just touching the metal sounded like a gigantic gong in the dark night. So we crawled about hundred metres eastwards where the bamboo-like grass was fairly thick. It had burned, but the long thin remaining sticks would afford some cover. Here we lay for the rest of the night, but the temperature had plummeted to a few degrees above zero. I had no shirt on and Diana only had my shirt wrapped around her and a light blouse. We froze and my jaw moved uncontrollably, making noises from clattering teeth. I turned to try to control the jaw movement, and eventually found that lying on my back with my neck lifted at a forty-five degree angle I could control the clattering. But I had no support under the back or head – a very tiring position. The sound of hyenas, a fearsome laugh from hell, added to our misery. Other animal sounds could also be heard. I tried to make some plan should a hyena emerge, but all I had was a metre-long stick picked up from the ground during our last move. While lying with my head in that awkward position I gradually sharpened the stick with my teeth so it could penetrate the body of an intruder. Fortunately that did not become necessary although we heard movements fairly close by on two occasions. Later in the day it was discovered that Tony, who initially had helped to open the hole in the fuselage, had run off as soon as the shooting had started and was hiding not very far from us. He had moved on, when we had moved, thinking our noises were caused by the killers or hyenas eating bodies. Dawn came very slowly after our longest night. Dogs barked in the distance and the sun rose gently as if nothing had changed, giving light to all in a misty smoke-filled environment. The crash had started a bush fire that had spread in all directions. Around nine o'clock we heard the first noise of searching aircraft, very faint and far away to the east. Some African children came close, but did not see us and did not enter the crash site. A few cows with bells around their necks came to drink water from a little muddy pond shaded by a large green tree twenty metres away. Their life had not been interrupted. Their time to have their throats cut and be eaten was to come another day. Many thoughts came and went and I argued with God. 'Give me a sign that higher powers do exist,' I requested silently. The 'answer' followed: 'You were invisible, not seen, and survived.' A brooding air of solemnity spread over the area and the warming rays of the sun increased. Still hearing aircraft flying far to the north east, Diana suggested that we try mental telepathy to direct the search party towards us. We had both experienced and read about 'other realities', out-of-body projection, mind-over-matter etc. for years, and had very strong convictions that the universal interconnected web was a fact. Like a fluid that encompasses all space, at all times, and that God-intelligence and wisdom or what we commonly refer to as 'GOD' somehow is 'that', and in that 'Pregnant Nothingness' the human consciousness inter-links to form The Universal Mind. In thought we entered the search plane, then entered the pilot's consciousness and directed him towards us. It worked. Five minutes later a Dakota was overhead. It passed, turned around and flew over us again dropping paratroopers, and circled until helicopters landed. We shakily emerged from our hiding place and a Rhodesian paratrooper established that we were not badly injured. He made us coffee while other paratroopers worked on the radio and investigated the area. Then Tony emerged from the bush and we shared a few words about what had happened and how he had fled when the shooting started. While waiting for the helicopter to fly us back to Kariba I wandered around and looked at the devastation in the glaring sunlight of day. The dismembered limbs and the scene of the massacre were painful. The little doll-like Asian girl now had a hole in her head – probably bayoneted. I addressed the Higher Reality, 'Through my eyes, the universal information web, see and understand what has taken place here and register it for ever, so the guilty and the perpetrators do not escape karmic justice.' A voice in my consciousness said, 'Amen.' Walking towards the helicopter, there in front of my eyes, glittering in the sunlight, I saw Diana's rings that had been removed earlier! I joined her near the helicopter, we boarded and flew off to Kariba. From the air the crash site was almost impossible to see because everything had been blackened by bush fires for kilometres in all directions and the air was very hazy and heavy with smoke. It so happened that by strange circumstance some weeks later we met the gentleman who was piloting the search Dakota, on that day. He had been trained as a pilot during the Second World War, and was on that fatal day using the usual grid pattern system to locate us. After being asked why he had abandoned the grid pattern search, he could only say that he suddenly had an inspiration that he should fly west, and since he had found nothing so far, why not? We did not elaborate because he was a nice practical 'normal' person and would possibly, like many humans, accept that intuition and inspiration exist but would find it difficult to accept the inter-linked mind-web system that links everything to everything else. But is that not the way healing and prayers work?

Many years later in the same country, now Zimbabwe, a friend asked us to accompany her to a spiritualist church where an African university lecturer was giving a talk followed by a clairvoyance session. His channelled sermon was very beautiful and uplifting and peppered with golden grains of love and compassion. He picked me out during the clairvoyance (we did not know anyone in the congregation except our one friend) and asked if I knew John and Brenda. I searched my memory and said, 'No, I know of no one by those names.' He elaborated and said that we had been involved in an accident, a big accident, together. I was still blank. Diana interrupted, 'John Hood was the pilot and Brenda the air hostess in the Viscount.' The clairvoyant continued to say that they were fine and they just wanted to say 'Hallo and Thanks'.

Being back in Kariba was like coming out of a sleeping nightmare. The last eighteen hours seemed unreal, but at the same time the door to 'Heaven' had been opened again, momentarily confirming my belief. My belief had been seen and experienced. The word 'God' seems meaningless unless one can have contact with 'It' and it would appear, as in deep meditation, that only by plummeting into the depths of darkness do we truly see the Light shine. But it also stands to reason that in darkness the light is more profound. The God-light of love is not a replacement of darkness or evil, although light dispels darkness. In the realm of God, darkness and evil cannot be.

In the hospital we bathed and our minor cuts were looked at. Bruno was overwhelmed to see us and so were Ulrich and Annette. They had heard that a helicopter had brought three survivors back to Kariba Hospital, only three out of the fifty-six passengers and crew! I saw the glow on their faces as they entered the hospital room and their gratitude that we had been spared, but I also saw others who turned away in uncontrollable tears. Their loved ones had been butchered or burned to unrecognisable ashes, never to be hugged or kissed again, and my heart cried out for them.

Numerous journalists and photographers came to the hospital, wanting stories for their respective papers and television channels. Later, back in our home, we refused to talk to those who thought that they had the automatic right to invade our life. Some phoned and made arrangements to meet us, and some came from Denmark. In most papers the story was related reasonably accurately, but some displayed a gleeful scorn – a serve-you-right attitude – as if I or ten young children or the rest of the passengers were responsible for Rhodesia's war with communist infiltrators. Hatred eventually destroys the fabric of society, so I will not even dwell on their stories. They are 'people of the lie' and they will have to live with their own world perception. In one story the name of the Granite Whamire hills where we had crashed was translated into 'From Here No One Returns'. Some well-wishing journalists thought we would be pleased by the news that the perpetrators had been 'brought to book', but we did not live in Oklahoma (bombing incident in 1996) and as far as I was concerned that was totally irrelevant and had nothing to do with true justice. Communist teenagers, brainwashed and trained to kill, will kill, especially when they are supplied with lethal weapons from countries that should know better. And when their leader Joshua Nkomo stood up in the US and other forums, and boasted about having shot down the plane with a Sam-7 missile, without even being told that his bestiality was totally unacceptable and outside civilised behaviour, it was too sad. I did not particularly want to see those teenagers killed because their action could not be compensated for by hanging them in the town square or sentencing them to jail. I was not that primitive, and it would not bring back the dead or console the bereaved either. I would have liked the world at large, especially the West, to have condemned the atrocity in strong terms and let it be understood that attacking soft targets, like civilian aircraft, is totally unacceptable, but that condemnation never came. As for Nkomo's young fighters and families, they were later (in Eighties in Zimbabwe) eliminated by the North Korean-trained Fifth Brigade under the pretext that they were dissidents. But that was part of the plan. Pol Pot of Cambodia is not one of a kind, others just manage to cover their tracks better. The lack of condemnation of the atrocity we had witnessed was to me the end of the civilised world and I considered most world leaders at that time to be nothing more than a bunch of hypocrites in cahoots with gangsters. My dream of whites and blacks in Africa, and humanity at large, holding hands in brotherhood, from the lower to the higher and merging with Heaven was temporarily shattered.

Diagram 4

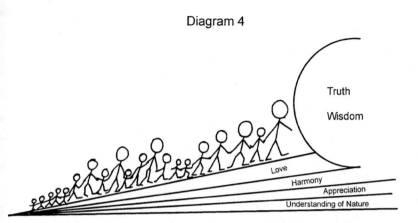

All of God is in all things, although not totally, but in some more abundantly and in others less. Because just as Divinity communicates with Nature, so one ascends to Divinity through Nature, as by means of a life resplendent in natural things, one rises to the Life that presides over them.

Bruno Giovanni, 1500

We thanked God for the songs of the birds and the warmth of the sun. We listened to Bach and Mozart and cried our hearts out. And we were overwhelmed with letters, flowers and gifts from well-wishers, many unknown to us. But the world leaders had died in my heart. No one could have said it better than The Very Revd J.R. da Costa at the memorial service in The Cathedral Church of St Mary and All Saints in Salisbury the following Friday, 8th September, 1978.

The Deafening Silence

'Clergymen', I am frequently told, 'should keep out of politics.' I thoroughly agree. For this reason, I will not allow politics to be preached in this cathedral. Clergy have to be reconcilers. That is no easy job. A minister of religion who has well-known political views, and allows them to come to the fore, cannot reconcile, but will alienate others, and fail in the chief part of his ministry. For this reason, I personally am surprised at there being two clergy in the Executive Council. It is my sincere prayer that they can act as Christ's ambassadors of reconciliation. My own ministry began in Ghana, where Kwame Nkruma preached: 'Seek ye first the political kingdoms, and all these things will be added to you.' We know what became of him. We are not to preach a political kingdom, but the kingdom of God.

Clergy are usually in the middle, shot at from both sides. It is not an enviable role. Yet times come when it is necessary to speak out, and in direct and forthright terms, like trumpets with unmistakable notes. I believe that this is one such time.

Nobody who holds sacred the dignity of human life can be anything but sickened at the event attending the crash of the Viscount 'Hunyani'. Survivors have the greatest call of sympathy and assistance of every other human being. The horror of the crash was bad enough, but that this should have been compounded by murder of the most savage and treacherous sort, leaves us stunned with disbelief and brings revulsion in the minds of anyone deserving the name 'human'. This bestiality, worse than anything in recent history, stinks in the nostrils of heaven.

But are we deafened with the voice of protest from nations which call themselves 'civilised'? We are not! Like men in the story of the Good Samaritan, they 'pass by, on the other side'. One listens for loud condemnation by Dr David Owen, himself a medical doctor, trained to extend mercy and help to all in need. One listens and the *silence is deafening*.

One listens for loud condemnation by the President of the United States, himself a man from the Bible-Baptist belt, and again the *silence is deafening*.

One listens for loud condemnation by the Pope, by the chief Rabbi, by the Archbishop of Canterbury, by all who love the name of God. Again the silence is deafening.

I do not believe in white supremacy. I do not believe in black supremacy either. I do not believe that anyone is better than another, until he has proven himself to be so. I believe those who govern or seek to govern must prove themselves worthy of the trust that will be placed in them. One looks for real leadership: one finds little in the Western World, how much less in Africa!

Who is to be blamed for this ghastly episode? Like Pontius Pilate, the world may ask 'What is Truth? What is to be believed?' That depends on what your prejudices will allow you to believe, for then no evidence will convince you otherwise.

So who is to be blamed? First, those who fired the guns. Youth and men who, as likely as not, were until recently in church schools. This is the first terrible fact. Men who went over to the other side and in a few months were so indoctrinated that all they had previously learned was obliterated. How could this happen if they had been given a truly Christian education?

Secondly, it is common knowledge that in large parts of the world violence is paraded on TV and cinema screens as entertainment. Films about war, murder, violence, rape, devil-possession and the like are 'good box-office'. Peak viewing time is set aside for murderers from Belfast, Palestine, Europe, Africa, and the rest, to speak before an audience of tens of millions. Thugs are given full treatment, as if deserving of respect. Not so their victims' relations.

Who else is to be blamed? I am sure that the United Nations and their church equivalent, the WCC, both bear blame in this. Each parades a pseudo-morality which, like all half-truths, is more dangerous that the lie direct. From the safety and comfort of New York and Geneva, high moral attitudes can safely be struck. For us in the sweat, the blood, the suffering, it is somewhat different.

Who else? The churches? Oh yes, I fear so! For too long, too many people have been allowed to call themselves 'believers' when they have been nothing of the kind. Those who believe must act. If you believe the car is going to crash, you attempt to get out. If you believe the house is on fire, you try to get help and move things quickly. If you believe a child has drunk poison, you rush him to a doctor. Belief must bring about action. If you believe in God, you must do something about it! Yet churches, even in our own dangerous time, are more than half-empty, all the time. We are surrounded by respectable heathens who equate belief in God with the Western way of life.

In many war areas, Africans are told to 'burn their Bibles'. If this call was made to us, what sort of Bibles would be handed in? Would they be dog-eared from constant use, well-thumbed and marked? Or would they be pristine in their virgin loveliness, in the same box in which they were first received?

There are tens of millions who call themselves believers, who never enter any house of prayer and praise. Many are folks who scream loudest against communism, yet do not themselves help to defeat these satanic forces, by means of prayer, and praise, and religious witness. For make no mistake, if our witness were as it ought to be, men would flock to join our ranks. As it is, we are bypassed by the world, as if irrelevant.

Is anyone else to be blamed for this ghastly episode near Kariba? I think so. Politicians throughout the world have made opportunist speeches from time to time. These add to the heap of blame worthiness, for a speech can cause wounds which may take years to heal. The ghastliness of this ill-fated flight from Kariba will be burned upon our memories for years to come. For others, far from our borders, it is an intellectual matter, not one which affects them deeply. Here is the tragedy! The especial danger of Marxism is its teaching that human life is cheap, expendable and of less importance than the well-being of the state.

But there are men who call themselves Christians who have the same contempt for other human beings, and who treat them as 'expendable'. Had we, who claim to love God, shown more real love and understanding in the past, more patience, more trust in others, the churches would not be vilified as they are today.

I have nothing but sympathy with those who are here today, and whose grief we share. I have nothing but revulsion for the less than human act of murder which has horrified us all. I have nothing but amazement at the silence of so many of the political leaders of the world. I have nothing but sadness that our churches have failed so badly to practise what we preach. May God forgive us all, and may He bring all those who died so suddenly and unprepared into the light of his glorious Presence. Amen.

The Very Revd J.R. da Costa
The Cathedral Church of St Mary & All Saints in Salisbury
Friday 8th September, 1978

Fishing in Kariba

After a week I was back at work – a way of returning to normality. We were determined to improve the fishing company and bring life back to normal. Catches increased to three tons per night, so suddenly it turned out to be a money spinner. We designed a building with office, storeroom, kitchen and toilet facilities and also a workshop with all the required equipment. The plans were submitted and approved by the local authority and construction commenced in January, 1979. We also had a new pontoon built in Salisbury named *Dudu*, meaning 'Insect' in Swahili. Due to economic sanctions certain parts were hard to come by but we improvised and never gave up, often using parts from scrapyards. For example, outboard gears were made from discarded differential axles of old cars. We had, in a very short time, re-established ourselves with a new business and began to love it. We planted flowers in the garden around the office, and irrigated the emerald green lawn. We often sailed out on to the lake in the service boat at midnight with a flask of coffee to check that crew and pontoon were okay, and would return gliding along on the dark water as the easterly sky began to gain morning light. Sometimes we would go camping with Bruno to one of the small islands, but crocodiles and spiders could be a problem.

Storms would occasionally make the water choppy and the boats would come into harbour, One evening after dinner the wind started howling and thrashing the trees ominously – heralding a fierce storm. That was the first night new *Dudu* was out fishing with a crew trained on *Huhu*. Because we lacked a universal joint, we had towed *Dudu* out to 'sea' and left her to fish in one location not far out of Andora harbour. I rushed to Ulrich's house and in a few minutes we had wound our way down the tarred looping mountain road. As we entered our harbour *Huhu*, meaning 'Hippo' in Batonga, moored. I took over command and with six crew sailed out of Andora Harbour again, with the two-cylinder Lister diesel engine working under full power against the howling warm wind and restless water. A rescue mission had begun. The lake was getting rougher. The strong wind blew from the west, forcing the water towards the Kariba side of the lake, creating, if it persisted, what old-timers called 'the bathtub effect'. That meant very high waves very closely spaced, giving a rough ride to the daring. Slowly but steadily, with directed spotlights, in the pitch black turbulent and foaming water, we closed in on the motorless pontoon. One moment they were below us and the next above us like two long-legged insects trying to copulate in a gale. After a few attempts Ulrich managed to throw the starting handle tied to a rope over on to the deck of *Dudu*, which the skipper promptly tied to the bow. At that very moment the anchor rope on *Dudu* broke. I did not have enough time or space to line up the two pontoons for the entry of Andora Harbour and decided to go out to ride the storm. Ulrich was busy covering the lighting plant to shelter it from waves breaking over the front of the pontoon. He also had another problem to handle. Some of the crew members got seasick and wanted to jump overboard into the boiling sea, taking off their life jackets in panic. I saw him tying them up with the help of one crew member. I lost my shirt moving around the rudder bar. It flew into the air. By lining up two lights on land I worked out that we were only maintaining our position. Ulrich saw my gestures and came close. Talking was of no use in the gale, but he somehow understood that we had to increase engine speed by adjusting the governor on the engine, which he did. That gave us a few knots' advantage over the elements. But at the same time we were being blown towards Zambia, which would be suicide. After an hour a position had been reached where by riding the waves I could possibly land the pontoons on a sheltered sandy little beach. But we had to pass moored yachts. I waved for Ulrich and shouted the idea into his ear. He reckoned that we should go a bit further toward Zambia before turning. After another hour I turned and headed for land. The speed increased to almost surfing speed, and just before hitting land, *Dudu*, being lighter because of the lack of an engine, overtook *Huhu* and swung around. As the ropes tightened she missed a yacht by a metre, but we had reached the sandy beach and our boats were saved. Many boats were smashed and lost that night. Walking away from the now-secured pontoon a yacht owner approached, greeting us. 'Well done, I watched you from the club all evening, you must come from the North Sea. I have taken a bet with someone…' We confirmed that we were Danish and indeed came from near the North Sea, leaving other parts of our African story out. 'I could tell,' he said and walked back to the club, inviting us to join him. We declined, because I had no shirt on, and my back was very bruised by constant battering on the railings behind the rudder bar. We never sent pontoons out again without self-sufficient engine power. And we did not have another storm. We developed a very good relationship with our African staff and a new legend of the Murungu who sailed out in the stormy night began.

We meet some wonderful people in Kariba and made friends for life. In small places like Kariba the shortage of people is compensated for by their eccentricity. Our friend

Dinah, coming home at night, would stamp the ground and clap her hands, shouting a warning to the snakes before entering her garden. The Kariba town clerk was eager to take bets on putting a postage stamp on the back of a black rhino. One day Ulrich and Annette went to Salisbury for a few days, so we undertook to water their garden. Under their big Marula tree the grass was sparse, and the spray of water made the soil muddy. For a wedding present someone had given them an elephant foot as a waste-paper basket. It was very well suited for making elephant footprints in the mud. To make the scenario appear realistic we went down the hill where we had seen elephant dung, heaps of it. Carefully, we uplifted the elephant excrement and carted it into the garden, leaving it in artistically arranged heaps. On her return Annette broadcast far and wide that elephants had stampeded in her garden. We did not have the heart to tell the truth, but one day Bruno unintentionally spilled the beans. This confirms that from children you hear the truth! Even with the extreme heat, which we combated by spraying the house and keeping the bath full of cold water for a quick dip, dust and dryness, and an odd earth tremor and the war, we were very happy in Kariba. We had dinner parties and discussed our favourite topics – the mysteries of life. I fished with Bruno between hippos, we found crystals and odd-shaped stones on our walks along the waterfront, we experimented cooking kapenta for breakfast and life was marvellous and filled with happiness.

Our life had returned to normal – we thought.

In October, an American connected to the International Pilot Association came to see us in Kariba, because obviously airline pilots world-wide were concerned that aircraft could be used as targets in political quests for power. If that type of terrorism were accepted in one country, it would become widespread in a world with many conflicts.

Newspaper headlines in 1979 read: 'US ENCOURAGES RHODESIA TERRORISTS' and 'WHY US HUSH ON TERRORISM?'

No wonder airline pilots were worried! Even the Soviet Union's commercial pilots joined with other civilian pilots of the world, condemning Nkomo's murder of civilian airline passengers and crew.

Our delightful and welcome American visitors, Ellie and George, were also interested in the spiritual side of man's life, possibly their main reason for coming to Rhodesia. Rhodesia was a haven for spiritual awareness. They were involved in, and learning to understand, the soul's journey in higher dimensions and believed that 'soul travel' is an art that can be developed and practised before physical death occurs. They left us some wonderful books on the subject. I am in full agreement with most of what that movement stands for. But that said, I believe all spiritual teaching to be of great value. We had good discussions while cruising on the lake in our little boat. They were particularly interested in 'The Blue Light' described earlier, which appeared during the shooting of the passengers after the crash. Later, in a letter, they wrote,

> *As a result of that talk, I have been notified that the ECK Mata Journal once-a-year international publication for Eckankar – would like to do a story about you both, and learn more about the blue light! Not so much from a political viewpoint, as from a spiritual viewpoint, for as you know the presence of a Master is very often seen as a blue light!*

They were very mystified and very concerned as to why a visa to the USA for Diana was refused. Why could Hans and Diana not come to the US together? they asked.

After the crash and massacre we had been approached by a group of American citizens, asking that we travel to the

USA to give talks on the subject. We accepted the invitation, but after repeated applications to the US consulate in Johannesburg, the visa for Diana was turned down on the grounds that she held a Rhodesian passport. What else could she hold? She had been born there! We gave up the US visit. The US consulate in Johannesburg requested that we furnish evidence of 'binding obligation which would establish beyond any reasonable doubt that it is your intention to return to Rhodesia', which we did. One bind was that Bruno would stay behind in Rhodesia, and secondly, there were my property/business interests. The visa was refused. Section 212 (a) (26) states that 'As the bearer of a Rhodesian passport, you are ineligible to receive a United States visa'. That Diana was possibly related to the renowned American-Indian Princess Pokahontas's lover or husband was of genealogical interest to us, not that it should have made any difference to the visa application. But why were they scared of us?

Joshua Nkomo, the external nationalist leader who proudly and laughingly had stated to the world press that he was behind the downing of our flight, had no problem entering the US on repeated visits. As a matter of fact he was there when I eventually did go alone.

On one such visit Nkomo said, 'Violence is the only answer,' a common attitude of frustrated criminals who only feel powerful when perpetrating atrocious deeds. He added that Britain and America dared not recognise the New Rhodesian government of the internal settlement headed by Bishop Abel Muzurewa because, he said, 'Any government... that will act in a manner regarded by us as hostile to the interests of our people will be branded an enemy... Your country is still healing the wounds of Vietnam. It does not need other wounds.' On the same visit Nkomo was also met by several religious leaders, among them C.T. Vivian and Rev. Ralph David Abernathy of the

Letter from US Consulate

CONSULATE GENERAL OF THE
UNITED STATES OF AMERICA

P.O. Box 2155 Johannesburg 2000

November 13, 1978

Mrs. D. Hansen
P.O. Box 16
Kariba.
Rhodesia

Dear Sir/Madam:

This office regrets to inform you that it is unable to issue you a visa because you have been found ineligible under the following section(s) of the Immigration and Nationality, as amended: (Only the checked items apply to your case)

/_/ Section 212(a)(15) which prohibits the issuance of a visa to anyone likely to become a public charge.

/_/ Section 221(g) which prohibits the issuance of a visa to anyone whose application does not comply with the provisions of the Immigration and Nationality Act or regulations issued pursuant thereto.

xxx/xx/ Section 212(a)(26) As the bearer of a Rhodesian passport, you are ineligible to receive a United States visa.

Further consideration will, however, be given to your visa application if you obtain and present to this office the following: A passport of another nationality. The Consulate General is able to issue a visa to your husband, since he holds a Danish passport. Please advise if you wish his visa issued. In the meantime, his passport will be retained in this office pending your reply. The documents enclosed with your letter are returned to you herewith. Your passport is also returned.

Very truly yours,

John D. O'Shaughnessy
Consul of the United States

Southern Christian Leadership Conference. His visit was called by Abernathy a 'great blessing'. Terrorism had triumphed and the black leaders of a band of guerrillas from Africa held the US administration to ransom! Or had the great US President Carter capitulated to yet another reverend's (Jim Jones) philosophy? 'Life is a gamble and I'd damn well rather gamble on the side of communism. You sure don't gamble on the side of capitalism when there's nuclear weapons bristling and you face the fact that half the world is suffering from starvation. I don't see that capitalism is the way to live. I look at what Castro has done, and I think he has done tremendous things. I wish I'd had his circumstances, being in an island, fighting a real battle, and winning a revolution, and had the challenge of building a society, a nice society. But some of us are not born with that opportunity. Now, being a foreigner in a country that can't be openly Marxist-Leninist is frustrating to me.' And speaking about himself he said, 'I take this goddamn church as a communist who believes in nothing. That is how religious I was (and still am)...' (AIM report – published by Accuracy In Media Inc. Vol VIII, February 1979, No.4.)

The same Nkomo who gave 'blessings' in Morehouse College, USA, and who professed to fight racism, has recently stated in Bulawayo, Zimbabwe, that Aids is an epidemic that was 'harvested by whites to obliterate black people'. Who may I ask sows seeds of hatred?

Since our visit to the US had not materialised, Diana and I visited Denmark, where we spent quality time with my ageing parents and played in the snow. While there we went to Copenhagen and paid a morning visit to a government ministerial department. I took the liberty of asking our host what people like Diana and I should do in the light of the Western world's governments' unrelenting desire to install a communist regime in Rhodesia. He did not answer, so I asked, 'Would you recommend that we head for Brazil?' With a slip of the tongue he said, 'Don't, they are next on the list.' I have often wondered what list he referred to. I can only speculate. Had communism not collapsed with Africa, South America would have been the next sacrificial lamb.

A second plane was shot down with the loss of fifty lives. This time no one survived. Two Sam-7 missiles were apparently used. Again there were no condemning words from the USA government. And again I was approached by concerned US citizens to travel to the USA to speak to senators and the news media. I agreed. I would go alone.

Boarding of the 747 in Salisbury was interrupted by a bomb scare while Diana and Bruno waited on the airport balcony. The plane was searched and two hours later we took off for London. Arriving in London, I discovered that my Pan Am flight had been cancelled. The ticket was changed to a TWA (not 800) flight arriving in New York, too late to catch my connection to Washington. Again I changed the ticket to some South American carrier that promised a short stop in Washington. On arrival at Dulles airport at one o'clock in the morning, no one was there to meet me as arranged. Pacing and telephoning produced results and by three in the morning, after thirty hours travelling, I could rest. I slept very well in Virginia.

It was a hectic programme. Numerous interviews and talks had been arranged for the following days, starting with a press conference on 16th February, 1979, and an address to sixty key members of the American Legion at their convention. There was a meeting with Senators Jepson, Humphrey, Shweiker, Hayakawa and twenty legislative assistants. That was followed by a thirty minute TV talk show. I addressed a luncheon given by Accuracy In Media. Next there was a tour to the State Department, where my sponsors and organisers pointed out someone in a corridor to whom I should talk. I introduced myself to the stranger, a middle-aged, smallish bald man – I was supposed to meet Hodding Carter. When I mentioned that I was a victim of terrorism from Rhodesia, Africa, and was there to appeal to the US government to help stop the downing of civilian commercial aircraft, he said, 'There is nothing we can do about it, we follow our plans. You are better off going home and not interfering.' I detected hostility and replied, 'You and your plans. Your hands are in blood up to your elbows, and it is only statistical to you.' We left and travelled a short distance by an electric underground van to a coffee bar.

If nothing else I had found that there was indeed a plan behind the madness. I had my deep-rooted suspicions confirmed. If states in Africa want to be communistic and tyrannical, which will invariably lead to chaos, let them, and they will likely drag their mentor, Russia, with them into the abyss of bankruptcy and despair. In the long term it will only serve to show that the USA has the ultimate right political philosophy, and its people will be content. Also, no Afro-American in the USA can say, 'Our Government opposed the "African liberation struggle" and therefore we have the right to burn down Los Angeles.' They can now look at TV and wonder what went wrong in Africa. During discussions and interviews I also discovered that when strong public opinion has been formed by the mass media on specific subjects, then governments will have to act on the assumption that that opinion is correct, even if it is a 'self-imposed monstrous guilt complex', because they can't change it. This is mass media democracy in a nutshell. The crucifixion of Jesus happened that way. Power of public opinion is all right, but if the public opinion is formed by an unscrupulous sensationalist mass media, then we have all become robots and lost the ability to see the truth from the semi-truth or direct lies. More on that later.

I went to the Pentagon and Crystal City. I attended dinner parties, a US Air Force dance, and went sightseeing.

America was great, made great by blacks and whites working together. Africa could have been great too, potentially even greater, but greed and political idiocy made that dream remote. Hatred destroys the haters' society.

My last talk was on a Larry King radio show at midnight on 28th February.

While in the USA someone suggested that I should enrol at a university and become a politician. On the way back to Rhodesia I stopped over in Denmark for a few days and during discussions with my father mentioned that suggestion. He was horrified and said that there are many ways to hell, but that that was surely the most direct! I did settle his horror by saying that I could never give up my free thinking by belonging to a rigid, formalised political party that in time would become a destroyer through its inability to change when circumstances required it.

Back in Rhodesia we received a vast amount of newspaper cuttings and letters from well-wishers in the USA, but not from the main opinion-making papers though. They were obviously following the same plan as the State Department. One such cutting from *The Atlanta Journal*, 15th October, 1978, written by George McLendon, reads:

> ...Another puzzler is, why is it that American blacks, especially American black leaders, wish that the only bi-racial government in all of Africa should fail? Is it possible that a successful bi-racial nation in Africa would be considered an embarrassment to the other totally black ruled nations? None of which is known for sound economies or individual liberty. I personally believe that American blacks are bigger than that. Co-operation and communication are what is working in America.

Have American blacks, and especially black leaders, searched their souls to find out what hoodwinked them into supporting African dictators and Marxist demigods? In Denmark we have a saying: 'Tell me who your friends are, then I will tell you who you are!' Only by seeing the truth can one grow. Hiding from responsibility and saying 'I am not the *one*' leads to domination by manipulators.

Another story came from *The Lima News*, 11th March, 1979, whose philosophy is as follows:

> The Lima News is directed to furnishing information to our readers so they can better promote and preserve their own freedom and encourage others to see its blessing. Only when man is free to control himself and all he produces can he develop to his utmost capabilities.
>
> We believe that freedom is a gift from God and not a political grant from government. Freedom is neither license nor anarchy. It is control and sovereignty of oneself, no more no less. It is thus consistent with the coveting Commandment.

Their article, written by Allan C. Brownfield, reads:

> Terrorism in Rhodesia on the part of the Marxist guerrillas of the Patriotic Front has become so widespread that we tend to overlook the human tragedies involved.
>
> Hitler said long ago that if you kill one man it is murder, while if you kill millions it simply becomes a statistic. To official Washington, the dead, both black and white, at the hands of terrorists in Rhodesia, have simply become statistics.
>
> The shocking barbarism of such terrorist activity becomes apparent, however, when one listens to the

firsthand report of a survivor, as this writer recently did.

That survivor is Hans Hansen who was one of the eight who lived through the crash of a Rhodesian airliner shot down by terrorists on September 3, 1978. After the aircraft was brought down by Soviet-made surface-to-air missiles, the terrorists murdered ten survivors, including women and children, in cold blood. Hansen, a native of Denmark, and his Rhodesian-born wife managed to crawl away to safety.

When the Hansens were invited to the US by the American Security Council to tell their story, the US Department of State refused to give Mrs Hansen a visa because she is a Rhodesian citizen and according to the department, 'We do not recognise Rhodesia.'

This, of course, has not kept the State Department from giving visas to the terrorist leaders of the Patriotic Front, Joshua Nkomo and Robert Mugabe. The double standard is clear and obvious.

Hans, travelling on a Danish passport, could not be legally prevented from coming to the US. After prodding from the American Security Council, he decided to leave his wife behind in the interest of letting Americans know about the terrorist groups their own government, the World Council of Churches and others in the West continue to support...

Since arriving in the US Hansen expressed surprise that the views of most Americans and that of the State Department were radically different. 'I came here', he said, 'because my wife insisted that if I told the American people the truth about terrorism in Rhodesia, they would cease their support for the Patriotic Front.' He states, 'Most Americans I speak with oppose terrorism totally. They, too, cannot understand why their government seems to embrace it.'

Yet the press has shown little interest in Hans Hansen's story. Phil Clark of the American Security Council reports, 'We held a press conference, but not one story has appeared in *The Washington Post*, *The New York Times* or any other major paper. The West German television was there, but not NBC, CBS or ABC. The Associated press sent a reporter, but I have seen no published story about the press conference.'

The refusal of the Carter administration to reject the barbaric terrorism which has been inflicted upon Rhodesia by the Soviet-supported Patriotic Front is shocking. The terrorists themselves do not hesitate to proclaim that their goal is an all-black, Marxist dictatorship for the future Zimbabwe.

It is Ian Smith, Bishop Muzurewa, Chief Chirau and other moderate black leaders who together are bringing Rhodesia to the 'majority rule' demanded by US policy. Yet the US rejects those who believe in democracy and a multiracial society and embraces the terrorists instead. Typical of the views of a Rhodesian terrorist is the statement made by an Angolan-trained Patriotic Front member who admitted killing twenty-one black civilians, including women and children. He told a conference of war correspondents in Salisbury, 'I am a ZIPPRA force guerrilla. I was trained to kill and I enjoyed killing. It was my job and I did it well...'

Why was the US State Department afraid to let Mrs Hansen accompany her husband and tell her story?

...Hans Hansen laments that if US policy reflected the views of the many Americans with whom he has spoken, it would be entirely different. In this he is surely correct. But encouraging our enemies has, somehow, become an axiom with many in this administration.

> Lima News
> 11th March, 1979

Yet another article read: 'COMMUNISM IN AFRICA. A BAD YEAR FOR RUSSIA,' (1979). Written by a special correspondent from the Sudan:

> You Westerners are too uncertain about your own values. That is one of the reasons you make communism appear to be a threat to you and to all of us. Communism in Africa would be as dead as a doornail if you were not keeping it alive by constantly writing about its power and danger.

> Extract from *To The Point*
> January, 1980

Although I found a colossal amount of sympathy and concern in the USA, I knew that the tide could not be reversed before a terrorist Marxist-Leninist government with its suppressive organs had been installed in Rhodesia. I had to be realistic and because of the exposure the crash, and now the American tour, had created, we had to look at our options. We were not just farmers or fishermen any more, we were survivors. We were advised by a newspaper notice to get out of Rhodesia before it became Zimbabwe. Not only had we survived against all odds, but that appeared to be a crime in itself.

The Unconstitutional Ruling Powers

In the evening before falling asleep I often asked myself, 'Why is it that the Western mind has to have an enemy?' If there is none, the state and media seem desperate to create one. That includes the Christian religion. Why invent a devil, who, according to traditional Christian teaching, is very powerful and to be feared? Surely evil is only in the minds of men and women (mainly men), and perpetrated by them? One can only assume that the reason was to make men fearful and therefore turn to the church of 'love' and comfort, and pay for that institution's protection. 'When God Died', according to *Time*, and conventional religion with it, a new fear reverberated through the Western world – 'the Russians are coming' – but the state institutions were quick to respond, offering protection. With the fear of terrorism firmly established, the public are assured of protection by their respective governmental institutions, who can now show good reason to implement new rules to control human behaviour. All playing into the hands of powerful manipulative government institutions – power wants more power!

Years ago in Denmark a local rat catcher was made redundant after many years of service. Asked why, he replied, 'I caught the rat.' Had the rat catcher been after long-term employment and power, he would have been breeding rats on the side, releasing them and asking the taxpayer for more money to finance a larger rat catching unit. This is just an illustration!

So, terrorism came to the Western world and government institutions offered protection. 'Everything is under control' they assure the public. The public knows no authority other than state institutions employing thousands to combat terrorism, just as the kings did in bygone days. Because of fear, the masses of people capitulate to state protection. The state now has total control. Elected government is quite happy with fear issues that deflect attention from real problems such as overpopulation, pollution and manipulation. New fears have been developed and again institutions come forth to offer protection. This is all a smoke screen for real problems for which politicians have no solutions. Ask most youngsters, and yes, they fear the 'Greys', black-eyed aliens from space. Why? A deliberately designed fear object! If that is not the grandest manipulation of minds since the invention of the devil, what is? If an intelligence has the ability and technology to build machines that can disobey known physical laws, fly millions of kilometres in galactic travel or appear in some other projected way, 'they' do not have to steal your eggs or sperm. 'They' will not crash either. 'They' will not be after your body or eat mutilated cattle in your backyard. That is all fabrication by the mass media and government agents to control your mind and to introduce fear so we all become dependent on bureaucratic governmental protection agencies. Meteors crashing into earth is another one – another institution will be created to protect you, but ultimately death still remains a certainty! Rejection by authority of a deliberately constructed lie often reinforces the belief in it.

In Vietnam and Rhodesia the authorities had programmes to 'win the hearts and minds' of the local population by persuasion and service. It should have been done by mission stations and the churches. That it did not succeed does not mean that the method was wrong. It failed because terror won.

Some have to be terrorised in the flesh for it to be effective in the minds of others. The terrorising of man's mind is an evil that all freethinkers have to do something about. It would be a very sad day if/when the real spiritual UFO light (which could be your Higher Self) comes into your life but, because of conditioning by mass media, government institutions and public opinion, you only see a devil with a long fork who is after body parts.

Later in 1979 a retired farmer bought our fishing business in Kariba. We made preparations to leave, not really knowing where to go. We thought Australia, maybe, but first had to go to South Africa from where we could hand in applications. Driving to South Africa with Bruno in the back seat practising his multiplication tables and little money in our pockets was not really what we wanted, after all I saw South Africa as having contributed to Rhodesia's destruction, but we did not have many choices. We arrived at a crossroad in the Cape Province. Not having a fixed destination, we flipped a coin and headed toward the Eastern Cape coast where we could have a bit of rest before taking up a new challenge in life. Later we would have to battle with yet another power-hungry governmental institution, namely that of Apartheid in South Africa. But that is another story.

I do not wish that anyone should go through even a part of what I have had to experience to learn life's many lessons. I do not believe that it is necessary or desirable. I believe the beautiful parts to be very desirable, freeing the spirit, but the negative part could scare one beyond redemption. I can count myself fortunate, for without the support of a wonderful wife and son, family and friends, I would probably not have had the strength and love that is required to endure such a complex life. The last chapter is a brief understanding of our earth's present position, which politicians will not reveal in truth because their jobs are at stake, and a method of meditation which I hope will lead to a greater appreciation of what life is all about. If it works, maybe some can be spared having to go through similar experiences to mine before knowing that there is more to life than being a naked hairless ape. Homo Sapiens are gods in the making, but in the process they can also perform horrendous devilish acts.

Finale: Meditation – Out of this World

Is not the ultimate goal, in this travel of life, to find some meaning in it all? We humans have tilled the lands for thousands of years, built factories and produced billions of consumer goods. Humans have over many years evolved political and religious systems, and other systems, which have grown out of history, such as philosophy, psychology, economics and science. More could be added. They have become our classical knowledge. We are almost like a snowball rolling down the mountain slope, picking up more and more snow as it turns, at the same time gathering momentum the greater it becomes.

We have built huge cathedrals with metre-thick walls to praise God. To worship and pray to the God that history has provided us with. Sometimes it is a God made in our image, at other times one that resembles a monster. We have fought wars for politician and priest in order that they give us security, glory, or eternal life. We have managed to solve mysteries, in some cases by moving the date of their occurrences so far back in time that even the sane capitulate. Some mysteries have been explained away by complexity, others by strange means that baffle the brain. I have heard it said that since nothing existed in the beginning, nothing exists today. Everything is a gigantic delusion. Others say an infinite number of possibilities exist so therefore everything exists in infinite numbers, and again others postulate a 'Big Bang' in nothingness and timelessness. In relative terms, that means the echo of a whisper behind a non-existing shadow 'burst the bubble'.

We have carved stones and erected long-lasting monuments to immortalise our visit here on this round ball in space, for reasons that defy rational economic reality and common sense.

We have ritualised our behaviour and called on the dead to leave us alone or to interfere in the running of our lives, Rituals have at times destroyed the very thing that makes us human. All for what agenda? Do we after all have a nagging desire to bring forth the hidden?

We have hated and loved and produced billions of humans, all like ourselves in appearance, who again make love and have billions of children, so that the earth can be filled, as the Christian Bible suggests, and most have the same fate, ultimate pain and suffering and goodbye. Few depart in a comfortable way, even fewer ascend in the glory of a ball of light.

Is it not time a question was put to the world? Are we not loving ourselves to death in our continuing cycles of existence? Are we not making so much love that the seams of the world are being torn apart and sustainability in question? And what is left is being eaten by the living hordes or consumed by ever-greater machines. A new wave of extinction will be caused by overpopulation. Our closed earth system is choking. The gutter is full.

The snowball is aiming for the valley, the speed is high. The unborn cannot suffer so why not let them stay where they are, in the bliss of nothingness? A place of ultimate understanding of unspeakable beautiful nothings that fill every cubic space with everything, which can be interpreted by the ones who have the minds that divine purpose intended, not by intellect but by intuition. We refer to that place as Nirvana, or Heaven.

That place is hidden and I cannot see it for you, but if you follow the directions and guidance below you may see it and interpret it in your own way. The unborn may even talk to you and say, 'Save me from your world of catastrophe, your world is doomed.'

Many claim that they can help you and me. I say escape is nigh.

Let us use our knowledge. Maybe there is a way to tap wisdom from the hidden kingdoms. Let us give it a try.

It is commonly known that the physical body reacts to suggestion. Hypnosis has proven the point. For example, if it is suggested to a person that he or she is burned by a cigarette the body might produce a blister in that spot. We also know that our mind and emotions react to suggestions or dreams, as in the rapid heartbeat during and following a nightmare. Also, during dreaming, if you come in contact with electrical wires, you will most likely wake up with something that feels like an electrical shock. Art can also be a trigger to activate emotions.

Our adventurous journey for new wisdom will take us well over the horizon of known science, not only in words and as a spectator, but as an observer and participator. It could shatter your present world view.

What we intend to do is to make the mind react to suggestions that will separate the mind body from the flesh body. Obviously the mind body will retain the conscious awareness.

Forget all previous conditioning and present world systems you are holding, and accept that your potential is far greater than the run-of-the-mill church, scientist or politician will ever tell you. This is a quotation from one who knows, believed to be Nelson Mandela:

> Our deepest fear is not that we are inadequate. Our deepest fear is that we are powerful beyond measure.

> It is our light, not our darkness, that most frightens us. We ask ourselves, 'who am I to be brilliant, gorgeous, talented, fabulous?' Actually who are you not to be? You are a child of God. Your playing small doesn't serve the world. There's nothing enlightened about shrinking so that other people won't feel insecure around you. We are all meant to shine as children do. We were born to make manifest the glory of God that is within us. It's not just in some of us; it's in everyone. And as we let our own light shine, we unconsciously give other people permission to do the same. As we're liberated from our own fears, our presence automatically liberates others.

I will assume that you are familiar with meditation techniques, a relaxation method whereby brain activity, thinking, is stilled sufficiently to allow the mind to follow the suggested journey without distraction from internal questioning or analysis.

No harm can arise from this experience. It is beautiful and enhances imagination. After the journey we will come back to our present home, our physical body, with a new experience that can only make us happier humans, realising that the mystery of existence is greater that we ever thought, and with a new insight to realms previously unknown.

The best way is just to follow our adventure, look at the detail, feel the surroundings and listen to spoken words. Pick up the 'vibes'.

From here you will need someone to read for you, or to read it aloud to a recorder and then play it back.

Sit comfortably or lie down, close your eyes (you see, you can't read any more), relax, still the mind, have no fear, try to listen to the silence. Let pictures form in your mind as we go on.

We see a mountain path. We are walking down the mountain path, just coming out of the mist belt. The top of the mountain is covered in mist. We are clad in golden brown robes like monks from a monastery, and feel very comfortable. Our path takes us downwards, a winding path. We are well below the mist now and sunlight is pouring into the valley, it is still very early in the morning, and the sun is a fiery red ball. We look back at the mist. Above it are the snow-covered mountain tops. The sunshine is slowly becoming brighter.

In front of us is a valley. A deep green valley. We see farmlands, cultivated fields, miniature fields, far down in the valley. Still further away we see a little village next to a blue, sunlit, glittering fjord. There is also a little harbour. Our path takes us past wild flowers, bluebells and anemones, and the smell is sweet and soothing. Moss and pebbles cover our path. We are thrilled by the beauty. Now we pass a little stone church. Stop and listen for a while. The Gregorian chant is causing the air around the church to shimmer, and generates in us a feeling of love for the valley. Above a lark sings with excitement. We are enchanted and at the same time filled with solemnity.

The setting is very peaceful and tranquil. We walk again and slowly descend. As we get further down we see farmers working on their lands. All plants seem to be full of loving response, swaying in a gentle breeze, content to carry the natural flow of energy that keeps the world alive.

We have arrived at the village and follow the road that takes us through the little village, down towards the harbour. The harbour area is clean and orderly. We notice men working on a wooden boat, seven men, also clad in robes, belted around the waist. The seven men are in the process of painting a fairly big boat, eighteen metres long and three metres wide. The boat is standing on land, supported by rafters while it is being painted.

We approach them and ask where they are going. They answer us that they are going to the northern light, beyond the western wind, and that they are waiting for two other companions, and suggest we join them. They ask where we come from. I point at the mountain. They nod with approval and inform us that they also came from the mountain mist.

A man holding a paint pot says, 'We are all Sons of Dawn. Welcome. Glory to The Holy One.' He hands us paint and brushes. The colour of the paint is yellow. We turn up our sleeves and assist in painting. The top of the boat is yellow, with only the name in blue. The boat builders of antiquity named it 'Mercy'. The very boat that has taken thousands of souls home, souls that have completed and overcome the tension of opposites – duality.

The lower part of the boat is painted royal blue, so it merges and blends with the water. We are all excited about the journey and work very hard to hasten departure. After thirty days of preparation and in-between rest in the Starlit Inn across the road, everything on the boat is ready. We push the boat into the water.

A golden yellow boat in blue water with a green background, a beautiful picture and a delight for the eyes.

Three days pass during which time we study the stars for navigation purposes from The Deva Room in Starlit Inn. From there we also have a good view of where we came from and are filled with appreciation and reverence for the unseen force that has selected us for the journey. Then, finally, nine of us set sail for the unknown. It is a long journey, we understand, but the fascination of the unknown fills us. We have no idea what to expect, yet somehow feel that it is all so very right, unfolding harmoniously.

We see hundreds of people, young and old, on the shoreline. Some would have liked to join us but they have duties and responsibilities to which they must attend. Others have no desire to go further than what they see and know, and love the local funfair and merry-go-round. That is their choice and maybe right for them.

We sit in our allocated places. There is room enough to lie down if rest is required.

Slowly, we glide out of the fjord with a slight breeze in the sail. We hear farewell songs from the shores. Harmonious songs that penetrate and resonate in our spines. We see singing people waving white handkerchiefs, all bidding us farewell.

We have mountains on either side and open ocean in front of us. The breeze fills our sail and the land slowly disappears.

After hours of silence the man at the rudder says, 'We are now far from the comfort of traditional thinking. We are open-minded, otherwise we would not be here. Will someone give a talk on light and darkness tonight? As we are the Children Of Dawn, it should not be difficult.'

Some time passes. The full moon emerges as the sun sets. The sky is clear of clouds. A youthful looking person stands up and says, 'My name is Darkness Once Removed, I am the product of reason and rational thinking. Here I am following what is totally uncertain, but so far, in doing that, my imagination ignites and darkness disappears, so am I right to assume that prolonged certainty can lead to darkness? That certainties can lock away imaginative thinking, that creativity eventually stagnates, and that hence there is darkness?'

'Well said,' replies the rudder man, and adds, 'Certainty can be death to a man's soul. Creative imaginative thinking is required by life – the force that life uses to propel evolution. The nature of stone has no preference between being a heap of rubble or a castle. A body of skin and bones cannot talk. But imagination makes the difference. Imagination creates structures out of randomness. In the world of physics it is known and accepted that the experimenter influences the experiment and that the outcome often resembles the desire or expectation of the experimenter. We see that especially in plant breeding, gardening and farming. The biological world is more attuned to our projected wishes and therefore reacts easily to them. In short, everything entropies given enough time, if not supported by a constant renewing influence. That is our faith, dead or alive, like it or not. Children of darkness only eat and devour, they give nothing back. Let someone talk to us about light.'

The man next to Darkness Once Removed stands up and says, 'My name is Point In-Awareness. I project thoughts, therefore I am. All light seen and unseen is vibrating energy, and it brings with it information about the sender. Look at the moon. Sunlight shining on the moon picks up the information of the moon and brings it to us. Look at the land of ice in front of us. Moonlight picks up the information about the land and sends it to us.' We notice the land in front. 'Likewise, when you look at me you see reflected light that carries my image. The universe is full of those vibrations, coming from all directions. Any point in the universe is full of vibration. The universe can well be compared to a gigantic shining vibrating crystal. When one place is knocked or shines it sends a ring of vibration everywhere. In a way it acts like a three-dimensional gong. But if the energy that vibrates is purified thought or one-poled love energy, spiritual energy, then the universal crystal becomes a superconductor. The energy moves instantaneously with no energy loss and the thought pattern or spiritual body will then have no locality, but be where its attention is put.'

'Well,' says the rudder man, 'as we can see from that talk, we live in an information bubble universe, where everything gives off information to everything else that it comes in contact with, and in the process exchanges energy. But what we have to understand is that the universe vibrates with all information, everywhere, all the time, and it is just for us to tune in, to focus correctly and pick out required information. It is all there for the taking. Synchronicity and interconnectedness is part of that system. We must remember we are souls, composed of spirit. We can be expanding souls, Gods in the making, and can be a great source of light. The land of ice is near. Let us shortly disembark.'

We feel no cold, actually we are warm. Gently the boat drifts towards the ice shelf, into a natural little mooring place. We leave the boat, and the rudder man gives the 'follow me' signal. No one talks. The silence is enormous, but just audible, we pick up the sound of bells and head towards it. The beautiful ringing and high-pitched notes are getting louder and louder as we near the source. It seems we no can longer distinguish from where the tones are coming. This blue-white ice field is strange. Without saying anything to one another, we call it, telepathically, 'The Land of Singing Ice', and we know by intuition that that which is not purified will not resonate with the singing ice. We are awe-struck, it is all so incredibly overwhelming. We want to stay for ever, but the rudder man points to a pillar of light that seems to emanate from a big hole surrounded by ice and white snow. We walk and it takes us a day or so to get to the hole where the violet light comes from. We have lost track of days because on reaching the Land of Singing Ice we have not seen any nights. We reach the rim of the hole. Deep down we see molten rock. Its temperature is very, very high. Anything that falls into that furnace is consumed and becomes a pillar of light. We look at one another and know that we have reached the Ring of No

Return, the lake of refiner's fire, also known as the Well of Siloam.

After a while we are ready for the final instruction. 'Listen, this is important,' says the rudder man. 'When you come out of the fire on the other side aim for the centre of the rainbow. Have no fear, relax, accept, and your joy will be great. We all have to do this alone and no further guidance can be given. You will see a small opening in the crystal, in the centre of the rainbow. When you come through you will be an eternal free spirit, flying like a swan through the eternal space. Others will be there too, to fly with you over the waves, and eternal ecstasy is yours and the sting of death will be known no more. Give your hand to the divine. Go with my love.

'Jump.'